China–India Relations

The question of whether China and India can cooperate is at the core of global geopolitics. As the two countries grow their economies, the potential for conflict is no longer simply a geopolitical one based on relative power, influence and traditional quarrels over land boundaries.

This book assesses the varying interests of China and India in economics, environment, energy and water, and addresses the possibility of cooperation in these domains. Containing analyses by leading authorities on China and India, it analyses the nature of existing and emerging conflict, describes the extent of cooperation, and suggests possibilities for collaboration in the future. While it is often suggested that conflict between the giants of Asia is the norm, there are a number of opportunities for cooperation in trade, international and regional financial institutions, renewable energy development and climate change, and shared rivers.

This book will be of interest to researchers in the fields of Asian studies, international relations and Asian politics.

Kanti Bajpai is Wilmar Professor of Asian Studies at the Lee Kuan Yew School of Public Policy, National University of Singapore.

Huang Jing is Lee Foundation Professor on US–China Relations and Director of the Centre on Asia and Globalisation at the Lee Kuan Yew School of Public Policy, National University of Singapore.

Kishore Mahbubani is Dean and Professor of Practice at the Lee Kuan Yew School of Public Policy, National University of Singapore.

Routledge Contemporary Asia Series

For a complete list of titles in this series, please visit www.routledge.com.

29 **Soft Power in Japan-China Relations**
State, sub-state and non-state relations
Utpal Vyas

30 **Enhancing Asia-Europe Co-operation through Educational Exchange**
Georg Wiessala

31 **History Textbooks and the Wars in Asia**
Divided memories
Edited by Gi-Wook Shin and Daniel C. Sneider

32 **The Politics of Religion in South and Southeast Asia**
Edited by Ishtiaq Ahmed

33 **The Chinese/Vietnamese Diaspora**
Revisiting the boatpeople
Edited by Yuk Wah Chan

34 **The Dynamics of Social Capital and Civic Engagement in Asia**
Vibrant societies
Edited by Amrita Daniere and Hy Van Luong

35 **Eurasia's Ascent in Energy and Geopolitics**
Rivalry or partnership for China, Russia and Central Asia?
Edited by Robert E. Bedeski and Niklas Swanström

36 **Asian Popular Culture in Transition**
Edited by John A. Lent and Lorna Fitzsimmons

37 **Sexual Diversity in Asia, c. 600–1950**
Edited by Raquel Reyes and William G. Clarence Smith

38 **Asia's Role in Governing Global Health**
Edited by Kelley Lee, Tikki Pang and Yeling Tan

39 **Asian Heritage Management**
Contexts, concerns, and prospects
Edited by Kapila D. Silva and Neel Kamal Chapagain

40 **Genocide and Mass Atrocities in Asia**
Legacies and prevention
Edited by Deborah Mayerson and Annie Pohlman

41 **Child Security in Asia**
The impact of armed conflict in Cambodia and Myanmar
Cecilia Jacob

42 **Vietnamese–Chinese Relationships at the Borderlands**
Trade, tourism and cultural politics
Yuk Wah Chan

43 **Asianism and the Politics of Regional Consciousness in Singapore**
Leong Yew

44 **Disaster Relief in the Asia Pacific**
Agency and resilience
Edited by Minako Sakai, Edwin Jurriëns, Jian Zhang and Alec Thornton

45 **Human Trafficking in Asia**
Forcing issues
Edited by Sallie Yea

46 **Democracy or Alternative Political Systems in Asia**
After the strongmen
Edited by Michael Hsin-Huang Hsiao

47 **European Studies in Asia**
Contours of a discipline
Georg Wiessala

48 **Corporate Social Responsibility and Human Rights in Asia**
Robert J. Hanlon

49 **Irregular Migration and Human Security in East Asia**
Edited by Jiyoung Song and Alistair D. B. Cook

50 **Renewable Energy in East Asia**
Towards a new developmentalism
Christopher M. Dent

51 **East Asian Development Model**
Twenty-first century perspectives
Edited by Shiping Hua and Ruihua Hu

52 **Land Grabs in Asia**
What role for the law?
Edited by Connie Carter and Andrew Harding

53 **Asia Struggles with Democracy**
Evidence from Indonesia, Korea and Thailand
Giovanna Maria Dora Dore

54 **China–Malaysia Relations and Foreign Policy**
Razak Abdullah

55 **Politics of the 'Other' in India and China**
Western concepts in non-Western contexts
Edited by Lion König and Bidisha Chaudhuri

56 **China–India Relations**
Cooperation and conflict
Edited by Kanti Bajpai, Huang Jing and Kishore Mahbubani

China–India Relations
Cooperation and conflict

Edited by Kanti Bajpai, Huang
Jing and Kishore Mahbubani

LONDON AND NEW YORK

First published 2016
by Routledge
2 Park Square, Milton Park, Abingdon, Oxon OX14 4RN

and by Routledge
711 Third Avenue, New York, NY 10017

Routledge is an imprint of the Taylor & Francis Group, an informa business

© 2016 Selection and editorial matter: Kanti Bajpai, Huang Jing and Kishore Mahbubani; individual chapters: the contributors.

The right of the editors to be identified as the authors of the editorial material, and of the authors for their individual chapters, has been asserted in accordance with sections 77 and 78 of the Copyright, Designs and Patents Act 1988.

All rights reserved. No part of this book may be reprinted or reproduced or utilised in any form or by any electronic, mechanical, or other means, now known or hereafter invented, including photocopying and recording, or in any information storage or retrieval system, without permission in writing from the publishers.

Trademark notice: Product or corporate names may be trademarks or registered trademarks, and are used only for identification and explanation without intent to infringe.

British Library Cataloguing in Publication Data
A catalogue record for this book is available from the British Library

Library of Congress Cataloging in Publication Data
China–India relations: cooperation and conflict / edited by Kanti Bajpai, Huang Jing, and Kishore Mahbubani.
pages cm. — (Routledge contemporary Asia series; 56)
Includes bibliographical references and index.
1. China—Relations—India. 2. India—Relations—China.
3. China—Foreign economic relations—India. 4. India—Foreign economic relations—China. 5. Environmental policy—China.
6. Environmental policy—India. 7. Energy policy—China. 8. Energy policy—India. 9. Water resources development—Government policy—China. 10. Water resources development—Government policy—India.
I. Bajpai, Kanti P., 1955- editor of compilation. II. Huang, Jing, 1956- editor of compilation. III. Mahbubani, Kishore, editor of compilation.
DS740.5.I5C4834 2016
337.51054—dc23
2015024823

ISBN: 978-1-138-95575-2 (hbk)
ISBN: 978-1-315-66610-5 (ebk)

Typeset in Times New Roman
by Swales & Willis Ltd, Exeter, Devon, UK

Contents

List of figures ix
List of tables x
List of contributors xi
Acknowledgements xiii

Introduction: the long peace, new areas of competition and opportunities for cooperation in China–India relations 1
KANTI BAJPAI, HUANG JING AND KISHORE MAHBUBANI

PART I
Economics 19

1 **Convergence and divergence in development: an Indian perspective** 21
PREM SHANKAR JHA

2 **Towards greater financial cooperation: a Chinese perspective** 37
ZHAO GANCHENG

3 **Bilateral trade and global economy: an Indian perspective** 52
SANJAYA BARU

4 **Competitive cooperation in trade: a Chinese perspective** 67
HU SHISHENG

PART II
Environment and energy   91

5   Working together towards an ecologically civilised world: a Chinese perspective   93
PAN JIAHUA

6   Cooperation on climate change mitigation: an Indian perspective   108
ARABINDA MISHRA AND NEHA PAHUJA

7   Sino-Indian interactions in energy in the 2000s: a Chinese perspective   130
ZHA DAOJIONG

8   What scope for resource cooperation? An Indian perspective   144
ARUNABHA GHOSH

PART III
Water   165

9   Towards riparian rationality: an Indian perspective   167
UTTAM KUMAR SINHA

10   A river flows through it: a Chinese perspective   182
SELINA HO

Conclusion: ways forward for China–India cooperation   198
KANTI BAJPAI, HUANG JING AND KISHORE MAHBUBANI

Index   218

Figures

4.1	Simple average of tariff rates for China, India and the world (for goods), 1992–2010	77
5.1	Territorial CO_2 emissions for the top three country emitters and the EU	95
6.1	CO_2 emissions in China and India (metric tons per capita)	110
6.2	GDP projections for China and India at market exchange rates (2014 US$ billions)	112
6.3	Primary energy demand projections for China and India (Mtoe)	113
6.4	GHG emissions by source in China (MtCO$_2$e)	114
6.5	GHG emissions by source in India (MtCO$_2$e)	115

Tables

3.1	China–India bilateral trade (US$ billion)	57
3.2	China–India trade balance	57
4.1	Top five commodities' share (%) in Chinese exports to India	69
4.2	Top five commodities' share (%) in Indian exports to China	70
4.3	Indian imports from China and the world (shares by commodity in % share of total all products)	71
4.4	Indian exports to China and the world (shares by commodity in % share of total all products)	72
4.5	Indian exports to China and the world (shares by commodity in % share of total all products)	73
4.6	India's trade with China (shares of commodity in % to shares of total all products)	73
4.7	Bilateral trade (in billions USD)	74
4.8	The structures of the Indian economy (% of GDP)	75
4.9	Trade balances (% of GDP)	75
4.10	India's trade balance with some of India's top trade partners in 2009–10 (Rs'000 Crore)	76
4.11	India's trade deficit (as % of Indian GDP) with China and with the rest of the world	77
5.1	Primary energy consumption for selected economies (Mtoe)	94
5.2	Fossil fuel production (Mtoe) reserves-to-production (R/P) ratios (years) for selected economies at end of 2011	96
5.3	Carbon emissions in 1990 and 2013	99
5.4	World steel production (2014)	101
5.5	Energy generation from renewable sources (wind, solar, geothermal, biomass and wastes), (Mtoe)	104
6.1	Top ten emitters	109
6.2	Key development indicators: a comparison	113
6.3	Top ten G20 countries in clean energy investment (2013)	120
8.1	India's resource nexus	149
8.2	Priorities for action, consequences of inaction	150
10.1	Existing Sino-Indian cooperation on transboundary rivers	190

Contributors

Kanti Bajpai is Wilmar Professor of Asian Studies at the Lee Kuan Yew School of Public Policy, National University of Singapore.

Sanjaya Baru is Director for Geo-economics and Strategy at the International Institute of Strategic Studies (IISS), UK.

Arunabha Ghosh is CEO and co-Founder of the Council on Energy, Environment and Water, New Delhi, India.

Selina Ho is Senior Research Fellow at the Centre on Asia and Globalisation at the Lee Kuan Yew School of Public Policy, National University of Singapore.

Hu Shisheng is Director of the Institute for South and Southeast Asian and Oceania Studies, China Institutes of Contemporary International Relations, China.

Huang Jing is Lee Foundation Professor on US–China Relations and Director of the Centre on Asia and Globalisation at the Lee Kuan Yew School of Public Policy, National University of Singapore.

Prem Shankar Jha is a columnist who writes on Indian and global political economy, a former editor of the *Financial Express* and the *Hindustan Times*, and a former media advisor to Prime Minister V.P. Singh.

Kishore Mahbubani is Dean and Professor in the Practice of Public Policy at the Lee Kuan Yew School of Public Policy, National University of Singapore.

Arabinda Mishra is Senior Social Scientist at the International Centre for Integrated Mountain Development (ICIMOD) in Kathmandu, Nepal.

Neha Pahuja is Fellow at The Energy and Resources Institute (TERI), New Delhi, India.

Pan Jiahua is Director of the Institute for Urban and Environmental Studies, Chinese Academy of Social Sciences, China.

Uttam Kumar Sinha is Fellow at the Institute for Defence Studies and Analyses in New Delhi, India.

Zha Daojiong is Professor of International Political Economy at the School of International Studies, Peking University, China.

Zhao Gancheng is Senior Fellow and Director, South Asia Studies, Shanghai Institute of International Studies, China.

Acknowledgements

This volume evolved from the conference 'China and India: Towards Cooperation between the Giants of Asia', held at the Lee Kuan Yew School of Public Policy on 26–27 April, 2013. We gratefully acknowledge funding from the Ministry of Education (MoE), Republic of Singapore, for supporting our project, also titled 'China and India: Towards Cooperation between the Giants of Asia' (MOE2011-T2-2-148). In addition, we wish to record our thanks to all the participants of the conference and especially our authors for their cooperation. Thanks are also due to those within the Lee Kuan Yew School of Public Policy who assisted us with the conference and publication of the book. They include the staff of the Research Support Unit (RSU), the research associates/assistants and staff of the Centre on Asia and Globalisation (CAG), but especially Varigonda Kesava Chandra and Libby Morgan Beri, who worked tirelessly and with great good humour on the manuscript and improved it in innumerable ways.

Introduction

The long peace, new areas of competition and opportunities for cooperation in China–India relations

Kanti Bajpai, Huang Jing and Kishore Mahbubani

This book is about the possibility of cooperation between China and India in economics, environment, energy, and water. The two giants of Asia are usually thought of as geopolitical rivals and as doomed to conflict even though they have not fought a war since 1962.[1] The long, if uneasy, peace between them indicates that they can cooperate in security matters, at least to the extent of avoiding hostilities. As the two grow their economies, however, the potential for conflict is moving beyond the geopolitical sphere. Even though there is a huge convergence of interests between the two countries in their efforts to modernise, the pattern of modernisation itself might lead them into new arenas of contention. This volume considers the prospects for conflict and cooperation in four areas – economics, environment, energy, and water. While the two countries have worked hard on security cooperation, they have done less to manage tensions in these other areas and to exploit the opportunities for common benefit.

The China–India relationship is steadily becoming one of the keys to peace and prosperity in Asia. If the relationship is managed well, then chances are that Asia will do well. If the relationship is managed badly, then Asia will do badly. As Asia is increasingly the geopolitical and economic nerve-centre of the world, China–India relations are crucial to world order. China and India's leaders have known this at least since 1949; the rest of the world is gradually becoming conscious of the fact. Not surprisingly, the China–India relationship is seen as a barometer of Asia's wellbeing – *a* barometer, not *the* barometer because the China–US and China–Japan relationships are also vital to Asian peace and prosperity. Diplomats and scholars alike are paying much greater attention to China–India relations. They are particularly focused on signs of discord and conflict rather than signs of concord and cooperation, although both are clearly important: discord but also concord, conflict but also cooperation. The question for the future is which way the balance tilts. Will China and India take advantage of more than half a century of peace and two decades of rapid economic growth to help build lasting peace and prosperity in Asia, or will they, as they did in the late 1950s and early 1960s, squander the opportunity?

With this context in mind, the Lee Kuan Yew School of Public Policy, National University of Singapore organised a conference on China–India interactions in economics, environment, energy, and water in April 2013. Six Chinese and six Indian participants contributed papers. Each author was asked to make an assessment of the conflicting and common interests of the two countries in relation to their issue area; to deal with the history of cooperation, if any; and to make suggestions on how the countries could cooperate in the future. Why economics, environment, energy, and water? It is no great intuition to see that peace and prosperity in Asia and elsewhere are intimately linked to economic interactions and arrangements, to a clean and healthful environment, to the price and supply of energy, and to the availability of freshwater. These are as basic as the security of the homeland.

The volume is divided into three sections. In the economics section, our authors deal with comparative development policy and the implications for cooperation (Prem Shankar Jha), the prospects of cooperation in investment and in restructuring the global financial order (Zhao Gancheng), and the China–India trade relationship (Sanjaya Baru and Hu Shisheng). The second section deals with environment and energy. It consists of two chapters on China and India's climate change policies and the prospects of cooperation (Pan Jiahua and Arabinda Mishra and Neha Pahuja) and two on energy policy and cooperation (Zha Daojiong and Arunabha Ghosh). The final section focuses on water conflict and cooperation (Uttam Kumar Sinha and Selina Ho). Each section features a Chinese and Indian author addressing more or less the same set of issues. Except for Ho, our authors are nationals of China and India. The authors were asked to present dispassionate, reasoned analyses of conflict and cooperation. While they certainly bring national perspectives to bear, it is important to note that they do not purport to endorse or represent official views on the subject; indeed, they are often critical of national policies and stances. At the same time, they are cognisant of the limits within which national policy must be made. Their recommendations and suggestions are therefore marked by a good understanding of what is feasible.

Our introduction begins by engaging the question of why and how China and India have stabilised bilateral security relations and maintained a 'long peace' since 1962. It then turns to the central concern of this volume, namely, the emergence of new challenges in the bilateral relationship as a result of their economic rise. We go on to summarise the state of cooperation between the two powers in the areas of economy, environment, energy, and water as a way of suggesting that the two powers are aware of the threat of conflict and the opportunities for gain in these areas, even if their record of collaboration so far is a modest one. Our broad argument is that four structural factors and four key policy pillars designed to prevent another war have produced the long peace; that as a function of economic growth in a globalised world order there are new areas of contention but also opportunities for cooperation; and that the record of cooperation in the newer areas thus far is modest but is poised to grow.

The long peace

China–India relations since the 1962 war have been marked by a cold peace, by which we mean that they feature a high degree of military stability even though there have been diplomatic ups and downs and brief moments of crisis. Not a single shot has been fired in anger since the border incident at Nathu La in 1967, and no serious military confrontations have occurred to match the Sumdurong Chu incident of 1986.[2] How did the two countries meliorate their hostility and construct a long (if cold) peace?

The first cause of the long peace between China and India is their acceptance of the status quo. Notwithstanding their formal positions to the contrary, the two powers have been fairly satisfied with the post-1962 alignment of the Line of Actual Control (LAC). This is a strong claim, but we would suggest that the historical record bears it out. While it is true that China and India have not concluded a border agreement, and while both officially claim territories under the other's control, there has long been recognition in the two governments that the actual points of difference are not as great as the rhetoric indicates.

Beijing has always held that it will not accept the McMahon Line in the so-called 'eastern sector', and since the late 1980s it has insisted that Tawang in Arunachal Pradesh belongs to China. In addition, it contemplates 'adjustments' in other areas along the Line of Actual Control.[3] Having said this, China has never seriously expected to get all of Arunachal Pradesh, or indeed all its claims in the other two sectors of the contested border, whatever it may say in public. New Delhi too has never seriously countenanced keeping every inch of Arunachal Pradesh or getting back the Aksai Chin in the western sector. On at least two occasions, China offered India a 'package deal' on the border. The deal envisaged a settlement along the LAC and would have 'swapped' Arunachal Pradesh for Aksai Chin. India twice rejected the deal (in 1960 and 1980), but in the 1980s came around to reopening the possibility with China.[4] The status quo more or less satisfies both powers, for quite good strategic reasons. For Beijing, invading Arunachal Pradesh and then integrating it into China would be a formidable military, social and political task, not the least because of the geographical obstacles posed by the Himalayan mountain ranges. For New Delhi, the Aksai Chin is of little economic or human value: as Jawaharlal Nehru said, not a blade of grass grows there, and it is almost completely uninhabited.[5]

A second reason for the long peace between China and India is that both powers have had numerous other challenges, both domestic and international, that were far more important than prosecution of the bilateral quarrel. China was beset by a series of domestic challenges – the Great Leap Forward; the Cultural Revolution; leadership upheavals after the death of Zhou Enlai and Mao Zedong; dramatic changes in economic direction under Deng Xiaoping; pro-democracy activism; separatism in Xinjiang and Tibet; and increasing social protests. India too was preoccupied by domestic challenges – most importantly, changes in leadership after Nehru's death; decline in the Congress Party's long-term organisational strength and electoral fortunes; widespread public protests against Indira Gandhi culminating in the Emergency declaration; Maoist insurgency in the 1960s and then again in the 2000s; religious, caste, and separatist violence; terrorism; economic reforms after the financial meltdown in 1990–91; and volatile coalition government at the central level since 1989.

Internationally, both China and India confronted a number of far more serious problems than those posed by the other country. For China, the biggest challenges were relations with the Soviet Union and the United States. In the end, Beijing determined that the Soviet Union was the greater enemy and a partnership with Washington became necessary in order to deal with Moscow. Yet the US remained in alliance with China's regional enemies, particularly Taiwan and Japan. In addition, after Vietnam's reunification in 1975, Beijing came to regard its southern neighbour as a threat – over a then-unresolved border dispute as well as Hanoi's closeness to Moscow.

For India, the greatest international challenges were Pakistan and the US. The breakup of Pakistan in 1971 ironically had the effect of reducing Islamabad's sense of vulnerability vis-à-vis India as well as increasing its determination to build its military power and its strategic ties with the US, China and the Muslim world. First in Punjab and then in Kashmir, where separatism raised its head in 1982 and 1989, respectively, Pakistan turned to asymmetric conflict, backing the insurgencies and helping destabilise India's borderlands. By 1986, Pakistan had developed nuclear weapons which protected it against any threat of Indian retaliation over the deepening crises in Punjab and Kashmir. India's relations with the US were at their lowest ebb in this period as well, even though India relied on American development aid. After 1971 and for the rest of the Cold War, New Delhi found itself arrayed against Washington and deeply opposed to its South Asia policy. Apart from Pakistan and the US, New Delhi also worried about its smaller South Asian neighbours whose domestic politics were volatile and who flirted strategically with China and the US.

A third cause of the long peace between China and India is conventional and nuclear deterrence. China had won the 1962 war convincingly and already had a battle-hardened military, but, with an eye on the Soviet Union, it embarked on a programme of military modernisation. Its modernisation programme was facilitated by rapprochement with the US in 1972 and access to Western technologies in the second half of the Cold War.[6] By the mid-1990s, China in addition had about 200 nuclear weapons and a three-legged deterrent, with land, air, and sea-based nuclear capability.[7] No power on earth would easily contemplate war with China; certainly India, in a relatively weak position, could not.

After the 1962 war, India embarked on a massive expansion of the Indian Army, increased its defence expenditures, and modernised its equipment primarily through arms imports from the Soviet Union. In 1974, it conducted a nuclear test, and by the early 1980s had enough fissile materials to produce several nuclear weapons.[8] By the 1990s, India was beginning to produce ballistic missiles and had bought European and Soviet aircraft capable of carrying nuclear weapons. The Indian Army fought the Pakistani Army to a standstill in 1965 and defeated it in 1971 in the Bangladesh war. It therefore had substantially regained its fighting spirit, and by the late 1970s was confident of defending itself against China.[9]

Fourth, the integration of the two economies into the global economic order has played a role in sustaining the long peace. China's economic reforms, leading to unprecedented rates of growth, began with the ascent to power of Deng Xiaoping in 1978. A major component of the country's growth was the dramatic expansion in trade and foreign investment and the acceptance of private property. Between 1978 and 2013, China's trade grew from US$ 21 billion to US$ 4.16 trillion, and it received investments worth about US$ 2.6 trillion.[10] Its economy grew at 9.85 per cent per annum on average.[11] These figures show just how quickly China integrated into the global economy. In 2001, it joined the World Trade Organization (WTO), a further indication of its desire to integrate. India's less dramatic integration in the global economy began in the wake of the 1990–91 foreign currency and fiscal crisis. Prime Minister Narasimha Rao was forced to open the economy to trade and investment and to carry out a programme of domestic reform to free the private sector. Between 1990 and 2014, India's trade grew from US$ 41.7 billion to US$ 777 billion, and it received investments worth about US$ 287 billion.[12] Unlike China, India was an original GATT and then WTO member, and in this sense was already integrated into a global set of norms and rules. Given their dependence on the foreign sector, both countries had and continue to have a stake in peaceful international relations. Hostilities between the two would disrupt their trade and would alarm foreign investors, and there is little doubt that both governments feel the need to reassure economic partners.

These four structural reasons for the long peace were supplemented by a conscious policy of conflict management and rapprochement. Here the turning point was 1988. From 1971 to 1988, India-China relations improved but at a glacial pace – the biggest breakthrough during this period was the decision to resume border negotiations in 1981 after a gap of 20 years. It was not until Rajiv Gandhi's visit to China in 1988 that the strategic deadlock was broken. During the visit, India agreed to normalise the relationship. China and India had restored full diplomatic ties in 1976, but economic interactions and people-to-people links had remained hostage to New Delhi's insistence that a full-bodied relationship was dependent on the return of all territories lost in the 1962 war.[13] With the softening of India's stand, China–India relations, and particularly economic relations, began to take off. The deepening of diplomatic and economic ties was briefly stopped by India's nuclear tests in 1998 and by New Delhi's pointing to the China 'threat' as justification for the tests.[14] Within months, however, the two sides had patched up and resumed economic and diplomatic interactions. When India and Pakistan found themselves at war in 1999 after Pakistani intrusions into the Kargil sector of Kashmir, China made it clear that it disapproved of Islamabad's adventurism.[15] This was another key moment in China–India relations.

In the 15 years since the Kargil war, China and India have increased the intensity of the relationship, and a high degree of stability has marked their interactions. The two countries have built the relationship around four pillars: high-level summits, border negotiations, confidence-building measures, and trade.

Since 1988, and particularly over the past decade, Chinese and Indian leaders at the highest level – president, prime minister, and foreign minister – have met more times than ever before in their history. These meetings have been held in bilateral, regional, and multilateral settings. The second pillar of stability has been the negotiations over the border. The two powers have been in almost continuous discussion since 1981, culminating in the "Agreement on the Political Parameters and Guiding Principles for the Settlement of the Boundary Question" that was signed in 2005.[16] The third pillar of stability has been a series of confidence-building measures – namely, the 1993 and 1996 agreements on the LAC, the establishment of the "Working Mechanism for Consultation and Coordination on India–China Border Affairs" signed in 2012, and, most recently, the "Border Defence Cooperation Agreement" of 2014. Beijing and New Delhi are reportedly in discussion on maritime security as well.[17] The two sides have also established a robust trade relationship that has made China amongst the top three trade partners of India and India amongst the 15 leading trade partners of China.[18] In doing so, China and India have explicitly linked trade to peace and stability in the hope that economic progress can hold the relationship steady until a strategic breakthrough becomes possible.[19]

While China–India relations have matured and stabilised, there are troubling trends. Arms acquisitions and development of military infrastructure along the LAC have engendered a security dilemma, with each side accusing the other of destabilising behaviour.[20] According to India, there has been a steady rate of border incursions by Chinese troops.[21] Indian officials have admitted that given the undefined nature of the Line of Actual Control, this is not altogether surprising. In addition, former Army Chief V.K. Singh and Defence Minister A.K. Antony have noted that Indian troops too have crossed the Line.[22] In April 2013 and then again in September 2014, Chinese and Indian troops confronted each other for two weeks in Ladakh. The two confrontations occurred just before the visits of Li Keqiang and Xi Jinping to India, thus overshadowing the visits themselves.[23] In the case of the September 2014 confrontation, India felt it necessary to rush 1,500 troops to the LAC in support of local border forces.[24] It remains unclear why these two incidents coincided with high-level Chinese visits to India.

Beyond the border quarrel, there is a history of mistrust arising from two other issues – India's hosting of the Dalai Lama and Tibetan refugees, and China's support of Pakistan. Here again the recent record is by no means all negative. While India has played host to the Dalai Lama and Tibetan refugees for over five decades, it has restricted their political activities. In addition, India has repeatedly stated that it sees Tibet as a part of China.[25] Yet China continues to worry about India's stand on Tibet, particularly at times of instability and in a post-Dalai future. With respect to Pakistan, since the 1980s, with an eye to regional stability, China has edged away from its full-throated support of Islamabad on issues such as Kashmir.[26] The continuing rise of Islamic extremism and terrorism in Pakistan is another worry for Beijing, which has become increasingly wary of its erstwhile ally.[27] As a result of this shift in China's stand, Beijing and New Delhi have begun discussions on the evolving situation in Pakistan.[28] While Pakistan has divided the two powers over the past 60 years, there is now a shared interest in containing the threats emanating from it. Still, India resents Beijing's military support of its South Asian rival and China's apparently deepening involvement in Pakistan's infrastructure plans, including port-building in Gwadar and road-building in Pakistani-occupied Kashmir.[29]

In sum, the period from 1988 has been largely stable in a security and diplomatic sense, though suspicions and doubts remain on both sides. Meanwhile, the two economies have grown dramatically, benefitting both countries but adding to the complexity of the bilateral relationship. To these new areas of competition we now turn.

New areas of competition

In dealing with each other, China and India face a series of new challenges arising from their economic growth over the past two decades. The rapid development of the two countries and their increasing integration into the global economic system has created a different set of problems in the bilateral relationship. In the long run, those problems could be substantial and lead to conflict.

With the opening of China and India's economies and the growth in bilateral trade, the (im)balance of trade has become a point of friction. China–India trade has grown from US $2.92 billion in 2000 to a high of US $73.9 billion in 2011.[30] Since then, it has declined to about US $66.57 billion, which partly reflects the downturn in the global economy and reduced demand everywhere.[31] China exports far more goods to India than it imports from India, and the trade deficit in 2013–14 was US $36.2 billion, roughly 55 per cent of total trade between the two countries. But this situation is not unique to China: India runs a trade deficit with 16 of its top 25 trade partners, and in some cases, the deficit as a proportion of total trade is as high as 90 per cent.[32] Nevertheless, the deficit with China catches the headlines and has alarmed some sections of Indian business. This has caused New Delhi to complain that Beijing unfairly blocks the entry of Indian goods and dumps cheap products in India, thus undermining Indian producers.[33] China has pointed out that it is India's weakness in manufacturing and more generally economically that is the problem.

As China and India have risen economically, their demand for various 'goods' has increased, including arms, international status, food, energy, clean environment, and water. Here we focus on the increasing demand for energy (specifically oil), clean environment, and water.

China and India's demand for oil is increasing with economic growth. It is oil, more than any other energy source, which could bring the two countries into conflict. From 1990 to 2013, China's primary energy consumption grew from 664.6 millions of tonnes of oil equivalent (MToe) to 2852.0 MToe, an increase of 429 per cent. Over the same period, India's primary energy consumption grew from 180.7 MToe to 595 MToe, an increase of 330 per cent.[34] In 2013, China consumed 10.76 million barrels of oil per day (12.1 per cent of global consumption) and India consumed 3.7 million barrels per day (4.2 per cent of global consumption). However, India's consumption grew at an average of 3 per cent in 2013 whereas China's reduced by 0.6 per cent.[35] China imported about 60 per cent of its oil needs in 2014.[36] Its imports could rise as high as

72 per cent of total consumption by 2040.[37] India imported about 73 per cent of its oil needs in 2013, and its dependence could rise to 87 per cent by 2040.[38]

Both countries import most of their oil from the Gulf and Middle East. If demand rises as it is projected to do and if they are unable to diversify supplies either from domestic or other international suppliers, they could come into conflict in this and other regions. There are already signs of competition if not conflict. During the mid-2000s, Chinese and Indian state-owned oil and gas companies competed to acquire overseas oil and gas fields. In the end, Indian state-owned companies were repeatedly outbid by Chinese state-owned oil and gas companies in Africa and Central Asia.[39]

In addition, as material consumption increases in both countries, they are polluting the air, water, and soil at home and perhaps abroad. The most serious problem in the long term is carbon emissions and global warming. The two countries are amongst the top three carbon emitters in the world.[40] By 2030, China's total emissions could rise to 10.6 billion tonnes, an increase of 34 per cent from current levels.[41] By 2031, India's total emissions will reach between 4.0 and 7.3 billion tonnes, roughly a tripling from 2009 levels.[42] China and India are also likely to be amongst the most affected by global warming: according to an assessment by Standard & Poor's, out of 116 countries, India ranks as the 16th most vulnerable country to climate change and China ranks 33rd.[43]

The effects of climate change will be global. As leading emitters, China and India will inevitably have to deal with each other on the issue. So far they have largely cooperated in the international negotiations on climate change, but this may change. Already, China has signed a separate deal with the US, thereby suggesting that Beijing and New Delhi may be on the brink of parting ways. China seems to be edging closer to committing to internationally verifiable limits on carbon, while India has steadfastly refused to do so.

The consequences of global warming could be devastating for all societies, even if the effects are differential. These include damage to crops, flooding and drought, rising sea levels along vulnerable coastlines, severe weather catastrophes, epidemics and increases in other public health problems, rising social and political conflict within societies, domestic and international out-migration, and massive economic disruption. It is easy enough to see that climate change could lead to bilateral tensions, particularly between neighbouring countries that cannot be insulated from developments across their borders. Already, some are arguing the case for 'coercive climate change' actions against those who refuse to reduce their carbon emissions.[44] In the case of China and India, both the direct and indirect consequences of carbon emissions and global warming could bring them into contention.

Water is another potential area of tension. In 1998, then Vice Premier Wen Jiabao asserted that the "survival of the Chinese nation" depended on dealing with the water crisis. And in 2007, Prime Minister Manmohan Singh made a forceful statement on dwindling water supplies in India.[45] The water statistics for China and India are daunting. Together the two countries consume 25 per cent of water withdrawals globally. By 2030, China's water demand is projected to grow by 200 billion cubic metres, representing a roughly 33 per cent increase. India's situation is worse. Its demand for water will grow by 798 billion cubic metres, a doubling over present consumption levels.[46] China and India both face the spectre of water shortages, though the availability is greater in China: per capita water availability for China is 2,138 cubic metres per person per year whereas it is only 1,719 cubic metres for India. By contrast, the United States can count on 10,231 cubic metres per capita, five to six times higher than the two Asian giants.[47] By 2050, it is estimated that China's per capita water availability will be less than 1,800 cubic metres and India's per capita water availability will have sunk to 1,140 cubic metres.[48] Between 1951 and 2050, India's per capita water availability will have reduced from 5,177 cubic metres to 1,140 cubic metres.[49]

Alarmists have suggested that China and India could go to war over water. In particular, worry is growing in India over China's hydrological plans. China is building a series of large dams on the Yarlung Tsangpo/Brahamputra River, and some Chinese experts have proposed the diversion of waters from the river as part of the great South-North diversions that Beijing has been planning for more than 60 years.[50] The Indian media and foreign commentators have claimed that the water flow to India could as a result be severely reduced. This has led to considerable resentment in China, which regards itself well within international law in utilising the Yarlung as it sees fit and which thinks that there has been a conscious attempt to misrepresent its motives and actions.

Opportunities for cooperation in economics, environment, energy and water

If there are grounds for thinking that China and India could be in contention over economics, environment, energy, and water even as they stabilise their border areas and military relationship, what is their record on cooperation in these areas?

The biggest bilateral economic problem confronting the Chinese and Indian governments is the trade deficit which, as noted earlier, is massively in China's favour and still growing. The Indian government has raised the issue with Beijing on several occasions, most recently at the summits of 2013, 2014, and 2015.[51] China has promised to help address the issue. In 2013, during his visit to India, Chinese Premier Li Keqiang said "We understand Indian concerns on trade imbalance. . . . The Chinese side is also willing to provide facilitation to more Indian products to access Chinese markets".[52] The two sides agreed to deepen their discussions on the deficit and set up three working groups to deal with it – the Services Trade Promotion Working Group, the Economic And Trade Planning Cooperation Group, and the Trade Statistical Analysis Group.[53] India has suggested that greater levels of Chinese investment could help offset the widening trade deficit. During Xi Jinping's visit to India in 2014, China pledged to invest up to $20 billion in India over the next five years. New Delhi in turn promised to open two industrial parks for Chinese investors.[54]

China and India are potential partners in various economic ventures relating to trade and investment. While China would like to sign a bilateral free trade agreement (FTA), India is reluctant to do so, fearing it may increase the deficit with China.[55] On the other hand, both countries are interested in reaching an accord on the Regional Comprehensive Economic Partnership (RCEP), which includes ASEAN and its six free trade partners (Australia, China, India, Japan, South Korea, and New Zealand). India has also indicated its interest in joining the Asia Pacific Economic Cooperation (APEC). President Xi invited India to attend the APEC meeting in China in November 2014, but India declined because it was invited as an observer member. Since then, the US has invited India to join the organisation, apparently as a full member.[56] APEC would bring China and India into yet another economic arrangement together.

China is also trying to interest India in its overland and maritime "One Belt, One Road" initiative that would connect Asia to Europe. The idea is still quite embryonic, but Beijing wants to encourage investment in infrastructure along the routes (including ports and railways), promote trade, provide Chinese technical assistance to local industry, and enhance cooperation on capital flows and currency use. New Delhi is undecided on its response to the initiative. It does not want to be left out of what could be a lucrative opportunity, nor does it want China by default to dominate the undertaking. It remains suspicious that Beijing's true intent is more political than economic.[57]

In addition, China and India have cooperated in BRICS, the grouping that brings Brazil, Russia, India, China, and South Africa together. At the Brazil summit in 2014, the grouping launched the New Development Bank. This was originally an Indian idea, but given Chinese currency reserves, China is the bank's linchpin. Prime Minister Narendra Modi finally agreed that China should contribute the largest amount to the Bank and that it should be headquartered in Shanghai. In return, China accepted that the first head of the Bank will be Indian.[58] The latest instance of economic cooperation is working together in the Asian Infrastructure Investment Bank (AIIB), which will have a capital fund of $100 billion. China invited India to join the bank in June 2014, and India became a founding member in April 2015. By April 2015, the AIIB had 57 members, including 37 from Asia. At least one reason India may have joined is to get funding for its coal projects, which the US-led World Bank has refused to fund on environmental grounds.[59]

Beijing and New Delhi have a decent record on climate change, where they have consulted fairly extensively, particularly in international climate change negotiations. Broadly speaking, their positions are the same – namely, that they support the original Kyoto Protocol agreement of "common but differentiated responsibility". Thus, they accept that all states must take on responsibilities to curb global warming but believe that those who have been the primary cause of carbon emissions and temperature rise should assume the leading role in mitigation.[60] Until now, they have both refused to commit to carbon emission limits and to international verification of any commitments they might make. Although Beijing and Washington announced a deal in 2014 that commits China to peaking its emissions by 2030, the deal does not limit Chinese emissions in the interim. India for its part refuses to countenance any emissions limits, on the plea of development imperatives.[61] China and India also agree that "the polluter must pay" and that the advanced countries have an obligation to transfer technologies as well as finance the adoption of technologies that will limit carbon dependency in poorer countries.[62]

China–India cooperation on energy is not quite so encouraging.[63] In 2006, the state-owned oil companies signed a Memorandum of Understanding to jointly acquire overseas assets.[64] Chinese and Indian companies successfully bid for oil fields in Syria and Colombia, and they have joint stakes in Sudan. These three are, however, the only examples of (moderately) successful cooperation. Chinese companies being far more adept at global oil and gas acquisitions than their Indian counterparts, and the utility of such acquisitions for their energy security being questionable (because the oil is mostly sold on the international market), the record of joint bidding and acquisitions so far has been a poor one.

Finally, sharing the waters of the Yarlung Tsangpo/Brahmaputra River may be one of the most challenging and fractious problems ahead of China and India. Recognising this, the two countries began negotiations on water issues in June 2001, after extensive flooding in Arunachal Pradesh along the Brahmaputra River and in Himachal Pradesh along the Sutlej River.[65] However, it was not until January 2002 that China and India signed a river water agreement dealing with the Brahmaputra flow. An MOU between the two ministries of water resources, signed on January 14, 2002, committed China to share hydrological information on flood season flows.[66] Thereafter, China and India have signed numerous agreements on principles governing hydrological issues and on actual data-sharing (from China to India). This is as far as things have progressed. In the meantime, New Delhi has accepted that China's big dams are run-of-the-river structures and will not affect downstream water flows. Beijing has strenuously denied that it is seeking to divert the Yarlung. New Delhi has not contradicted Beijing in this matter either. Partly in response to public pressure in India, however, it continues to raise river issues with China.

In sum, the two governments have recognised the need to deal with emerging areas of contestation in economics, environment, energy, and water and to explore the possibility of cooperation. A degree of cooperation is already established. There is recognition in Beijing and New Delhi that more can and should be done. It is from this perspective that the present volume makes its intervention.

Conclusion: poised for cooperation?

How China and India deal with each other in the decades ahead will affect the welfare and security of nearly three billion people. Since the welfare and security of these nearly three billion souls is intimately tied to the prospects of prosperity and stability in the rest of Asia and indeed the world beyond Asia, the China–India relationship is a pivotal one. China and India unwisely fought a war in 1962 and have regarded each other with suspicion since then. At the same time, with perseverance and good sense they have built a structure of cooperation to deal with security issues and establish a peace that has endured for over five decades. Economic change in both countries and the linking of their production and finance to the global economy, ironically, has given rise to newer areas of contention and suspicion that could destabilise the long peace. To their credit, the leaderships in both countries have recognised the possibility of conflict in these newer areas and the need therefore to cooperate, and have begun a modest record of cooperation in economics, environment, energy, and water. Can they cooperate beyond the rather sluggish present effort? The chapters that follow this introduction attempt to answer that question.

Acknowledgements

We wish to record our thanks to Varigonda Kesava Chandra and Libby Morgan Beri for their valuable inputs in this chapter.

Notes

1 See for instance John W. Garver, *Protracted Contest: Sino-Indian Rivalry in the Twentieth Century*, Seattle: University of Washington Press, 2001, and Mohan Malik, *China and India: Great Power Rivals*, New Delhi: Viva Books, 2012.
2 On the Nathu La and Sumdurong Chu crises, see Ranjit Singh Kalha, *India-China Boundary Issues: Quest for Settlement,* New Delhi: Indian Council of World Affairs, 2014, pp. 182 and 199–205, respectively.
3 On these issues, see Mohan Guruswamy and Zorawar Daulat Singh, *India-China Relations: The Border Issue and Beyond*, New Delhi: Viva Books and Observer Research Foundation, 2009, pp. 118–123. For a categorical Chinese statement on the McMahon Line, see Rong Ying, "Remembering a War: The 1962 India-China War", *rediff.com*, 20 December 2002, http://www.rediff.com/news/2002/dec/20chin.htm: "The Chinese government did not recognise the [McMahon] line yesterday; it does not recognise the line today, nor will it recognise the line tomorrow".
4 On the 1960 and 1980 swap offer, see Guruswamy and Singh, *India-China Relations*, p. 71 and p. 94, respectively.
5 Nehru's statement is quoted in B.G. Verghese, "The Truth of 1962: The War We Lost", *Tehelka Magazine,* 13 October 2012, http://archive.tehelka.com/story_main54.asp?filename=Ne131012Coverstory.asp. According to Srinath Raghavan,, the actual phrase was "[a] barren uninhabited region without a vestige of grass". See Srinath Raghavan, *War and Peace in Modern India: A Strategic History of the Nehru Years*, New Delhi: Permanent Black, 2010, p. 253. New Delhi remains interested in the swap. See Saurabh Shukla, "India 'Ready to Let China Keep Aksai Chin' if Neighbour Country Drops Claim to Arunachal Pradesh", *Mail Online India*, 28 November 2013, http://www.dailymail.co.uk/indiahome/indianews/article-2515187/India-ready-let-China-Aksai-Chin-neighbour-country-drops-claim-Arunachal-Pradesh.html.
6 On China–US cooperation, see Andrew Small, *The China–Pakistan Axis: Asia's New Geopolitics,* Oxford: Oxford University Press, 2015, pp. 34–39.
7 It is estimated that China had 232 nuclear warheads in 1990. See Robert S. Norris and Hans M. Kristensen, "Global Nuclear Weapons Inventories, 1945–2010", *Bulletin of the Atomic Scientists*, July/August 2010, p. 82.
8 Nuclear Weapon Archive, "India's Nuclear Weapons Program Present Capabilities", Nuclearweaponarchive.com, 5 April 2001, http://nuclearweaponarchive.org/India/IndiaArsenal.html.

9 The military balance between China and India is reinforced by geography. Any thought of war between China and India is complicated by the massive constraints that the Himalaya and the Tibetan Plateau pose on extended hostilities. The modernisation of equipment notwithstanding, any large-scale conflict seems improbable given the difficulties of terrain and elevation.
10 Rui Pan, "China in the WTO: A Chinese Perspective", in Ka Zeng and Wei Liang, eds., *China and the Global Trade Governance: China's First Decade in the World Trade Organization*, Oxford: Routledge, 2013, p. 26; Jamil Anderlini and Lucy Hornby, "China 'Overtakes' US as World's Largest Goods Trader", *BBC*, 10 January 2014, http://www.bbc.com/news/business-25678415. Foreign Direct Investment (FDI) measured from 1982 to 2013. See The World Bank, *World DataBank*, http://databank.worldbank.org/.
11 The World Bank, *World DataBank*, http://databank.worldbank.org/.
12 United Nations, *UN Comtrade Database*, http://comtrade.un.org/data/; The World Bank, *World DataBank*, http://databank.worldbank.org/.
13 See R. S. Kalha, *Xi's Visit and the Boundary Issues*, IDSA Comment, Institute for Defence Studies and Analyses, New Delhi, 24 September 2014, http://idsa.in/idsacomments/XIsvisitandtheboundaryissues_rskalha_240914.html. See also Kalha, *India-China Boundary Issues*, p. 206.
14 Guruswamy and Singh, *India-China Relations*, pp. 98–99.
15 According to Srikanth Kondapalli, "[The] Chinese response to the visits of Pakistan's Foreign Minister Sartaz Aziz and Prime Minister Nawaz Sharif to Beijing on June 11 and 29 respectively, in the midst of the Kargil conundrum, reportedly was cautious . . . China has told Pakistan to abide by the LoC and requested it to negotiate with India on the basis of the Simla Agreement . . . ". See Srikanth Kondapalli, "China's Response to the Kargil Incident," *Strategic Analysis* 23/6, 1999, pp. 1039–1044. "When General Musharraf visited China . . . the Chinese leadership made it clear to him that locking horns with India was no sane decision and ultimately Pakistan will have to call back its troops". See Mussarat J. Cheema, "International Community on Kargil Conflict", *South Asian Studies*, 28/1, 2013, pp. 85–96. See also Small, *The China–Pakistan Axis*, pp. 57–59.
16 For the text of the 2005 agreement, see Ministry of External Affairs, Government of India, "Agreement between the Government of the Republic of India and the Government of the People's Republic of China on the Political Parameters and Guiding Principles for the Settlement of the India-China Boundary Question", 11 April 2005, http://www.mea.gov.in/bilateral-documents.htm?dtl/6534/Agreement+between+the+Government+of+the+Republic+of+India+and+the+Government+of+the+Peoples+Republic+of+China+on+the+Political+Parameters+and+Guiding+Principles+for+the+Settlement+of+the+IndiaChina+Boundary+Question.
17 "China, India Held Military Talks", *CCTV.com English*, 25 February 2014, http://english.cntv.cn/program/newsupdate/20140225/101299.shtml. The report notes that maritime security talks were held but does not say that naval confidence-building measures were discussed.
18 On China's rank in India's trade, see "China Emerges as India's Top Trading Partner: Study", *The Times of India*, 2 March 2014, http://timesofindia.indiatimes.com/business/india-business/China-emerges-as-Indias-top-trading-partner-Study/articleshow/31268526.cms. On India's rank in China's trade, see Embassy of India, Beijing, "India-China Bilateral Relations", http://www.indianembassy.org.cn/DynamicContent.aspx?MenuId=3&SubMenuId=0.

19 During his official visit to India, President Xi Jinping cited growing bilateral trade as evidence of closer relations between China and India, stating, "Relations between China and India have made significant progress in the new century... China has become India's largest trading partner, with their bilateral trade volume increasing from less than US$ 3 billion early this century to nearly US$ 70 billion". At the same time, he also stated that "Progress has been made in the negotiations on the boundary question, and the two sides have worked together to maintain peace and tranquility in the border area". See Xi Jinping, "Towards an Asian Century of Prosperity", *The Hindu*, 17 September 2014, http://www.thehindu.com/opinion/op-ed/towards-an-asian-century-of-prosperity/article6416553.ece.

20 On how both sides see road building along the border, see, for instance, Subir Bhaumik, "Why India is Planning a New Road Near the China Border", *BBC*, 16 October 2014, http://www.bbc.com/news/world-asia-india-29639950.

21 Some Indian sources allege more than 600 incursions by Chinese troops between 2010 and 2013. See Rajat Pandit, "600 Border Violations by China along LAC Since 2010", 23 April 2013, http://timesofindia.indiatimes.com/india/600-border-violations-by-China-along-LAC-since-2010/articleshow/19687928.cms.

22 On Antony's admission of Indian transgressions across the Line of Actual Control, see Guruswamy and Singh, *India-China Relations*, p. 117. On General V.K. Singh's admission, see Ritu Sharma and Avinash Paliwal, "Border Intrusions May Continue Till India-China Boundary Issue is Resolved", *Tehelka*, 10 January 2011, http://archive.tehelka.com/story_main48.asp?filename=Ws100111INTERNATIONAL.asp.

23 On the 2013 confrontation, see Gardiner Harris and Edward Wong, "Where China Meets India in a High-Altitude Desert, Push Comes to Shove", *New York Times*, 2 May 2013, http://www.nytimes.com/2013/05/03/world/asia/where-china-meets-india-push-comes-to-shove.html?_r=0. On the 2014 confrontation, see Rajat Pandit, "Ahead of Chinese president's visit, confrontations along border in Ladakh," *The Times of India*, 15 September 2014, http://timesofindia.indiatimes.com/india/Ahead-of-Chinese-presidents-visit-confrontations-along-border-in-Ladakh/articleshow/42554530.cms.

24 Sanjeev Miglani and Fayaz Bukhari, "Chinese and Indian Troops in Himalayan Standoff", *Reuters*, 23 September 2014, http://in.reuters.com/article/2014/09/23/india-china-idINKCN0HI10C20140923.

25 Between 1988 and 2006, all key joint statements contained reference to India's recognition of Tibet as part of China. Since 2008, however, India has been more circumspect and has refused to repeat the reference.

26 John Garver, *Protracted Contest: Sino-Indian Rivalry in the Twentieth Century*, Seattle: University of Washington Press, 2001, pp. 216–242. Also see Small, *The China–Pakistan Axis*, pp. 47–60 on China's changing attitude to the Kashmir dispute and to the India–Pakistan relationship.

27 Jason Dean and Jeremy Page, "Beijing Points to Pakistan after Ethnic Violence", *The Wall Street Journal*, 1 August 2011. Much of Andrew Small's book, *The China–Pakistan Axis*, is devoted to China's worry of extremism from Pakistan and Afghanistan, especially chapters 4–7 and the Epilogue.

28 In the security roundtables held at the Lee Kuan Yew School of Public Policy in 2014 and 2015, participants from both sides repeatedly referred to the ongoing discussion on Pakistan among Chinese and Indian officials. See also Indrani Bagchi, "PM Manmohan Singh to China's Wen Jiabao: Back off on South China Sea", *The Times of India*, 19 November 2011, http://timesofindia.indiatimes.com/india/PM-Manmohan-Singh-to-Chinas-Wen-Jiabao-Back-off-on-South-China-Sea/articleshow/10786454.cms.

29 Charu Sudan Kasturi, "Xi Trip to Pak Bothers Delhi", *The Telegraph*, 18 April 2015, http://www.telegraphindia.com/1150418/jsp/nation/story_15284.jsp#.VWvV0EaK5ME.
30 Embassy of India, Beijing, "Trade and Commercial Relations", http://www.indianembassy.org.cn/DynamicContent.aspx?MenuId=3&SubMenuId=0.
31 Ibid.
32 Amitendu Palit, "Paranoid about the Deficit", *Indian Express*, 23 September 2014 http://indianexpress.com/article/opinion/columns/paranoid-about-the-deficit/2/.
33 "Steel Ministry Bats for Higher Duty to Check China 'Dumping'", *Times of India*, See 2 April, 2015, http://timesofindia.indiatimes.com/india/Steel-ministry-bats-for-higher-duty-to-check-China-dumping/articleshow/46785628.cms; and Raja Murthy, "India, China Lead Global Anti-dumping Dance", *Asia Times Online*, 5 May 2009.
34 See BP, *BP Statistical Review of World Energy*, June 2014, http://www.bp.com/statisticalreview.
35 Eric Yep, "India Outpacing China's Oil Demand", *Wall Street Journal*, 1 September 2014, http://blogs.wsj.com/moneybeat/2014/09/01/india-outpacing-chinas-oil-demand/.
36 "China's Dependency on Foreign Oil Nears 60 pct in 2014: Report", *Xinhua*, 28 January 2015 http://news.xinhuanet.com/english/china/2015-01/28/c_133953934.htm.
37 "China's Oil Demand is Growing, US agency says", *ChinaDaily USA*, 6 June 2014, http://usa.chinadaily.com.cn/epaper/2014-02/06/content_17269251.htm.
38 "India's Oil Supply and Demand Gap Widening", *The Maritime Executive*, 1 July 2014, http://www.maritime-executive.com/article/Indias-Oil-Supply-and-Demand-Gap-Widening-2014-07-01.
39 "China and India's Growing Energy Rivalry", *Bloomberg Business*, 16 December 2010, http://www.businessweek.com/globalbiz/content/dec2010/gb20101215_795065.htm#p2.
40 In 2013, China was the number 1 emitter, followed by the US and India in that order. See Global Carbon Atlas, "Emissions", http://www.globalcarbonatlas.org/?q=en/emissions.
41 "China CO2 emissions to rise by one third before 2030 peak – study", *Reuters*, 14 November 2014, http://www.reuters.com/article/2014/11/14/china-carbon-idUSL3N0T41EY20141114. These figures are from a report written by Tsinghua University, Beijing.
42 See Press Information Bureau, Government of India, "India's Per Capita GHG Emissions in 2031 to be Well Below Global Average in 2005", 2 September 2009, http://pib.nic.in/newsite/erelease.aspx?relid=52329; and US Energy Information Administration (EIA), "International Energy Statistics", http://www.eia.gov/cfapps/ipdbproject/iedindex3.cfm?tid=90&pid=44&aid=8.
43 See "Climate Change Is a Global Mega-Trend For Sovereign Risk", *S&P Capital IQ, Global Credit Portal*, 15 May 2014, https://www.globalcreditportal.com/ratingsdirect/renderArticle.do?articleId=1318252&SctArtId=236925&from=CM&nsl_code=LIME&sourceObjectId=8606813&sourceRevId=1&fee_ind=N&exp_date=20240514-20:34:43.
44 Bruce Gilley and David Kinsella, "Coercing Climate Change", *Survival*, 57/ 2, April 2015, pp. 7–28.
45 For the two statements, see Nazia Hussain, "Water: The New Dimension in India-China Relations", Centre for Peace and Development Studies (CPDS), http://www.cdpsindia.org/pdf/Water%20war.pdf.
46 Eluvangal quotes a study by the International Water Management Institute (IWMI). See Sreejiraj Eluvangal, "India Will Have Water and Food Crises by 2030: Study", *DNA*, 18 April 2011, http://www.dnaindia.com/india/report-india-will-have-water-and-food-crises-by-2030-study-1533439.

47 The figures for China, India, and the US are taken from Peter H. Gleick, "China and Water", in Peter H. Gleick, Heather Corley, Michael J. Cohen, Mari Morikawa, Jason Morrison, and Meena Palaniappan, eds., *The World's Water 2008–2009: The Biennial Report on Freshwater Resources*, p. 84, http://www2.worldwater.org/data20082009/ch05.pdf.

48 On China, see Aquastat, Food and Agriculture Organisation of the United Nations (FAO) "China", http://www.fao.org/nr/water/aquastat/countries_regions/chn/index.stm. On India, see UNICEF, FAO, AND SaciWATERS, *Water in India: Situation and Prospects*, 2013, p. 4, http://coin.fao.org/coin-static/cms/media/15/13607355018130/water_in_india_report.pdf.

49 Narayan G. Hegde, "Water Scarcity and Security in India", 2012, p. 4, http://www.indiawaterportal.org/sites/indiawaterportal.org/files/Water_scarcity_security_India_NGHegde_BAIFDRF_2012.pdf. Hegde cites the Ministry of Water Resources, Government of India, from 2009, for these figures.

50 There is a growing literature on China–India river water issues, particularly the Yarlung/Brahmaputra. See Brahma Chellaney, *Water: Asia's New Battleground*, New Delhi: HarperCollins Publishers India, 2011, pp. 129–197.

51 On the Manmohan Singh-Li Keqiang interactions on the trade deficit, see "China, India Agree on Roadmap to Balance Trade Ties," *Business World*, 20 May 2013, http://www.businessworld.in/news/economy/india/china-india-agree-on-roadmap-to-balance-trade-ties/901668/page-1.html. On the Xi-Modi interactions, see "Border, Trade Deficit Figure in Modi-Xi Summit Talks", *Business Standard*, 14 May 2015, http://www.business-standard.com/article/news-ians/border-trade-deficit-figure-in-modi-xi-summit-talks-115051400927_1.html.

52 Will Davies, "Beijing Vows to Ease Imbalance With India", *Wall Street Journal*, 22 May 2013.

53 "China, India Agree on Roadmap to Balance Trade Ties".

54 Ministry of External Affairs, Government of India, "Joint Statement between the Republic of India and the People's Republic of China on Building a Closer Developmental Partnership", 19 September 2014, http://www.mea.gov.in/bilateral-documents.htm?dtl/24022/Joint+Statement+between+the+Republic+of+India+and+the+Peoples+Republic+of+China+on+Building+a+Closer+Developmental+Partnership.

55 On India's reluctance to sign an FTA, see Rupesh Janve and Rituparna Bhuyan, "Commerce Ministry Opposes China FTA", *Business Standard*, 9 February 2008, http://www.business-standard.com/article/economy-policy/commerce-ministry-opposes-china-fta-108020901016_1.html.

56 See Amitendu Palit, "India and APEC: Not Yet There, But Getting Closer", *PECC Discussion Forum*, 16 July 2014, http://www.pecc.org/blog/entry/india-and-apec-not-yet-there-but-getting-closer. On why India chose not to attend, see "India Should Join APEC to Avoid Isolation: China", *Zee News*, 17 November 2014, http://zeenews.india.com/business/news/international/india-should-join-apec-to-avoid-isolation-china_112072.html. On the US's softening towards India's APEC membership, see Alyssa Ayres, "Next Steps with India", *Forbes Asia*, 6 February 2015, http://www.forbes.com/sites/alyssaayres/2015/02/06/next-steps-with-india/.

57 See Shannon Tiezzi, "China's 'New Silk Road' Vision Revealed", *The Diplomat*, 9 May, 2014, http://thediplomat.com/2014/05/chinas-new-silk-road-vision-revealed/.

58 "New BRICS Bank to be Based in China, India to Have Presidency", *The Economic Times*, 16 July 2014, http://economictimes.indiatimes.com/articleshow/38442417.cms?utm_source=contentofinterest&utm_medium=text&utm_campaign=cppst.

59 Rupa Subramanya, "Is the Asian Infrastructure Investment Bank Good for India?", *Foreign Policy*, 15 April 2015, https://foreignpolicy.com/2015/04/15/is-the-asian-infrastructure-investment-bank-good-for-india-coal-china/.
60 Watts, "China and India Agree to Cooperate on Climate Change Policy".
61 On China's commitments after the deal with the US in 2014, see Lenore Taylor and Tania Branigan, "US and China Strike Deal on Carbon Cuts in Push for Global Climate Change Pact", *Guardian*, 12 November 2014, http://www.theguardian.com/environment/2014/nov/12/china-and-us-make-carbon-pledge. On India's continuing refusal to commit to carbon limits, see "India Can't Follow China's Emissions Pledge, Says Negotiator", *India Climate Dialogue*, 12 November 2014, http://indiaclimatedialogue.net/2014/11/12/india-cant-follow-chinas-emissions-pledge-says-negotiator/. On the other hand, India under Narendra Modi has stopped harping on "common but differentiated responsibility", the standard phrase used by New Delhi to put the onus for carbon cuts on the industrialized countries. See Dhanasree Jayaram, "India Subtly Shifts on Climate Change Agreements, but Power Gap Persists", *Global Times*, 5 February 2015, http://www.globaltimes.cn/content/906198.shtml.
62 China and India called on the advanced countries to honour their commitment to $100 billion in funding for developing countries to make the shift to cleaner technologies. See Press Information Bureau, Prime Minister's Office, Government of India, "Joint Statement on Climate Change between India and China during Prime Minister's visit to China". See also "China and India Call on Rich Countries to Step up Climate Change Efforts", *Guardian*, 15 May 2015, http://www.theguardian.com/environment/2015/may/15/china-and-india-call-on-rich-countries-to-step-up-climate-change-efforts.
63 See Jonathan Hoslag, *China and India: Prospects for Peace*, New York: Columbia University Press, 2010, pp. 99–102.
64 On China–India climate change cooperation, see Press Information Bureau, Prime Minister's Office, Government of India, "Joint Statement on Climate Change between India and China during Prime Minister's visit to China", 15 May 2015, http://pib.nic.in/newsite/PrintRelease.aspx?relid=121754. Their cooperation dates back to 2009 in the run-up to the Copenhagen summit on climate change. See Jonathan Watts, "China and India Agree to Cooperate on Climate Change Policy", *Guardian*, 22 October 2009, http://www.theguardian.com/environment/2009/oct/22/china-india-climate-change-cooperation.
65 Ministry of Water Resources, Government of India, *Annual Report 2001–2*, from http://wrmin.nic.in/forms/list.aspx?lid=462, p. 57.
66 Ibid., p. 50.

Part I
Economics

1 Convergence and divergence in development

An Indian perspective

Prem Shankar Jha

For more than two decades, China and India have been the fastest growing economies in the world. It is now taken for granted that by the middle of this century, at the latest, these will be the two largest economies in the world. This projection assumes that the growth will not only continue, but also that both countries will remain politically stable. Recent experience shows, however, that this stability cannot be taken for granted because both countries are experiencing deepening currents of social unrest.[1]

The root cause of the unrest is that, despite considerable efforts, neither country has been able to reconcile its rapid economic growth with social equity. In both China and India, social discontent has risen because of rising inequalities in income, an increasingly blatant corruption of the elite, and above all the growing insecurity in increasingly market-dominated economies. To understand why even unprecedentedly rapid growth has not delivered political stability, it is necessary to move beyond an analysis of economic performance and examine the interaction, in both countries, between economic growth and political power.

The key to understanding this paradox is that despite very different starting points, both China and India are in the early to middle stages of their transformation into capitalist economies. This is a period in which the income gap between the owners of property and the owners of labour widens rapidly, and the latter are particularly vulnerable to economic fluctuations because they enjoy no social security. In the economic literature of the past two decades, China and India are held up as cases of successful transition from command to market economies. A closer look at their respective trajectories of development shows that this conclusion is misleading. In China, there is virtually no correlation between the *progress* of reforms and the *acceleration* of growth. The country's GDP growth rate jumped to 11 per cent in 1981, within two years of the start of the reforms, when the dismantling of centralised planning and price controls had barely begun and Premier Zhu Rongji's privatisation drive was more than a decade away.

Clearly, some other force had been unleashed. This, it turned out, was the granting of freedom to invest to the lower rungs of the state. In 1978, at the start of China's transformation, there were 83,700 state-owned industrial enterprises in the country, employing 31.39 million workers. By 1996, the number had grown to 113,800 industrial SOEs employing 42.77 million workers. This rate of expansion was dwarfed by the growth in the number of enterprises run by local administrations. The number of these 'non-state' enterprises, or collectives, grew from 244,700 in 1978 to 7.87 million in 1996.[2]

India's development reflects the opposite trend. In 1947, it had a well-integrated national market, a well-developed financial system, a robust private sector, and a sizable industrial base. The First Census of Manufactures, held in 1946, identified 29 sectors in which industrialisation had taken place.[3] These included cotton and jute textiles, steel, sugar, vegetable oils, tea, coal, paper and paper pulp, tobacco and matches, and general engineering that produced consumer goods for mass consumption such as bicycles and lamp bulbs. Best of all, these industries had been built by private enterprise, entirely without the benefit of tariff protection, and were therefore highly efficient. Yet in spite of all these advantages, between 1951 and 1981 India recorded one of the slowest growth rates of the world.

Economists have blamed India's failure to seize its initial advantages on the adoption of a rigid and inefficient model of centrally planned industrialisation. A closer examination shows that while the public sector was indeed inefficient, it made up far too small a proportion of the economy to be held responsible for this abysmal performance.[4] Therefore, one needs to look for another cause for India's economic stagnation. That cause was the deliberate adoption of polices that were supposedly pro-poor but whose effect was to strangle growth in the private sector for three decades, from the mid-1950s till the mid-1980s.

This chapter sketches the larger context within which China and India charted their economic development giving rise to high rates of growth in the 1980s and beyond. These high rates of growth were achieved on the back of various economic, political, and social reforms but also by the use of higher levels of natural resources, especially energy. In turn, economic growth spurred a higher demand for energy resources and water. As China and India grew economically and used more resources, they fouled the atmosphere with carbon emissions and polluted the soil and water. Today, their patterns of development and the consequences of this development confront China and India with some difficult choices, internally as well as externally. If the two countries carry on using resources at the current rate, they could well come into conflict. On the other hand, they could search for ways to cooperate in resource use and in dealing with air, soil, and water pollution. The view of this chapter is that patterns of national development will bear upon the chances of both conflict and cooperation.

The chapter is broadly divided into five sections. The first two sections look at the role of the state in driving or impeding economic development in China and India during the initial years. The third section examines the reforms and economic changes that led to a spurt in growth. The fourth analyses the challenges the countries faced in recent years in maintaining growth, particularly with the financial crisis of 2008 and the subsequent global recession. The fifth section attempts briefly to answer the question of whether or not the two countries can learn from each other and how they might cooperate.

Class conflict in early capitalism: China's intermediate regime

Strange as it may seem at first sight, the completely opposite economic results in China and India spring from the same root cause – namely, in the early stages of capitalism the central line of conflict that defines the struggle for power lies not between capitalists and workers but rather between two emergent strata of the capitalists themselves.[5] In China, these are the party cadres that man the central government and its state-owned enterprises (SOEs) and those that man five tiers of 'local' government and enterprise. In India, the two strata are the bourgeoisie already in place at the time of independence, whose leaders were dubbed the 'Large Industrial Houses', and a new 'intermediate' stratum of small and medium bourgeoisie that came into being almost overnight in the late 1950s, when an acute foreign exchange crisis forced the government to put a complete ban upon the import of consumer goods imports. This created a vacant space in the market that the former importers of consumer goods and other small investors quickly moved into.

In China, the competition between the central and local cadres of the Communist Party erupted when the winding up of centralised planning and price controls between 1981 and 1984 devolved the power to plan and finance investment, collect taxes, take loans from the banks, and assign land for development projects, by default, to the provincial and local governments. This set off a race between provinces, prefectures, counties, and townships to outdo each other in finding new ways of meeting and exceeding various development targets.[6] Greater autonomy also increased local cadres' temptation to use their control of the supply of labour, land, and key raw materials to personally make money out of their deployment. The fusion of the two motives set off an investment spree in provincial and local government agencies that threatened to wrest control of economic resources – notably land, capital, and markets – from the central government. This in turn triggered an unacknowledged struggle for control between the central and local cadres that remains unresolved to this day. The local cadres initially took advantage of four instruments in their battle to control investment. These were their control over taxation, over bank credit, over land, and, as growth slowed down in the mid-1990s, over access to provincial markets. The central government responded with legislative changes, made in the name of reform, which wrested economic control back from the provinces.[7]

The most important of these were the taxation reform of 1994 and the banking reform of 1998. The former was triggered by the central government's loss of control over its tax revenues, and the latter by its loss of control over lending by the local branches of the giant state-owned banks. Between 1978 and 1993, the buoyancy of central tax revenues fell from 0.78 to 0.53 and the central government's share of tax revenues from 35 per cent to 11 per cent.[8] As a result, by 1993 the central government was running an ever-increasing budget deficit. The main purpose of the 1994 tax reforms was therefore to restore the fiscal dominance of the centre. It did so by reducing the provinces' share of total tax revenues from 78 per cent in 1993 to 44.3 per cent in 1994 and raised those of the centre from

22 to 55.7 per cent.[9] The result was that the provinces were plunged into a fiscal deficit that was aggravated by the centre's directive that henceforth local governments would be responsible not for just five but nine years of education.

The central government tried to compensate by devolving a share of its revenues upon the provinces. This only partially ameliorated the local governments' fiscal crisis because it replaced a bottom-up distribution of tax revenues with a top-down one that allowed each tier of government to retain whatever it felt it needed before passing on the balance to the next lower tier. To fill the gap in their revenues, township and village authorities imposed scores of ad hoc taxes, fees, and fines upon the rural population, and floated rural credit funds and credit societies that offered very high rates of interest to mobilise the savings of the peasants.[10]

The timing of these initiatives could not have been more unfortunate, for it coincided with the beginning of China's first prolonged slowdown in growth.[11] As demand shrank, township administrations that had invested hugely in new enterprises during the post-Tiananmen boom years found their profits turning into losses. Since they lacked the power to declare bankruptcy and lay off their workers, they did the next best thing: they simply handed over the plants to the workers and asked them to run them as best as they could. A study of 670 township and village enterprises located in 15 randomly selected counties in Zhejiang and Jiangsu provinces showed that while only 8 per cent of these were privatised in the above manner in 1993, 30 per cent were privatised during the two worst recession years, 1997 and 1998.[12] It was not, therefore, entirely by design that Premier Zhu Rongji launched a privatisation drive in 1997. On the contrary, like the introduction of the Household Responsibility System in agriculture in 1979, privatisation was born in the provinces out of sheer necessity and was only retroactively given the status of a national policy by the central government.

A large proportion of the collectives that were privatised during these years did not survive. Between 1993 and 2002, the number of collective enterprises declined from 5,156,000 to 1,885,000, but the total number of private enterprises rose from 237,000 to 2,435,300.[13] Thus, at the very least, 1.1 million collectives that had been privatised did not survive the recession and simply disappeared.[14] Since some of the rise in the number of private ventures must have been accounted for by fresh start-ups, the true number of privatised collectives that failed must have been substantially higher than this number.

At the township and village levels, in particular, the failure of these enterprises also meant that the funds the local administration had borrowed from the rural credit funds and societies could not be paid back. Thus, millions of peasants and small local entrepreneurs lost their savings. For a little while the local administration tried to meet its payments by running a Ponzi scheme – using fresh borrowing to service existing debt – but by 1998 not only were the state-owned banks saddled with large amounts of unrecoverable loans but the country was also in the grip of a full-blooded rural banking crisis as well.

This crisis was largely responsible for the banking reforms of 1998, which banned the setting up of rural credit societies and merged the rural credit funds into the state banking system. The combined effect of the tax and banking reforms was to further deepen the fiscal crisis of the local governments and increase their predatory extractions from the poor.

The brunt of the recession was not borne by local government officials, who were salary earners, but rather by peasants and small entrepreneurs in the villages and townships and by the workers who lost their jobs. They had the right to work on the land and were entitled to food rations. However, the supply of both land and food was limited, so their loss of industrial employment was reflected in deepening poverty for the entire family. Their poverty was not shared by the cadres who sanctioned the setting up of the plants, for these were salary earners who had run no entrepreneurial risk. Most of them had also received their share of the kickbacks that went with the setting up of other enterprises. Thus, the burden of recession, which fell almost entirely upon the shoulders of the displaced workers and their families, was worsened by a simmering resentment of the corruption of the party cadres. The convergence of impoverishment and growing predatory extraction by cadre elites drove a deep wedge between the Chinese Communist Party and the peasants.[15]

Class conflict in early capitalism: India's intermediate regime

In contrast to China, India's new aspirants to economic power came from outside the political power structure. They were insecure small capitalists who were investing their own money or money borrowed at prohibitive rates of interest and therefore faced a high level of entrepreneurial risk. This risk had been low immediately after the ban was imposed on consumer goods imports. A decade later, though, the space in the domestic market created by the ban had been filled and the market itself was growing more slowly because of a sharp slowdown in annual growth from 4.1 per cent (between 1951 and 1965) to 3.2 per cent (between 1965 and 1981).[16] The large business houses had therefore begun to squeeze the small manufacturers.

To survive, the latter had to persuade the government to put up hurdles to the unrestricted expansion of 'big business'. However, they needed to acquire political influence first. The struggle between them and the large industrial houses therefore morphed into a struggle for political power. That struggle may well have ended the way Marx and Engels had foreseen, but for a fortuitous development which came to the small manufacturers' aid in the 1960s. Between 1967 and 1970, the government of Indira Gandhi first restricted and then banned corporations from donating money to political parties. At the same time, it did not replace private funding with a state financing system. This decision created a gap in party finances that the intermediate stratum was able to step into with relative ease. It used its newly acquired influence within the ruling party to get a succession of laws passed that restricted the right of the Large Industrial Houses (LIHs), and of big business in general, to invest in consumer goods industries, and limited the annual growth of established manufacturers to five per cent a year.[17] As a result, the annual growth rate fell even further over the next decade, from an average of 3.43 per cent between 1957 and 1966 to an average of 3.15 per cent between the next eight years.[18]

These laws blocked investment by the LIHs in consumer goods industries except in niche markets (such as tourism, hotels, and shipping lines) that were utterly unconnected to their main areas of competence. Yet the protagonists of the intermediate class were still not satisfied. A fourth enactment, the Foreign Exchange Regulation Act, put an end to foreign direct investment. The cumulative impact of these enactments was to turn India into a stagnant island of obsolete industry at the precise moment when foreign private investment and invaluable technology and managerial expertise were flooding into East and Southeast Asia.[19] This 'achievement', by a government that never missed a day without reaffirming its commitment to the poor, would have been comic had its consequences not been so tragic.

It was only in 1974, when the Indian economy plunged into another foreign exchange crisis by the combined effect of a poor harvest (1972–73) and a fourfold rise in oil prices (December 1973), that New Delhi began to relax the restrictions on large private industry that were choking economic growth. During the next 17 years, successive governments incrementally relaxed import controls, devalued the rupee, eased the strictures of industrial licensing by defining commodity groups more broadly, and raised the floor level of investment for the definition of a monopoly, culminating in the more ambitious reforms of 1991 under Narasimha Rao.[20]

These measures were designed not to end but rather to defend the intermediate regime. The small and medium sized enterprises that were its backbone were essentially parasitic. The permanent economic shortages they thrived on were slowly choking the economy. The government therefore relaxed controls, but only to let the economy breathe more freely and revive. It lifted import bans but replaced them with high protective tariffs; devalued the rupee but did not free the exchange rate; eased but did not lift import licensing; raised the investment ceiling for small-scale industries and the floor for defining monopolies but did not repeal either the reservation of consumer goods for small-scale industries or the Monopolies and Restrictive Trade Practices Act.[21]

In the end, India's intermediate regime consumed itself. The cumulative relaxations of the late 1970s and 1980s lifted the growth rate to 5.9 per cent between 1985–86 and 1990–91,[22] but the overvalued rupee, made possible by very high tariffs, severely hampered the growth of exports and prevented these from keeping pace with the rise in imports. As a result, the balance of payments deficit widened. Indian policymakers saw the writing on the wall but did not have the courage to dismantle the command economy.[23] Instead, from 1987 they increasingly resorted to short-term borrowing to cover their balance of payments deficit.

It took a fifth and final foreign exchange crisis in 1990–91, triggered by Iraq's invasion of Kuwait, to finally pry the government loose from the coattails of the intermediate regime. The change did not come a moment too soon. An entire generation of protected profit margins had created a cash-rich, medium-scale, entrepreneurial class that had begun to chafe at the restrictions that the laws, which had been designed to protect its earlier growth, now placed upon its further expansion. In 1991, the convergence of these two pressures tilted the balance against another dose of incremental reforms, in favour of sweeping change.

Capitalism's inexorable logic: similarities of the post-reform period

As China had done in the 1980s, India too adopted a process of gradual reform that it was unable to complete. Both countries more or less succeeded in freeing their product markets from government controls, but were only partially successful in freeing their factor markets. In India, most consumer goods industries outside the telecom and IT sectors remained reserved for small-scale industries until well after the turn of the century. A succession of governments also did virtually nothing to make hiring and firing labour, or employing it seasonally, any easier than it used to be. Despite this, by 2003 India had swept all but a few vestiges of the command economy out of industry, mining, infrastructure, foreign trade, and finance. The spurt in growth that followed economic liberalisation was electrifying. India's growth rate recovered from a little over one per cent in 1991–92 to an average of 7.2 per cent between 1992–93 and 1996–97 and then, after a recessionary hiatus of five years, to 8.5 per cent from 2002–3 until 2010–11.[24]

The qualitative change that competition was making to Indian industry and finance was equally impressive. India's steel plants re-emerged as among the most efficient in the world. Its construction industry began to compete in speed and quality of work with the best in the world. The nationalised Indian banks shed a third of their staff and computerised their operations to the point where they were able to offer banking services comparable to those offered by foreign banks at a fraction of their cost; the Bombay and National Stock Exchanges were fully computerised and brought under stringent regulation by a newly constituted Security and Exchange Board of India (SEBI).[25]

Mobile telephony spread by leaps and bounds, and by 2012 more than 80 per cent of the Indian population was connected by telephone.[26] A large middle class sprang up almost overnight. While estimates of its size depend upon the yardsticks chosen, one indication is that according to the 2011 census of India, more than 25 per cent of households in the country – 62 out of 247 million – relied upon private, motorised vehicles – cars and two-wheelers – for transport.[27]

In both countries the burst of growth reached its peak in the first half of 2008. China's magnificent handling of the Beijing Olympics made the world acknowledge that a new superpower had arisen in the east. Its economy had not only recovered from the recession of 1996–2001 but was also in its fifth year of double-digit growth. Its exports had trebled in the previous four years, and its foreign exchange reserves were in excess of US$ 2 trillion.[28] In March 2008, India completed its fifth year of eight per cent average growth. Its GDP had risen by two-thirds in the previous five years, and its external account was almost perfectly balanced, with an average current account deficit of a mere 0.3 per cent of GDP. Its foreign exchange reserves exceeded US$ 312 billion,[29] and about half of these were non-debt reserves.[30] Its exchange rate reflected this strength and had appreciated by more than five per cent in the previous five years. Best of all, the rate of growth of employment in the non-agricultural sector healthily exceeded the rate of growth of job seekers.[31] The future looked bright.

Maintaining high growth in difficult times

Underneath the surface, however, cracks had begun to develop in both economies. In China, the provincial administrations had again run away with investment. During the first half of 2003, investment under the purview of local government increased 41.5 per cent, while central government projects actually decreased nearly 8 per cent.[32] By the end of the year, following an extremely rapid increase in investment, especially in the housing sector, a bubble economy had begun to form. The central bank raised its deposit reserve ratio from six to seven per cent as early as June 2003 and raised it six more times between then and 2007 till it had nearly doubled.[33] It also resorted to informal controls on lending but all to no avail. Investment grew by 48 per cent in the first half of 2004 and was still growing at 37 per cent in 2007.[34]

As a result, when the global recession began, China once again found itself confronting the problem it had faced in 1996. After five years of hectic, uncoordinated investment by central, state, and local agencies, it was again saddled with excess capacity in virtually every industry. This had already begun to curb the country's growth. To make matters worse, while in 1996 its exports had been booming, by the middle of 2008 these had begun to falter. It therefore found itself faced with a simultaneous fall in both domestic and external demand.

China's response was to announce a two-year, four trillion yuan (US$ 586 billion) fiscal stimulus package that astonished the world.[35] Only nine per cent of the package was devoted to stimulating consumption directly.[36] Two thirds of the rest was slated for industrial modernisation and infrastructure projects, i.e. for investment. The actual stimulus administered turned out to be much larger, and a disproportionate share went into unwanted real estate, for investment once again ran amok. Within one month of Beijing's announcement of a small relaxation of investment controls on provincial governments, the National Reform and Development Commission was overwhelmed by 25 trillion yuan worth of investment proposals.[37] What is more, provincial authorities did not wait for the NRDC's approval. As a result, the increase in bank lending during the first quarter of 2009 over the increase that had taken place in the same quarter of 2008 – a fairly reliable measure of the increase in investment – amounted to 4.6 trillion yuan.[38]

Thus, despite its best intentions, by the end of 2010 China had ended its fiscal stimulus with an even greater excess capacity than it had had in 2008, without significantly ameliorating the condition of the country's peasantry and urban migrant labour. And this time there were no quick fixes left: in July 2012 Premier Wen Jiabao ruled out another fiscal stimulus, pointing out forcefully that there was already excess capacity in 21 industrial sectors.[39] This was the legacy that President Xi Jinping and Premier Li Keqiang inherited.

India, too, was already facing a slackening of demand and industrial growth when the world went into recession. Its cause was the opposite of China's. While China had invested too much, India had concentrated upon increasing the purchasing power of the poor to the virtual exclusion of investment. This had spooked the Reserve Bank of India (RBI), so that by July 2008 it had pushed up the average lending rate.[40]

When the global recession hit India, the RBI hurriedly halved interest rates, but with the next general election only eight months away, Manmohan Singh's government also announced a fiscal stimulus programme and spent US$ 100 billion on it by April 2010. The two moves together increased India's annual budget deficit from 2.5 per cent to an unsustainable 6 per cent of GDP.[41]

The contents of the two fiscal stimulus programmes were, however, the exact opposite of what each country needed. In 2009, China needed to stimulate domestic consumption to absorb the excess capacity it had created during the investment boom of the previous six years, but it did the opposite. India desperately needed to increase investment in order to remove severe infrastructure bottlenecks that were threatening future growth. However, of the US$ 100 billion fiscal stimulus, it allocated only US$ 2.5 billion to investment. The balance went into fiscal giveaways, such as a US$ 10.5 billion loan waiver to farmers and a 40 per cent increase in the salaries of its civil servants.[42] The resulting consumption boost raised the growth rate back to its pre-recession level of 8.6 per cent in 2009–10 and took it even higher, to 9.3 per cent, in 2010–11, but it also made the fiscal deficit unsustainable.[43] As a result, when inflation rose to 10 per cent once more in 2010, the RBI began to raise interest rates again.[44]

The RBI's misgivings about the fiscal stimulus were understandable. This time, it made a serious error. The inflation in 2010 had not been caused by an excess of demand, but by a sharp rise in world oil and commodity prices caused by China's investment spree and an indiscriminate export of rice and vegetables from India. The increase in interest rates had absolutely no effect on the rate of inflation, but industrial growth collapsed from 13.5 per cent between July 2009 and June 2011 to just less than 1 per cent between November 2011 and March 2014.[45] Worst of all, employment in the non-agricultural sector stagnated. In all, 35 million young people who might have had jobs if the economy had not been driven into stagflation in 2011 joined the ranks of the unemployed.[46]

In both countries, the sharp dip in economic growth, a drying up of new employment opportunities and, consequently, a sudden return of insecurity to the middle class and the poor have once again brought simmering discontent to the surface. In market economies, recession invariably exposes the difference in economic power between the strong and the weak, between those who own property and those who own only their labour. When, as is the case in China and India, the economic power of the propertied class is protected and reinforced by its control of political power, the predatory nature of the state is immediately exposed. The anger that is unleashed shakes the legitimacy of the political system.[47]

This is what global recession and misguided responses have triggered in both countries. In China, recession unleashed a fear of loss of legitimacy in the eyes of the people that had been mounting ever since a giant survey of popular opinion in 1999, involving 300,000 respondents, had shocked the party. The survey revealed the depths of disillusionment in the people with the moral decay of the party cadres.[48] The expulsion from power of Bo Xilai brought the internal struggles within the party into the open. The extent of the turmoil unleashed within the party was reflected in the tenor of the editorials that appeared in *Peoples' Daily*, *Xinhua* and various party organs in the month that followed Bo Xilai's downfall. These sternly exhorted party cadres to:

> [r]esolutely implement the party's disciples [disciplines?], follow the laws of the state, not forget one's origin when in prominent position, ... not abandon the role of public servants once in public post, not use power for personal gains, ... not overstep the bottom line of the law, discipline, and morality under any circumstance, and have a keen sense of living up to the people's trust, guarding against wrong doing, and holding oneself to higher standards ... remain incorruptible as an official, behave like a decent human being, and do things in a law-abiding manner.[49]

In India, a wave of anger suddenly erupted in October 2010 when it was found that government officials had been taking kickbacks systematically on the construction and other work entailed in hosting the 2010 Commonwealth Games. This was followed by a spate of similar disclosures, many from the government's own reports, which would have attracted relatively little attention had the loss of the government's legitimacy in the eyes of the people not been so acute.[50] The revelations led to the formation of a nationwide 'India against corruption' movement that eventually forced the government to create an ombudsman with the power to investigate allegations of corruption against not only civil servants but also hitherto immune members of parliament.[51]

Clearly, economic remedies alone will no longer suffice to restore legitimacy in either country. To remain politically stable, therefore, both governments will need to supplement economic remedies with political measures that empower the poor and restore accountability of the decision makers. In the latter pursuit, India enjoys a distinct advantage over China because its democratic system permits the people to express their displeasure and change the government every five years. They did so in no uncertain terms in the national election of May 2014, in which they not only threw out Manmohan Singh's Congress-led government, but also brought back the Bharatiya Janata Party with an absolute majority in parliament – the first that any national party has obtained since 1984.[52]

In China, this struggle has so far been confined to within the Communist Party. The need to purge the party of corrupt cadres and severely limit the arbitrary taxation and punitive fining power of local governments and cadres over peasants and migrant workers is widely recognised, and was signalled in no uncertain terms by President Hu Jintao's Socialist Harmonious Society programme and his drastic purge of corrupt elements in the party in 2006. However, as the sharp rise in mass protests that has followed, and the struggle within the party exposed by the expulsion, conviction, and imprisonment of Bo Xilai has shown, the task of purification is far from over.[53] As for devolving some measure of political power to people outside the party, there has not yet been any serious discussion on even the initial question of the political structure within which this can be done.

Can China and India help each other?

Both countries therefore face an uncertain future. The problems they must resolve are not only economic but also political. Can they learn from each other's experience? Better still, can they take advantage of the complementarity that is developing between their economies and the convergence of views on key international issues that has been visible in the last three summit meetings of BRICS? These questions are answered in greater depth and detail in the ensuing chapters of the book. Here I offer a few brief and tentative thoughts.

While each country has to resolve the incipient domestic class conflict it faces in its own way, closer cooperation on economic and international issues can ease the challenge both countries face. For India, the immediate effect of China's economic slowdown has been a drastic fall in its exports to China – notably of iron ore, other minerals, and chemicals. This has created a very considerable asymmetry in India's trade with China. In 2012–13, China's exports to India were nearly four times its imports, and the gap has not closed in 2013–14.[54] India has tried to limit the imbalance by levying a variety of anti-dumping duties and putting up other short-term trade barriers against China's exports. Indian policy has not gone down well in Beijing, which has pointed out that balancing bilateral trade is increasingly unrealistic in a globalised world market. A far better way to restore the balance would be for China to invest heavily in India's development plans. China has been doing this throughout Africa and Asia because its constant tendency to over-invest has left it very few profitable avenues of investment at home for the surpluses its companies are generating.

One possible use of these surpluses, suggested recently by Indian Prime Minister Narendra Modi to his Chinese counterpart Li Keqiang, is for China to invest in India's infrastructure, where decades of underinvestment have created a golden opportunity for investment in infrastructure and industrial modernisation. India is constrained by a shortage of domestic savings and an absence of investment banking institutions. It is also inhibited by the fear of triggering a foreign exchange crisis if it steps up infrastructure investment too rapidly.[55] The former Indian Prime Minister, Manmohan Singh, acknowledged this by setting an investment target of more than US$ 1 trillion for infrastructure during the 12th Five-Year Plan.

India is a far more alluring prospect for investment than Africa – where Chinese companies have been increasingly active in recent years – because it has a large middle class and a highly integrated market structure. However, to make Chinese investment possible, India needs to accept that Chinese investors need, for linguistic and disciplinary reasons, to import the bulk of their labour force from China. This requires a substantial change in India's labour laws that no government has had the temerity to propose so far.

Another area for cooperation is energy security. Today, despite having launched ambitious renewable energy programmes, both countries are scrambling to secure stakes in existing and newly discovered oil and gas reserves because they do not believe that renewables can ever supplant fossil fuels. Energy competition can become a potential source of conflict as the rate of discovery of new reserves falls. An even more immediate threat is posed by the gradually developing race to pre-empt, on the basis of first-user rights, as much of the waters of the Brahmaputra river as possible. As of 2014, the two countries plan to generate 97,000 MW of power from more than 40 large and medium sized hydroelectric projects located in the Brahmaputra river basin, the most seismically unstable part of the above-sea-level portion of the earth's crust.[56]

With a solar thermal power plant at Fuentes de Andalucía supplying 20 MW of power to the town 24 hours a day since 2011, and several similar but much larger plants coming on stream in the US in 2013 and 2014, solar thermal power can now do all that the mammoth hydro-projects planned for the Brahmaputra can do without disturbing the earth's balance. What is more, it can do so in less than 3 years, against the 12 to 15 years that even Chinese hydro-projects take, for that is the time solar thermal power plants take to set up.[57] China and India have already signed an agreement in which China has undertaken not to disturb the flow of water to India and Bangladesh. But a far better and more fruitful initiative would be to use the breakthroughs in storing solar power, embodied by the Andalucía and California plants, to eliminate the possibility of conflict altogether. Solar energy currently makes up less than one per cent of India's energy mix, but India is working to increase this and has set ambitious targets for solar energy investment.[58]

There are promising signs of cooperation with China in these areas. During President Xi Jinping's September 2014 visit to India, China pledged to invest US$ 20 billion in India over the next five years.[59] China also plans to invest extensively into India's energy sector, both in the manufacture of components and the construction of solar power plants.[60]

Conclusion

Economic development in China and India was, in the initial years, driven by competition between two emerging strands of capitalists: the established large industrial houses and the newly emergent small and medium enterprises in the case of India, and the party cadres of the central government and the provincial cadres in the case of China. In both countries, the state was central to the trajectory of the country's development. In India, for instance, a series of government-enacted laws essentially restricted both foreign investment into the country and investment by the country's private industrial houses. By the time the government began opening up in 1991, the national economy was in tatters. The sudden rise in economic growth seen in the post-liberalisation era is again being hampered by the importance given by the state to fiscal policies and its negligence of infrastructure development.

In the case of China, while the competition between the central and provincial strata of the state gave rise to rapid development, the economic recession of the 1990s impacted the ability of state enterprises to repay loans and the ability of banks to lend, thereby impeding further investment and economic growth. However, in recent years, over-investment in infrastructure capabilities has far exceeded consumption, giving rise to increasing debts and overcapacity.

There exist several prospects of mutually beneficial economic cooperation between the two countries. India urgently needs investment to increase its infrastructure capacity, whereas the prospect of over-investment due to a fiscal surplus remains a pressing issue in China. China could therefore utilise its fiscal surpluses to invest in India's infrastructure industry, be it in the power, renewable energy, or transport sectors.

Notes

1 In China, surveys of public opinion have shown that those born after 1980 feel markedly lower levels of trust in their leaders than those born before. See Zhengxu Wang, "Generational Shift and Its Impacts on Regime Legitimacy in China", Discussion Paper 64, *The University of Nottingham China Policy Institute*, June 2010. Quoted by Yu Liu and Chen Dingding, "Why China will Democratize", *The Washington Quarterly*, 35/1, 2012, p. 48.
2 Ibid., p. 81.
3 Jagdish N. Bhagwati and Padma Desai, *India – Planning for Industrialization: Industrialization and Trade Policies Since* 1951, New Delhi: Oxford University Press, 1970.
4 Even in the mid-1970s, after a spate of nationalisations of banks, coal mines, petroleum companies, and external trade, the public sector contributed less than 20 per cent to GDP. Agriculture, the bulk of industrial production including virtually all consumer goods, and all services industries except banking and external trade, remained entirely in private hands.
5 Karl Marx and Friedrich Engels did not develop a theory of class conflict in early capitalism, because they were convinced that this conflict would be dissolved by the relentless march of technology and constantly increasing scale of production. The possibility that this might not happen, and that the 'lower strata' of the bourgeoisie might achieve dominance and succeed in 'holding back the wheel of history' for a considerable length of time, was raised by the Polish economist Michal Kalecki in a short essay titled "Social and Economic Aspects of Intermediate regimes". See Michal Kalecki, *Selected Essays on the Economic Growth of the Socialist and the Mixed Economy*, Cambridge: Cambridge University Press, 1972, pp. 162–169. For a fuller description of the nature of class conflict in early capitalism, see Chapter 4 of Prem Shankar Jha, *Crouching Dragon, Hidden Tiger: Can China and India Dominate the West?* New York: Softskull Press, 2010. This was published in India as Prem Shankar Jha, *India and China: The Struggle between Soft and Hard Power*, New Delhi: Penguin/Viking Press, 2010.
6 For a detailed description of this tug of war, see Jha, *Crouching Dragon, Hidden Tiger*.
7 Ibid.

8 Roy Bahl, *Fiscal Policy in China: Taxation and Inter-Governmental Fiscal Relations*, San Francisco: The 1990 Institute, 1999.
9 Lynette H. Ong, "The Political Economy of Township Government Debt, Township Enterprises, and Rural Financial Institutions in China", *The China Quarterly*, 186, 2006, pp. 377–400.
10 See Jha, Crouching Dragon, Hidden Tiger.
11 Officially, the growth rate fell to an average of eight per cent in the period 1997–2000, but data on prices, employment and inputs, especially of energy, suggest a much steeper fall. See Jha, *Crouching Dragon, Hidden Tiger*.
12 Hongbin Li and Scott Rozelle, "Privatizing Rural China: Insider Privatization, Innovative Contracts and the Performance of Township Enterprises", *The China Quarterly*, 176, 2003, pp. 981–1005.
13 Joseph Fewsmith, "Continuing Pressures on Social Order", *China Leadership Monitor*, 10, 2004.
14 This would have been relatively easy in the non-state sector, where contract work was the rule, and there were no commitments of the state to its employees safeguarded by the constitution of the PRC.
15 One, but by no means the sole, indication of growing discontent was the rapid rise in incidents of mass protest, from 8,700 in 1993 to 87,000 in 2005. See Christian Gobel and Lynette Ong, *Social Unrest in China*, London: Europe China Research and Advice Network (ECRAN), 2012, p. 8.
16 Arvind Panagariya, *India: The Emerging Giant*, New York: Oxford University Press, 2008, p. 5.
17 Between 1970 and 1973, four new enactments tightened the government's stranglehold on private industry, until it almost ceased to grow. See Jha, *Crouching Dragon, Hidden Tiger*, pp. 151–175.
18 Jha, *Crouching Dragon, Hidden Tiger*, p. 180.
19 See Jha, *Crouching Dragon, Hidden Tiger*, pp. 175–180.
20 Jha, *Crouching Dragon, Hidden Tiger*, p. 183.
21 Panagariya, *India: The Emerging Giant*, pp. 67, 78–94.
22 Ibid.
23 This ambivalence was reflected in a long-term fiscal policy announced by Rajiv Gandhi's government in 1985. For further details of the policies of Rajiv Gandhi's government, see Panagariya, *India: The Emerging Giant*, pp. 83–84.
24 Averaged from data for individual years in the GOI *Economic Survey 2012–13*. See Jha, *Crouching Dragon, Hidden Tiger*, p.180.
25 Organisation for Economic Co-operation and Development (OECD), *OECD Economic Surveys: India*, OECD, 2007, pp. 146–152.
26 Nielsen, "The Mobile Consumer: A Global Snapshot", February 2013, p. 6, http://www.nielsen.com/content/dam/corporate/uk/en/documents/Mobile-Consumer-Report-2013.pdf.
27 See DevInfo, "CensusInfo India 2011", http://www.devinfo.org/indiacensus2011/libraries/aspx/home.aspx.
28 He Langsha and Liu Chang, "China Should Keep Sufficient Foreign Exchange Reserves", *People's Daily*, 9 October 2011, http://en.people.cn/90780/7612542.html.
29 Reserve Bank of India, "Appendix Table 20: India's Foreign Exchange Reserves", http://rbidocs.rbi.org.in/rdocs/AnnualReport/PDFs/20T_AN23082012.pdf.
30 The average external debt stock between 2003 and 2008 was US$ 156 billion. See Reserve Bank of India, "Annual Report: Macroeconomic and Financial Indicators", http://www.rbi.org.in/scripts/AnnualReportPublications.aspx?Id=1052.

31 The 66th round of the National Sample Survey estimated that 37.6 million jobs had been created between 2004 and 2009. See National Sample Survey Office, *Employment and Unemployment Survey: NSS 66th Round: July 2009- June 2010, Eighth Quinquennial Survey*, 18 March 2013.
32 Barry Naughton, "An Economic Bubble? Chinese Policy Adapts to Rapidly Changing Conditions", *China Leadership Monitor*, 9, 2004.
33 Guonan Ma, Yan Xiandong and Liu Xi, "China's evolving reserve requirements", *BIS Working Papers*, 360, November 2011, p. 2, http://www.bis.org/publ/work360.pdf.
34 Cary Huang and Jane Cai, "Central Bank Lifts Reserve Ratio to 10.5pc; PBOC Moves to Tighten Money Supply", *South China Morning Post*, 6 April 2007, http://www.scmp.com/article/587994/central-bank-lifts-reserve-ratio-105pc.
35 This was essentially a repeat of what Premier Zhu Rongji had done in 1996, on a scale ten times larger but over a much shorter period. However, the true extra spending envisaged was closer to 3 trillion yuan, because a quarter of the stimulus package had already been sanctioned to repair the damage caused by the Sichuan earthquake. The balance consisted of new investment. See Barry Naughton, "Understanding the Chinese Stimulus Package", *China Leadership Monitor*, 28, 2009.
36 Ibid.
37 Ibid.
38 Ibid.
39 See Barry Naughton, "The Political Consequences of Economic Challenges", *China Leadership Monitor*, 39, 2012.
40 Reserve Bank of India, 2009 and 2010 Annual Reports, https://www.rbi.org.in/scripts/AnnualReportPublications.aspx.
41 See Ministry of Finance, Government of India, *Economic Survey 2008–2009*, p. 21, http://indiabudget.nic.in/es2008-09/esmain.htm.
42 For details of spending, see Shankar Acharya, *India and the Global Crisis*, New Delhi: Academic Foundation, 2009.
43 Ministry of Finance, Government of India, *State of the Economy and Prospects*, p. 1, http://indiabudget.nic.in/es2012-13/echap-01.pdf.
44 Ibid.
45 Prem Shankar Jha, "An Economic Road Map for the Modi Sarkar", *Tehelka*, 28/11, 12 July 2014, http://www.tehelka.com/an-economic-roadmap-for-the-modi-sarkar/.
46 This estimate is obtained from the data in the National Sample Survey and the Ministry of Labor and Employment. See National Sample Survey Office, *Employment and Unemployment Survey: NSS 66th Round: July 2009-June 2010, Eighth Quinquennial Survey*, 18 March 2013; and Ministry of Labour and Employment, Government of India, *Quarterly Report on Changes in Employment in Selected Sectors (January, 2013 to March, 2013)*, Chandigarh: Labour Bureau, May 2013, http://labourbureau.nic.in/QES_JUNE13.pdf.
47 By another coincidence, this has happened in both countries in the same year, 2011. India saw the rise of the 'India Against Corruption' movement led by Anna Hazare. China saw the Communist Party convulsed by the Bo Xilai affair.
48 Joseph Fewsmith, "Social Issues Move to Center Stage", *China Leadership Monitor*, 3, 2002.
49 James Mulvenon, "The Bo Xilai Affair and the PLA", *China Leadership Monitor*, 38, 2012.
50 Two, in particular, proved especially damaging. These were the reports of the Comptroller and Auditor General (CAG) of India on the sale of mobile telephone

licenses for 2G spectrum in 2010 and the allocation of coal mining concessions to private bidders. Both moves were severely criticised by the CAG on the grounds of loss of government revenue because of undue favour having been shown in the award process. See Rohit Prasad, "The CAG and the 2G spectrum," *The Economic Times*, 29 November 2012, http://articles.economictimes.indiatimes.com/2012-11-29/news/35432953_1_cag-s-2g-uas-licences-mhz.

51 Parliament passed the bill on December 18, 2013. It took three fasts unto death by a veteran, highly respected Gandhian reformer, Anna Hazare, to force the bill through the two houses of parliament.

52 In a lower house of parliament of 544 members, the Congress' numbers fell from 206 in the May 2009 elections to 44 in 2014. Its vote share fell by 40 per cent, from just under 29 per cent in 2009 to 18 per cent in 2014. For details, see Election Commission of India, "General Election 2014", http://eci.nic.in/eci_main1/GE2014/ge.html. The BJP won 282 seats in 2014, against 117 in 2009.

53 Christian Gobel and Lynette Ong estimate that protests increased from 87,000 in 2005 to between 180,000 and 230,000 protests in 2010. See Christian Gobel and Lynette Ong, *Social Unrest In China*, London: Europe China Research and Advice Network (ECRAN), 2012, pp. 7–8.

54 "Indian, Chinese Firms Ink 15 MoUs," *Business Standard*, 23 September 2013, http://www.business-standard.com/article/news-ians/indian-chinese-firms-ink-15-mous-113092300751_1.html.

55 Federation of Indian Chambers of Commerce and Industry (FICCI) and Ernst & Young, *India Infrastructure Summit 2012*, 2012.

56 Prem Shankar Jha, "Why India and China should leave the Brahmaputra alone", In *Brahmaputra: Towards Unity*, thethirdpole.net, 2014, pp. 22–27, http://www.thethirdpole.net/wp-content/uploads/2014/02/Brahmaputra-Towards-Unity1.pdf.

57 Ibid.

58 "India's Modi Raises Solar Investment Target to $100 bln by 2022", *Reuters*, 2 January, 2015, http://www.reuters.com/article/2015/01/02/india-solar-idUSL3N0UG13H20150102.

59 "China to invest $20 Billion in India in the Next 5 Years, Much Less than Japan's Offer of $35 billion", *The Times of India*, 18 September 2014, http://timesofindia.indiatimes.com/india/China-to-invest-20-billion-in-India-in-next-5-years-much-less-than-Japans-offer-of-35-billion/articleshow/42814025.cms.

60 Anupama Airy and Arnab Mitra, "China, UK Cos to Invest Billions in Solar, Wind energy", *Hindustan Times*, 17 February 2015, http://www.hindustantimes.com/business-news/china-uk-cos-to-make-in-india-invest-billions-of-dollars-in-solar-energy-wind-energy/article1-1317526.aspx.

2 Towards greater financial cooperation
A Chinese perspective

Zhao Gancheng

In recent years, China–India relations have come to be seen in Beijing as one of the most important and complex bilateral relationships. That importance and complexity has many aspects. While some aspects exhibit quite negative features like distrust and suspicion, there are other aspects such as economic exchange and trade that are marked by positive trends.

In statistical terms, China is now India's biggest trading partner. Compared to the trade volume at the beginning of this century, bilateral trade has witnessed a huge rise beyond the expectation of most observers. When Chinese premier Zhu Rongji visited Delhi in January 2002, he depicted the two economies as complementary, and therefore he announced that the bilateral trading volume might eventually surpass the target of US$ 10 billion.[1] Eight years later, in 2010, Chinese premier Wen Jiabao declared in Delhi that bilateral trade was expected to reach US$ 100 billion by 2015.[2] The pace of development of trade between China and India is significant in understanding the complexities that surround the relationship between the two giants of Asia.

Trade is one of the areas in which the two nations have seen the benefits of cooperation. Trading linkages lead to other developments, because increasing trade requires other facets of the relationship to mature. Trade also produces more opportunities for both sides, such as mutual investment and financial collaboration, which would in turn help the two nations to expand their cooperation in the international arena. This chapter argues that, as rising powers, China and India share a lot in common. However, common ground, no matter how big, does not automatically ensure cooperative initiatives. Cooperation between China and India will require them to make use of existing dynamics that favour their interests and to avoid issues on which the two sides find it hard to stand on similar ground. Mutual investment and the restructuring of the global financial order may be precisely the areas where the two sides have to move both positively and cautiously.

The two rising powers: more cooperation necessary

The year 2008 was a dramatic turning point. The international financial crisis led to profound changes in the international environment. Crises occurred in most developed countries, greatly reducing their capacity to dominate global affairs.

And the developing countries, especially the rising powers represented by both China and India, tried to adapt to the new situation by working more closely together. The BRICS summit reflects the new status of the developing countries in the world system.

When the BRIC concept was first put forward by Jim O'Neill of Goldman Sachs, the nature of this new group was not very clear. They were emerging markets, or newly industrialising nations, or rising powers. Each of the labels seemed apt but was not predictive enough about how these countries would behave. It was not until the first BRIC summit, held in Yekaterinburg, Russia, in June 2009, that self-awareness of their new status in the international system was evident. By this time, they were identified as rising powers. Since then, the status of rising powers has been more or less confirmed in the international system. Their identities are different from that of the developed countries, even though they themselves are quite different from each other. Among the rising powers (now BRICS, with South Africa added in 2011), China and India are representative.

As rising powers, China and India have a lot in common, including being the most populous nations and being poised at the initial stages of an economic take-off. One of the interesting issues is their relative status in the international arena. China is one of the permanent members of the UN Security Council, and its economy is much larger than that of India, ranking as the second largest economy in the world in annual GDP terms, while India ranks tenth.[3] The argument that both China and India share similar status in the international system does not therefore look terribly persuasive.

The crucial issue is that, as countries of rapid growth, will China and India compete with each other or will they develop more cooperation in the years to come? Nobody really knows the answer because the two powers face many complex issues. There are analysts who hold quite pessimistic views on the future of China–India relations. For instance, China–India relations could be interpreted as a 'protracted contest'.[4] Mutual suspicion in bilateral ties has been one of the features of the relationship. This has led to the question: if the two sides do not trust each other, will it still be possible to build up cooperative linkages in crucial areas like global finance and international institutions?

On the other hand, there are positive views of bilateral ties. Some people on both sides believe that, despite the complexities, the two Asian powers will manage to develop a new type of relationship because they share much in common and they pursue similar kinds of goals in the international arena. Some are so optimistic that they describe China–India relations in the future as 'Chindia', a combination word used to signify the extent to which the countries might cooperate.[5] Judging from the current situation, there is little doubt that debates on what will happen in China–India relations will continue to be vigorous.

The difficulty in defining whether China and India become cooperators or competitors arises from some critical factors. One of them is the unresolved territorial dispute and the historical legacy of the war between the two countries more than 50 years ago. Another more general issue is how to judge the simultaneous rise of the two developing powers. That could be even more crucial for the two countries because they are rising in a system that was not created by them but in which they have to live until a new balance of power is created. During that complex process of adjustment, the status quo powers that created the system will do everything possible to prevent the system from changing in directions that might not benefit them, and the rising powers are likely to face various strategic choices.

Developing cooperation between themselves is just one of those choices, and in some cases it may not be the best option, because their rise, though simultaneous, will not be a symmetric one. The experience of both China and India has shown that imbalanced growth does not help build positive perceptions of each other.

Despite the difficulties of making accurate judgments about the nature of bilateral ties, there are areas showing clear signs of mutual benefit and common ground. One of them is trade. Bilateral trade started at a very low level, something like US $2 billion at the beginning of the century, and grew faster than most expected. For instance, when Chinese premier Zhu Rongji visited Delhi in January 2002, he made a seemingly optimistic estimate that, as the two economies were complementary, with China's strength in hardware and India's in software development, annual bilateral trade would reach US $10 billion.[6] Bilateral trade broke the targeted level much sooner than expected. It surpassed the goal of US$ 10 billion by 2004–5, and, after that, the pace of bilateral trade development was even faster.[7] When Chinese Premier Wen Jiabao visited Delhi in December 2010, he expected that the target of bilateral trade would be US$ 100 billion by the year 2015.[8] Given the sluggish global economic recovery, it is unlikely that this target will be reached, but the trading relationship between the two countries continues to be strong.[9]

In the bilateral relationship, in addition to trade, there are also other dimensions showing cooperative trends. With the increase in trade, mutual investment has become a new area that the business communities of both sides are trying to explore. China and India began investment in each other's economy after the normalisation process began in the late 1980s. During the 1990s, although the political relationship was already on track, trade and economic relations were not. It was not until 2003, when Indian Prime Minister Vajpayee paid a milestone visit to China in the wake of India's nuclear tests (which had caused a serious setback to bilateral ties) that bilateral economic exchanges increased significantly, and the business communities of both sides began to think about new prospects.

According to statistics released by the Indian Embassy in China, mutual investment started at a very low level. In 2007, Chinese investment in India only reached US$ 16 million, and Indian investment in China was US$ 34 million. The year 2008 saw a jump, with Chinese investment in India reaching US$ 49.1 million and Indian investment in China rising to US$ 257 million; by the end of 2011, the accumulated investment of China in India was US$ 575.7 million and India in China US$ 441.7 million.[10] From these figures, one may conclude that mutual investment between China and India has risen. If, however, we compare these figures with China and India's investments in the US and Japan, we can see that China–India investments have a long way to go.[11] There is much potential to be explored. However, the trend is already clear – mutual investment will be another area in which China and India will develop more cooperation in the future, despite existing difficulties.

As Zhang Xiaoqiang, Vice-Chairman of China's National Development and Reform Commission, observed at a Chinese investment forum held in Beijing in February 2013:

> Great progress has been achieved in trade in recent years. Yet the mutual investment is still low. Both sides have to objectively and rationally recognize, face and solve the challenges and difficulties in the investment in India by the Chinese companies. On one hand, enterprises of both sides should further intensify the exchanges, positively adapting to the market in the other country, making full use of their advantages, innovating cooperation modes and improving adaptabilities to changes. On the other hand, both the governments should intensify communications, coordination and promotion through relevant platforms such as the India-China Strategic Economic Dialogue (SED) mechanism so as to create a more open and more convenient investment environment.[12]

China–India collaboration in the international context

In the global arena, China and India are also uncertain about the question of whether they are cooperators or competitors. As rising powers, their role in the international system appears rather similar. However, as the international system evolves in a gradual way, there will be variables in the process. One of them is the changing perception of the status quo power that dominates the system, and another is the different rate of development of the rising powers that will determine their respective status in the system. As for China and India, since the two countries adopted similar kinds of reforms and began to pursue similar goals, it is natural enough to think of their common interests in the international system.

However, the rise of the two powers has not been symmetrical. In fact, when the two countries started down the track of reform, their status in the international system was already different. In terms of economic power, however, the difference was not very big. Both were listed in the category of low income countries, and both featured large populations and low per capita GDP. But after three decades, the situation is completely different. For instance, in terms of annual GDP, India's now is just a little over one-fourth that of China.[13] That disparity severely challenges the assumption of common ground in the international system. India may increasingly see China as a status quo power rather than a developing power that demands changes in the international system. In fact, in Indian academia, it is not rare to find that kind of argument.

It is precisely in this context that the two nations may have to explore new possibilities for cooperation in the international arena. Enhancing mutual investment and making a greater effort to restructure the global financial order are ways of improving China–India cooperation that would in turn reduce the existing disparity between the two countries. Through mutual investments, the two sides would make better use of the complementarities between their economies. Investments from the private sectors would play a particularly key role in this regard.

Working together in international financial institutions would certainly enhance their status in the global economy. Due to historical and political reasons, there was little progress in this area when they began their diplomatic normalisation in the 1990s. In retrospect, one may argue that the two sides may have focused too much on geopolitical and strategic issues, especially on attempts to solve the boundary disputes. Efforts in other fields were not as robust and extended. For example, the agreements reached in the 1990s were all on the boundary issue and relevant confidence-building-measures.[14] These were important, but the emphasis on the boundary meant that the two sides did not pay enough attention to trade, investment, and international cooperation, areas that could have improved bilateral ties in other ways. The shortcomings are now being realised when the two countries are on a track of fast growth.

Despite difficulties, China and India are continuing to rise in their own way, and their interactions with the international system are increasing rapidly as well. In the wake of the global financial crisis in 2008, the two rising powers managed to reduce the negative impacts of the crisis and to achieve relatively high growth. In the Chinese case, during the peak of the crisis, China became the second largest economy in the world in GDP terms in 2010.[15] Though India did not achieve similar progress, its situation in general was also much better than most developed countries. In that context, the so-called geopolitical competition between China and India has been replaced by the simultaneous rise of the developing powers. And the new mechanism of collaboration between them is not only about China and India but also Brazil, Russia and South Africa, namely, BRICS.

Since the first summit in Russia in 2009, the members of BRICS host the summit by rotation every year. The mechanism has become the most important framework for the five developing powers, and China–India relations have gone to a new level, even though frictions and differences still exist. As Chinese President Xi Jinping recently argued, "cooperation among the BRICS countries will help promote a more balanced global economy, improve global economic management and more democratic international relations".[16] As for China–India relations, the new Chinese leader listed five areas for cooperation:

- Keeping strategic communications.
- Promoting collaboration in infrastructure building and mutual investment.
- Enhancing cultural exchanges.
- Expanding cooperation and consultation in multilateral areas to defend legitimate interests of developing countries and handling global issues.
- Caring for each other's sensitivities to properly deal with existing problems and differences.[17]

From Xi Jinping's view of China–India relations, we can say that the focus is apparently on bilateral issues. However, the global areas where China and India may cooperate include multilateral consultation for the interests of developing countries, implying that China perceives its own status in the world as similar to that of India. That perception is important in evaluating Chinese intentions in the international system, and also the prospect of cooperation between China and other developing countries in the international arena including international financial institutions. This has been seen as one of the most important areas for the evolution of the international system in the wake of the 2008 financial crisis.

As members of the current international financial institutions, neither China nor India took a critical position until very recently, even though their economic capabilities witnessed a great increase. In fact, the financial system represented by the IMF and World Bank was by no means created for meeting the demands of developing countries, or for this matter, the demands of the world economy as a whole. The creation of the Bretton Woods institutions served the purpose of US-led industrialised economies after World War II, and the financial system in the post-war period was thus established. The system played a decisive role in stabilising the financial order and also to a certain extent in providing financial aid with its loans to some developing countries to help them with infrastructure construction and social advancement.

However, the work done by the IMF and World Bank did not have much relevance to either China or India until they decided to integrate their economies more deeply into the global system. That happened after they went down the track of reform and opened up to the outside world. Since then (in the Chinese case, the early 1980s, and in the Indian case, the early 1990s) both China and India have developed closer cooperation with the two institutions and played a larger role. Compared with the role of the developed nations in the institutions, both China and India did not have a high profile, nor did they have a decisive say over important issues, because the decision-making regime of the institutions determined the country's status, which was no longer commensurate with their increasing capabilities. This is one of the important areas where China and India could have consulted each other more, even though they have cooperated on issues such as the selection of the heads of these institutions as well as reform of voting regimes related to their special drawing rights (SDR) in the IMF and shares in the World Bank.[18] There is little doubt that China and India have to cooperate in this regard.

Attempts to restructure the financial order

China and India's continued economic growth and growing international stature, even in the midst of a slow global economic recovery, have highlighted the growing obsolescence of the current financial order, including its regimes, structures, rules, and operations. The financial storm indicates the shortcomings of the management system of global finance, including the lack of sufficient monitoring. As a result, the impacts of the crisis are spreading globally, not only destroying the banking system in developed countries but also affecting the financial situation in developing countries. Despite facing such challenges, however, the developing countries do not have much say in terms of improving the functioning of the global financial system given the current regime and norms of the governing institutions. Countries like China and India are big stakeholders, and if the global financial order collapsed, they would suffer enormously. By the same token, if they could take a more proactive part in revitalising institutions, in greater consultation with the developed countries that still dominate the institutions, there would be greater hope of promoting universal prosperity. As Kishore Mahbubani argues, a rising Asia should take on more responsibilities to promote the vitality of international organisations, financial institutions included.[19]

In terms of their current status in the IMF and World Bank, both China and India are likely to perceive reform of the two institutions – particularly in voting rights and decision-making processes – as necessary. In an effort to enhance their stature and ability to function within the organisation, China, India and other rising powers have raised the issue of enhancing their quota in the IMF as their continued economic growth has increased their relative positions. Quotas are denominated in special drawing rights:

> based broadly on the country's economic position relative to other members. The size of a country's quota takes into account its GDP, current account transactions, and official reserves. Quotas determine members' capital subscriptions to the Fund, voting power, and the amount of financial assistance available to them from the Fund.[20]

In October 2010, the G20 finance ministerial meeting decided to change the current quota distribution by increasing the quotas of China, India, Brazil, and other rising powers accordingly.[21] The reform has stalled due to the failure of the US Congress to approve the reform (which is required as the US holds the largest voting share and is the only member with veto power), but the developing powers are expected to continue their attempts to push forward this process.

Another reform is the way to select the heads of both the IMF and World Bank. Since their establishment, the president of the IMF has been a European and that of the World Bank an American. That reflects the reality of the dominance of the developed countries in the contemporary global financial order. However, with the fast development of financial activities and more engagement in the global management of finance by the rising powers, represented by the BRICS members, the legitimacy of the selection process is under challenge.

In 2011, when the scandal surrounding Dominique Strauss-Kahn, Managing Director and Chairman of the Executive Board of IMF, burst into view, selecting the successor was on the agenda. It was India that proposed the emerging economies might put forward a candidate other than a European to campaign for the post.[22] Though Christine Lagarde from France finally secured the post, the intention of the rising powers to change the established rules in the current system was clear.

In this regard, the Chinese attitude was not specifically supportive of the Indian initiative. Nevertheless, China too was expecting meaningful reforms. According to the Chinese foreign affairs spokesman, selection of the IMF head must be done through democratic consultation. The spokesman argued that the process was also part of the reform of international financial institutions. According to the consensus reached in the G20 summits, the selection of the management of international financial institutions should follow the principles of openness, transparency, and merit, and should help enhance the representation of the emerging economies to reflect changes in the global economic structure.[23] The Chinese official statement clearly matched the view of Indian officials. The case illustrates the trend of more common ground between China and India.

Meanwhile, China continues to play a proactive role in the multilateral consultations among the developing countries such as the BRICS summit and the G20 summit. As far as China–India cooperation in this regard is concerned, there is no particular obstacle to either side moving ahead. In most cases, the two nations can also use existing bilateral mechanisms to discuss what they want to see in the international arena such as the China–India Finance Dialogue and the China–India Strategic and Economic Dialogue.[24]

Although the focus of these bilateral mechanisms between China and India is bilateral issues, because this is the reason they were set up, how to strengthen cooperation in international institutions is always a key subject of discussion. As Montek Singh Ahluwalia, Vice Chairman of Indian Economic Planning Commission, said during the second Strategic Economic Dialogue, the economic growth of both India and China would have an important impact on the formation of the global economic order, and India would like to enhance collaboration and cooperation with China in international settings like the G20 and BRICS. If India and China work together to promote exchanges in economic, trade, investment, and policy areas, the two countries will play a more influential role in the international arena.[25]

At this point, the Chinese position seems to be in favour of collaborating with not only other rising powers like India and Brazil but also with the status quo powers like the United States. In fact, China seeks cooperation with the United States in various areas, and financial issues in particular, through a number of dialogue mechanisms. At the same time, both India and China have been active in the development of new financial institutions that are seen, by some, as potential challengers to the current system: the BRICS New Development Bank, initially proposed by India, and the Chinese-led Asian Infrastructure Investment Bank (AIIB).

In March 2012, when India hosted the Fourth BRICS summit, New Delhi initiated the idea of establishing a 'BRICS-led South-South Development Bank', which would aim at providing loans to developing countries, especially in the areas of infrastructure construction, because current international finance institutions do not effectively provide sufficient loans to developing countries.[26] Since the donating countries are now facing severe challenges, their capabilities to do so are greatly confined, according to anonymous Indian officials.[27] The decision to establish the New Development Bank was finally taken at the sixth BRICS summit in July 2014. The bank will be headquartered in Shanghai and its first director will be from India.[28]

The Chinese-initiated Asian Infrastructure Investment Bank (AIIB), which is expected to be established by the end of 2015 after being proposed in 2013, will focus on infrastructure projects in Asia and will be headquartered in Beijing. Despite objections by the United States and Japan, who view the AIIB as a rival to the World Bank, IMF and Asian Development Bank, and have raised concerns over governance, nearly 60 countries, including the UK, France, and Germany, applied to join the bank as founding members. The AIIB's composition – with an estimated 75 per cent of shares reserved for Asian countries, and China and India serving as the two largest shareholders – represents a significant shift from the governance structures of the currently dominant financial institutions.[29]

Both initiatives appear to have won broad support, particularly among BRICS members and developing countries, precisely because a global bank largely funded by developing countries and working for them would naturally carry political implications. The Indian argument is that the current financial institutions, mainly represented by the IMF and World Bank, are far from sufficient. The establishment of these new banks raises the prospect of competition between them and the Western-dominated institutions, perhaps implying a challenge to the existing system.

Given that China and India have huge foreign reserves, there is no reason why they cannot build up their own global banks for infrastructure loans and other development aid. If that is the case, then one may expect to see more competition in the global financial system in the future, and one of the possibilities is that there might be parallel institutions for global finance.

The issue of restructuring the global financial order will be on the agenda soon enough now that the banks have been established and will soon take on obligations to aid developing countries. Although it is too early to say the banks would be a replacement for the World Bank, the fact that they would take on loaning responsibilities to developing countries, which has been a big part of the World Bank's functions, is likely to reduce the significance of the World Bank. This is the reason why both initiatives drew great attention globally and represent very important areas for China–India cooperation in the international arena.

Problems to be addressed

As fast-growing powers, it is natural enough to see problems arising between China and India even in cooperative areas like trade and investment, which are seen as the most positive aspects of bilateral ties. One of the issues that is emerging and is often debated on both sides is whether politics should enter into non-political issues.

On the Chinese side, there are complaints about the political interruption of business exchanges. China believes that India's anti-China sentiments often play a negative role in China–India business activities. The Indian government generally denies this. China's telecommunication companies' involvement in the Indian market is a well-known case. On some occasions, complaints from Chinese companies have gone to the highest policymakers in China. In 2009, when the Huawei Corporation, the Chinese IT giant, took part in an international bid to provide equipment to BSNL, the largest Indian telecommunication service provider, the Chinese bid was turned down due to the accusation that Huawei had a Chinese military background. The accusation came from the Indian intelligence and defence departments, which led to strong complaints from the company and the Chinese media who argued that this was a political intervention rather than normal business operations.[30] Such cases have occurred repeatedly over the years.

Also, as mentioned above, the level of mutual investment between China and India is quite low. There are many reasons for this, and both sides want to improve the situation. The Second China–India SED touched upon the issue. Both sides apparently believe that:

> it is necessary to explore potential effects existing in the areas where the two sides are complementary, and to improve the trading and investment environment by eliminating market barriers, strengthening cooperation in project contracts, promoting communications and encouraging mutual investment more extensively.[31]

Apparently, investment is not an isolated issue. It is part of a more general problem in China–India economic ties despite the fast pace of growth in trade. Most analysts believe that the lack of political trust constitutes an obstacle to China–India ties in other areas because political concerns are also related to national interests.

However, failing to solve the problem does not mean that the two sides cannot move forward in areas like trade and investment. The fast growth of bilateral trade is an example. From that experience, one may argue that mutual investment is more or less a technical problem rather than a politically rooted one. If so, the two sides should make more attempts to address problems like the unfavourable environment for investment, the lack of knowledge of the legal conditions in each other's country, and so on.

As far as China's investments in India are concerned, Chinese complaints are mostly focused on the unfriendly atmosphere and unfavourable environment in India. Chinese references to the unfriendly atmosphere relate to political and nationalistic sentiments directed against China. In the first decade of the century, when bilateral trade developed dramatically, Chinese companies in infrastructure construction developed a global reputation for their relatively low cost and great efficiency. At the same time, India began to pay more attention to the demands of infrastructure including the reconstruction and building of power plants, communications, and ports and roads.

However, it is clear that Chinese companies, even though they want to invest and participate in such projects at the national level in India, will meet severe challenges not only from similar Indian companies who complain about the competitiveness of Chinese companies but also from other sectors which use national security as a reason to block Chinese companies. Some analysts argue that India will use other means to protect their own companies when trade protectionism does not work. This could be called security protectionism.[32] India's effort is to effectively block Chinese investment in India, especially in those areas where Chinese companies do enjoy advantages.

On the Indian side, there are complaints about the lack of transparency and shortcomings of the legal system in the Chinese market that constitute hurdles for potential Indian investors. The pharmaceutical industry is a case that is frequently mentioned.[33] The Indian pharmaceutical industry enjoys many advantages, and the Chinese market is enormous, which has already attracted huge investment from Western transnationals operating in China. There is little doubt that Indian companies would like to enter the market. But so far there has been very little investment from India. The complaints from India focus on too many regulations and non-tariff barriers in the Chinese market. Chinese authorities usually deny this, arguing that market access in China has to be the same for all pharmaceutical companies in China and that Chinese regulations are consistent with international practice. The problem for Indian companies is that competing with Western transnationals in China is too tough. Investing in the pharmaceutical industry requires huge inputs before the products can enter the market. It is the cost of entry that blocks Indian investment, and there is little that the Chinese authorities can do to ease the situation for Indian companies. These sorts of debates and disputes continue between the two countries.

However, the good news is that both sides are clearly aware of the need to improve mutual investment. In fact, how to enhance investment in each other's economy has become a serious agenda item whenever the leaders of the two nations meet. It is also one of the most important subjects for the bilateral strategic and economic dialogue, as seen in the last two rounds of dialogue. It can therefore be safely predicted that mutual investment between China and India will grow regardless of the existing barriers. Crucially, the business communities of the two countries have understood that there exist great opportunities in each other's markets. While the Chinese market does have some hurdles for potential Indian investors, and while the Indian market could be more open to Chinese investors, it is the lack of understanding of each other's investment environment and legal system that is the most challenging problem.

As for cooperation in international institutions, both sides seem to have more confidence in going forward here compared with cooperation in bilateral areas. In the bilateral areas, there are still mutual suspicions. The issue of whether the two countries are competitors or cooperators has not really been clarified. While China does have a more significant status in the international community, India will continue to strive for a global position as described by Jawaharlal Nehru more than sixty decades ago. It is not China that wants to contain India, for China is not a status quo power that wants to defend the current system.

By the same token, it is not India that wants to compete with China in the international system, for China does not control the system, and China, like India, has little say in the system. Therefore, it is a perception problem between the two countries, though addressing the perception problem is a tough challenge. Now that the two countries are in the forefront of the international system and multilateral institutions, they will have to find ways to work together and not to confront each other. How they are going to do it will be tested in their interactions in a number of multilateral institutions like the BRICS summit, the G20 summit, the IMF, and the World Bank. The BRICS Durban Summit in March 2013 revealed a new dynamic of cooperation in international finance between the rising powers, and the establishment of the New Development Bank is an example of successful cooperation between the two countries. Even though the goal of a BRICS bank is not intended to replace current international institutions, the fact that the developing powers are trying to decrease their dependence on these institutions will significantly impact the way international finance has to operate.

Conclusion

The simultaneous rise of China and India is the most important phenomenon in contemporary international political economy. Looking at the 20th century, one may learn a number of negative lessons from the rise of both the United States and Germany. It is partially because of the 20th century experience that China proposed the theory of 'peaceful rise'.[34] The theory does not solve the problems resulting from China's rise, but it does help understand China's position in the world. That position, still described by Chinese leaders as that of a developing country, should help consolidate China's cooperative approach to other countries.

Based on that position, China's India policy will move towards greater accommodation – that is, China will do its best to avoid open friction and confrontation over mutual differences, trying hard to consult India to arrive at solutions to their differences, and working out possible means to cooperate with India. It is not that India is a particular friend of China, but rather that confronting India does not fit China's interests at all. In this sense, one may have a relatively optimistic view of the future of China–India relations. China and India will be likely to work together in developing trade and mutual investment, and in proactively looking for common ground in the reform of international financial institutions, which at the end of the day may help restructure the global financial order.

Notes

1 "Zhu Rongji Delivered Important Speech at Lunch by India Industrial & Business Communities", Article in Chinese, *Renmin Wang*, 17 January 2002, http://www.people.com.cn/GB/shizheng/16/20020117/649797.html.
2 Ministry of External Affairs, Government of India, "Joint Communique of the Republic of India and the People's Republic of China", 16 December 2010, http://mea.gov.in/bilateral-documents.htm?dtl/5158/Joint+Communiqu+of+the+Republic+of+India+and+the+Peoples+Republic+of+China.
3 In 2013, India's GDP (in current US$) was US $1.875 trillion and China's was US$ 9.240 trillion. In PPP terms, the situation is totally different: The United States and China are nearly on par, and India ranks third. Data obtained from The World Bank, "Data", http://data.worldbank.org/country.
4 This is also the title of a monograph by John W. Garver, one of the leading analysts of China-India relations, who wrote the book *Protracted Contest: Sino-Indian Rivalry in*

the Twentieth Century. In the book, Garver depicts China–India relations as that characterised more by conflict than by friendship with frequent disagreements over national and international policies. See John W. Garver, *Protracted Contest: Sino-Indian Rivalry in the Twentieth Century*, Seattle: University of Washington Press, 2001.

5 Jairam Ramesh, who is both a senior official in the Congress-led government and a scholar, had a book published with the title *Making Sense of Chindia: Reflections on China and India,* with a forward by Strobe Talbott, President of the Brookings Institution, who was the chief American negotiator with India after India's nuclear test. The book was translated and published in China by Ningxia People's Publishing House in 2006. See Jairam Ramesh, *Making Sense of Chindia: Reflections on China and India*, Translated into Chinese, Yinchuan: Ningxia renmin chubanshe, 2006.

6 "China-India should collaborate not compete: Zhu Rongji", *Rediff*, 16 January 2002, http://www.rediff.com/news/2002/jan/16zhu.htm.

7 United Nations Commodity (UN Comtrade) Trade Statistics Database, http://comtrade.un.org/db/.

8 "India and China set $100bn trade target by 2015", *BBC News*, 16 December 2010, http://www.bbc.com/news/world-south-asia-12006092.

9 Ananth Krishnan, "India-China trade: record $31 bn deficit in 2013", *The Hindu*, 10 January 2014, http://www.thehindu.com/business/indiachina-trade-record-31-bn-deficit-in-2013/article5562569.ece.

10 Embassy of India, Beijing, "India-China Bilateral Relations: Trade and Commercial Relations", http://www.indianembassy.org.cn/Sub_DynamicContent.aspx?MenuId=35&SubMenuId=0.

11 From 2007–2011, mutual investment figures were as follows: US$ 39.9bn (China–Japan), US$ 15.9bn (India–Japan), US$20.6 bn (China–US), and US$ 20.3bn (India–US). Details on US FDI inflows and outflows are available at https://stats.oecd.org; details on Japanese FDI inflows and outflows are available at http://www.jetro.go.jp/en/reports/statistics/.

12 Embassy of India, Beijing, "Press Release – India-China Investment Forum", 26 February 2013, http://www.indianembassy.org.cn/EventsDetails.aspx?NewsId=397.

13 In 2013, India's GDP (in current US$) was US $1.875 trillion and China's was US$ 9.240 trillion. The World Bank lists India as lower middle income country and China as an upper middle income country. It is also worth mentioning that India's population by 2013 was 1.252 billion and China's was 1.357 billion. Thus, the disparity is not only in totality but also in per capita terms. See The World Bank, "Data: India", http://data.worldbank.org/country/india; The World Bank, "Data: China", http://data.worldbank.org/country/china.

14 There were two agreements signed in the 1990s. One was the Agreement to Maintain Peace and Tranquility in the Areas of LAC (Line of Actual Control) signed on September 7, 1993, and the other was the Agreement to Promote Confidence Building Measures in Military Areas around Boundary Areas of LAC signed on November 29, 1996. See Swaran Singh, "Three Agreements and Five Principles between India and China", in Tan Chung eds., *Across the Himalayan Gap*, New Delhi: Gyan Publishing House, 1998, p. 56.

15 "China's GDP Surpasses Japan, Capping Three-Decade Rise", *Bloomberg Business*, 16 August 2010, http://www.bloomberg.com/news/articles/2010-08-16/china-economy-passes-japan-s-in-second-quarter-capping-three-decade-rise.

16 "Xi: BRICS Cooperation Benefits World Economy", *China.org.cn*, 20 March 2013, http://china.org.cn/world/2013-03/20/content_28298069.htm.

17 A Joint Interview with Chinese President Xi Jinping by News Reporters from BRICS Countries. See Ministry of Foreign Affairs of the People's Republic of China, "Interview with Xi Jinping by media from BRIC countries", Website in Chinese, 19 March 2013, http://www.fmprc.gov.cn/mfa_chn/zyxw_602251/t1022932.shtml.
18 "India, China for early inclusion of IMF quota reforms", *The Economic Times*, 28 September 2013, http://articles.economictimes.indiatimes.com/2013-09-28/news/424 81748_1_imf-quota-brics-development-bank-china-and-india.
19 Kishore Mahbubani, The Great Convergence: Asia, the West and the Logic of One World, New York: Public Affairs, 2013.
20 International Monetary Fund, "Glossary of Selected Financial Terms", 31 October 2006, http://www.imf.org/external/np/exr/glossary/showTerm.asp#top.
21 According to the consensus, China's quota will rise from the current less than four per cent to more than six per cent, making China the third largest quota in IMF, and India's from the current 11th to 8th position. Brazil and Russia will have roughly the same rise. See "China IMF Share Rose to Third Place from Sixth Place below Germany, France and England", Website in Chinese, *China.com.cn*, 24 October 2010, http://www.china.com.cn/economic/txt/2010-10/24/content_21185554.htm.
22 Two anonymous Indian officials from the Ministry of Finance proposed the idea to other emerging economies, and got a positive response from the latter, though it was not discussed publicly. As quoted in, *Cankao Xiaoxi*, Newspaper written in Chinese, May 25, 2011.
23 "China Calls for IMF Chief to be Selected through Democratic Consultation", *Xinhuanet*, 26 May 2011, http://news.xinhuanet.com/english2010/china/2011-05/26/c_13895415.htm.
24 The China–India Finance Dialogue was initiated during Chinese premier Wen Jiabao's visit to Delhi in 2005. The first dialogue was held in 2006, and there have already been six rounds conducted. The China–India Strategic and Economic Dialogue was agreed upon when Chinese premier Wen Jiabao visited Delhi in 2010. The first dialogue was held in Beijing in 2011, the second in December 2012 in Delhi, and the third in March 2014 in Beijing. Both dialogues are at the ministerial level. See Embassy of India, Beijing, "Trade and Commercial Relations", http://www.indianembassy.org.cn/DynamicContent.aspx?MenuId=3&SubMenuId=0; Embassy of India, Beijing, "India-China Economic Relations", http://www.indianembassy.org.cn/DynamicContent.aspx?MenuId=86&SubMenuId=0.
25 "2nd Meeting of China-India Strategic Economic Dialog Held in New Delhi", *Xinhuanet*, 27 November 2012, http://www.gov.cn/jrzg/2012-11/27/content_2275907.htm.
26 Kester Kenn Klomegah, "BRICS bank could change the money game", *Al Jazeera*, 23 March 2012, http://www.aljazeera.com/indepth/features/2012/03/2012322743028880.html.
27 Anastasia Ustinova, "BRICS Bank to be Discussed at March Summit, Russia Official Says", *Bloomberg*, 27 February 2012, http://www.bloomberg.com/news/2012-02-23/india-said-to-propose-brics-bank-to-finance-developing-nations-projects.html.
28 Stephen Gibbs, "BRICS Development Bank announced, headquarters in Shanghai, India the 1st president", *CCTV.com*, 16 July 2014, http://english.cntv.cn/2014/07/16/VIDE1405484642161796.shtml.
29 Shannon Tiezzi, "A Big Step Forward for China's AIIB", 23 May 2015, http://thediplomat.com/2015/05/a-big-step-forward-for-chinas-aiib/.
30 "India Ban on Chinese Telecom Manufacturers Exposed", *People's Daily*, 8 July 2010, http://en.people.cn/90001/90778/90861/7057990.html.

31 "Special Report about India-China SED", Article in Chinese, Beijing: Embassy of India, November 2012.
32 Lora Saalman, "India's Security Protectionism and China", Article in Chinese, *South Asia Studies*, No. 2, 2013, Beijing, p. 19.
33 "China should open up to Indian generic drugs: Experts", *The Economic Times*, 16 September 2014, http://articles.economictimes.indiatimes.com/2014-09-16/news/53983182_1_indian-companies-indian-pharmaceutical-apis.
34 Zheng Bijian, a major policy adviser to the Chinese leadership, who was vice president of China Central Party School, first proposed the theory in 2003. His major arguments are in his article: Zheng Bijian, "China's 'Peaceful Rise' to Great-Power Status", *Foreign Affairs*, September/October 2005, pp. 18–24, http://www.foreignaffairs.com/articles/61015/zheng-bijian/chinas-peaceful-rise-to-great-power-status.

3 Bilateral trade and global economy
An Indian perspective

Sanjaya Baru

The movement of people, ideas, and goods are the most important forms of interaction between nations. Asia's biggest neighbours and two of the oldest living civilisations, China and India, have had such contact for centuries. Yet, bilateral economic relations as understood in the modern world are a relatively recent phenomenon. By 2014, China has become India's biggest trade partner.[1] However, this rapidly growing trade is skewed, with India mainly exporting raw materials to China and importing manufactured goods. The political dissonance that the burgeoning trade deficit has caused needs to be addressed. China and India have been able to find common cause on a variety of international issues and are likely to be equally concerned about regionalism in world trade, with the United States seeking to establish a trans-Pacific and trans-Atlantic free trade area that would exclude both countries. China–India economic relations will be characterised by, according to Prime Minister Manmohan Singh, elements of "coordination, cooperation and competition".[2] It is easy to see why the economic relationship between the two continental neighbours has been limited and sporadic over the centuries and till recently. It is equally easy to predict that the recent spurt in this relationship will continue in the foreseeable future. However, the two countries will have to address new challenges that have come up at the bilateral, regional, and global level.

Historical background

As the world's dominant economic entities till well into the 16th century, China and India accounted for almost half of the world's gross domestic product (GDP) in 1500, but their bilateral trade was largely confined to cross-border trade, both across land borders and across maritime regions.[3] Border trade through the Nathu La pass in the eastern Himalayas was one of the many arms of the so-called 'Silk Route' that connected ancient China with Europe, Central and West Asia, and India. For centuries, both countries also carried on seaborne trade.

While Fernand Braudel drew attention to the dominating presence of China and India, along with Arab traders, in the Indian Ocean region and through the Straits of Malacca, bilateral trade between Chinese and Indian traders was limited.[4] In his masterly and majestic survey of world history, Braudel refers to India and East Asia as the "greatest of all the world economies" of the pre-industrial, pre-capitalist era.[5]

Braudel defines the Far East as comprising "three gigantic world-economies":

> "Islam, overlooking the Indian Ocean from the Red Sea and the Persian Gulf, and controlling the endless chain of deserts stretching across Asia from Arabia to China; India, whose influence extended throughout the Indian Ocean, both east and west of Cape Comorin; and China, at once a great territorial power – striking deep into the heart of Asia – and a maritime force, controlling the seas and countries bordering the Pacific. And so it had been for many hundreds of years.[6]

According to Braudel:

> The relationship between these huge areas was the result of a series of pendulum movements of greater or lesser strength, either side of the centrally positioned Indian subcontinent. The swing might benefit first the East and then the West, redistributing functions, power and political or economic advance. Through all these vicissitudes however, India maintained her central position: her merchants in Gujarat and on the Malabar and Coromandel coasts prevailed for centuries against their many competitors – the Arab traders of the Red Sea, the Persian merchants of the Gulf, or the Chinese merchants familiar with the Indonesian seas to which their junks were now regular visitors.[7]

Historian Ashin Das Gupta notes how Chinese and Indian traders exchanged goods at Malacca, with neither venturing much across the waters in each other's direction, but both making their presence felt in the Indo-China region. "There can be no doubt", says Das Gupta, "that the emergence of Malacca as an *entrepot* where the Indian, Chinese and Javanese met to exchange their wares was the most important development in the history of the Indian Ocean during the fifteenth century".[8] Das Gupta concludes that "the main aim of both the Indians and the Chinese was to buy spices from the Indonesians, but some trade took place between them as well. . . . It does not seem that trade between India and China at Malacca was considerable".[9] Indian traders imported Chinese porcelain and silk and exchanged these for opium, sandalwood, and pepper.

An important constraint on Chinese maritime trading activity was the official policy of the Ming emperors to withdraw from the seas and remain a land-based power. While cross-border trade across land continued, especially across the eastern Himalayas, and a sizeable Chinese trading community became resident in Calcutta, the arrival of European trading powers in Asia further reduced China–India trade until the export of opium from India by the British. Through the entire colonial period, maritime trade was dominated by European merchants with direct China–India contact being restricted to cross-border trade. Calcutta remained an important outlet for Chinese goods from south-western China and to that extent some bilateral trade continued.

By the time India and China became sovereign republics, in 1947 and 1949 respectively, their bilateral trade was insignificant.

From inward to outward orientation

In the 1950s, there was considerable interest in reviving bilateral economic relations, though India's attention was focused more on its immediate Asian neighbourhood, on the Soviet Union, and the United States. China was not seen as a major trading or economic partner even though the bilateral relationship was good.[10]

In subsequent decades, the disruption of the bilateral relationship due to the border conflict in 1962 and the pursuit of inward-oriented and import-substituting industrialisation by both countries meant that neither side paid much attention to the potential for bilateral trade and investment relations. It is helpful to recall, however, that even through this period of import-substituting industrialisation China was a bigger trading nation, with foreign trade (goods and services) accounting for eight per cent of GDP in China in 1973, as opposed to four per cent in India.[11]

China's opening up to world trade, around 1980, began a decade before India's in 1991. In 1980 both countries had less than one per cent share each in world trade. China's vigorous pursuit of trade-oriented industrialisation in the 1980s sharply increased her share of world trade and the share of trade in national income. Thus, by 1990, China's share of world trade had increased to 1.7 per cent compared to India's lowly 0.5 per cent. By 2000, China's share of world trade was 3.6 per cent, while India's share remained below 1 per cent. As shares of national income, by the early 2000s, trade accounted for 30 per cent of China's national income and 15 per cent of India's.[12] Equally important, China emerged both as an exporting and an importing nation, importing both raw materials and machinery and components.

An important geo-economic dimension to China's rise as an exporting and importing power was its growing trade relationship with other Asian economies. In South Asia, while India traditionally had a larger share of the foreign trade of its immediate neighbours, barring Myanmar and Pakistan, by 1997 China overtook India in the trade share of all South Asian economies, except Sri Lanka and Bhutan.[13]

India's 'Look East Policy', launched by the government of P.V. Narasimha Rao in 1992, was aimed at restoring India's traditional political and economic links with Southeast Asian countries that had been disrupted by the geopolitics of the Cold War era. An important consequence of India's renewed focus on the countries to its east, especially after India had itself opened up its economy to increased flows of trade and investment, was to increase the share of the Southeast Asian economies in India's external trade. However, here too, India came up against the competitive pressure exerted by China. China's mercantilist trade policy, to gain access to new markets, and non-transparent fiscal and industrial policy towards this end, became a subject of contention.[14]

Fully aware of the emergent competitive pressure from an export-oriented China pursuing a mercantilist trade policy, India nevertheless supported China's accession to the World Trade Organisation (WTO).[15] India was wary of China's entry into the WTO, but her support for China's membership was defined both by an interest in strengthening the voice of the developing world within the multilateral trading regime and in seeking to bring China into the discipline of a multilateral regime, aimed at making Chinese policy more transparent and bringing China within the ambit of the WTO's dispute settlement mechanism.

The main reason for India's wariness was on account of the competition India knew it would face from increased Chinese exports in developed country markets. While China's trade liberalisation measures undertaken to qualify for WTO membership proved very helpful in boosting bilateral trade between the two countries, the rapid improvement in China's competitiveness posed a threat to other developing country exporters who found their developed country markets taken away from them by a more competitive China. Bhat, Guha, and Paul note the implications of China's WTO membership for India in a study commissioned by the Indian Planning Commission:

> Main gainers [from China's WTO entry] are developed countries, newly industrializing Asian economies such as South Korea, and Singapore and least developed countries. Because of the similar resources endowments, South Asian and South East Asian countries like Thailand, Malaysia, Indonesia and the Philippines may face keener competition in labor-intensive and low priced products. Low wages are the main source of China's comparative advantage. China has developed a strong comparative advantage in the assembly stage of technology/ capital intensive products and processing trade for a number of products. Further, it has improved its capacity in the production of components. The supply of skilled labour is high in China, which increases its potential to produce skill-intensive products. The developing countries that export labor-intensive products and assembly operations will be subjected to more of "competition effects" of China than "complementarities effects". On this basis, South Asia, Africa and Latin America may suffer from [the] competition effects of China.[16]

The new bilateral economic relationship

The normalisation of bilateral political relations in the late 1980s and India's own economic liberalisation programme launched in 1991 helped revive the bilateral economic relationship. India and China officially resumed trade in 1978, and in 1984 they signed the Most Favoured Nation Agreement. Border trade picked up after the Nathu La pass was reopened in July 1992, after a hiatus of more than thirty years, and consulates were re-opened in Mumbai and Shanghai in December 1992. By 1994, several agreements were signed in the areas of science and technology, civil aviation, and banking, and simplified procedures were adopted for granting visas. India's information technology and software revolution and role in handling the global Y2K problem enabled the country to register its presence in global services trade. India's emergence as a software services provider alerted China to the prospect of a synergy between the IT sectors of the two economies. As Chinese premier Zhu Rongji put it, during his 2002 visit to India: "You are the first in software, and we are the first in hardware. When we put these two together, we can become the world's number one".[17]

China followed up Zhu's policy by inviting Indian software companies to set up shop in China. Tata Consultancy Services (TCS), Infosys, Wipro, and Satyam started operations and training bases in China, and NIIT and Zensar set up learning centres that offered software services training to thousands of Chinese students.[18]

Despite such a promising beginning, the bilateral trade relationship was fraught. Indian companies, especially in the manufacturing sector and in food processing and pharmaceuticals, complain of a lack of policy transparency and 'unfair' competition from 'subsidised' Chinese goods. As editor of *The Financial Express*, I ran a series of news reports in 2001 on the 'dumping' of Chinese goods in the Indian market and the use of unfair trade practices by Chinese companies. These were news reports based on interviews with Indian companies that had been hurt by Chinese imports. However, by 2003, there were enough positive stories about Indian companies entering the Chinese market that enabled me to run a new series titled "Beyond the Great Wall".

It is a measure of how rapidly both countries responded to opportunities presented by the other that the US$ 10 billion bilateral trade target referenced during Chinese Prime Minister Zhu Rongji's 2002 visit to India was easily reached. A new target of US$ 20 billion was set during the visit of Prime Minister Wen Jiabao in April 2005. That too was met by 2008. In November 2006, during the visit of President Hu Jintao, the revised target was US$ 40 billion, and this was reached by 2009. By 2010, China emerged as India's biggest trading partner, overtaking the United States. In 2010, the two countries identified a trade target of US$ 100 billion for the year 2015, with total bilateral trade valued at more than US$ 66 billion in 2012 (Tables 3.1 and 3.2). A series of bilateral agreements were signed to encourage trade and business between the two countries.[19] In 2012, India became China's 15th largest trading partner and its 19th largest exporter, with a share of 2.03 per cent in China's overall foreign trade and a share of 1.1 per cent in imports into China.[20] India was China's 7th largest export destination, with a share of 2.33 per cent of total Chinese exports to the world.[21]

While the overall numbers are impressive, the structure of the trade has been less than encouraging, with India exporting mainly raw materials to China, and Indian manufactures and agri-exports facing the problem of market access. In 2012, India's major exports to China included ores, slag and ash (iron, chromium and zinc ore), cotton yarn (not carded/combed cotton), organic chemicals (cyclic alcohols), precious stones, and metals and iron and steel.[22] India's major imports from China were electrical machinery (with line telephony accounting for a major share), machinery (steam generating boilers and other types of boilers, steam turbines, office machine parts, cranes, air conditioning machinery, converters, ladles,

Table 3.1 China–India bilateral trade (US$ billion)

Year	Export	Import	Trade	Trade balance
2000–01	0.8	1.5	2.3	0.7
2001–02	1.0	2.0	3.0	−1.0
2002–03	2.0	2.8	4.8	−0.8
2003–04	3.0	4.1	7.0	−1.1
2004–05	5.6	7.1	12.7	−1.5
2005–06	6.8	10.9	17.6	−4.1
2006–07	8.3	17.5	25.8	−9.2
2007–08	10.9	27.1	38.0	−16.3
2008–09	9.4	32.5	41.9	−23.1
2009–10	11.6	30.8	42.4	−19.2
2010–11	14.2	43.5	57.6	−29.3
2011–12	18.1	55.3	73.4	−37.2
2012–13	13.5	52.2	65.8	−38.7
2013–14	14.8	51.0	65.9	−36.2

Source: Department of Commerce, Government of India, "Export Import Data Bank", http://commerce.nic.in/eidb/default.asp.

ingot moulds, and casting machines, and so on), organic chemicals (antibiotics and heterocyclic compounds), and iron and steel products.[23]

Apart from the skewed structure of trade, market access issues continue to come up in official and ministerial level meetings.[24] Both governments have blamed each other for continuing non-tariff barriers to trade, but given the huge trade deficit in China's favour India believes that it is up to the Chinese government to address these issues first. Formal consultative structures have been created, including a Strategic Economic Dialogue (SED) between the two governments. For India and China to cooperate at the regional and global level, it is essential that these bilateral issues be resolved. This has gained greater urgency given the deceleration of growth in both countries.

Table 3.2 China–India trade balance

(US$ billion & %)	2010	2011	2012
Total India–China trade	61.74	73.90	66.57
Percentage growth	42.66	19.71	−9.93
India's exports to China	20.86	23.41	18.82
Percentage growth	52.19	12.26	−19.61
China's exports to India	40.88	50.49	47.75
Percentage growth	38.25	23.50	−5.40
Trade balance for India	−20.02	−27.08	−28.93

Source: Embassy of India, Beijing, "Trade and Commercial Relations", http://www.indianembassy.org.cn/DynamicContent.aspx?MenuId=3&SubMenuId=0.

In the case of China, the trade deficit and market access issues are viewed not merely as economic problems but also as political problems mainly because of the lack of transparency in Chinese policy. For this reason, more than any other, the trade deficit problem has been consistently raised by Indian officials and business associations with their Chinese counterparts.[25] More recently, India's commerce minister Anand Sharma and external affairs minister Salman Khurshid have both drawn attention to the trade deficit during their visits to Beijing, and pointed especially to market access problems faced in China by Indian exporters of pharmaceuticals, agricultural products, buffalo meat, and information technology services.[26]

The recent ballooning of India's overall trade deficit and the current account deficit, which has increased from an average of less than two per cent of GDP in the decade before 2008 to over four per cent by 2012 and sharply higher in 2013, has raised the spectre of an external payments crisis.[27] Under the circumstances, India has had to adopt import compression measures. The need to address the China–India trade deficit has, therefore, gained even greater urgency. While India's recent decision to resume the export of iron ore may help reduce the trade deficit with China, the structure of trade would then only revert to the earlier pattern in which India exported raw materials to China and imported finished products from China.

The only way this structure can be altered is if China's rising cost of manufacturing, especially on account of rising wage costs, helps make Indian manufactured exports more competitive, or if China invests in the manufacturing sector in India. The foreign direct investment (FDI) route has the potential to reduce the trade gap and the current account deficit as well as change the structure of bilateral trade. While China has to address the issue of market access, India's decision to be more welcoming of FDI from China is one important way in which the trade deficit can be addressed, if such FDI is import-substituting or export-promoting in nature.[28]

Here, there are some problems. First India has had a problem with Chinese FDI in sensitive sectors like telecommunications, primarily for security reasons. While China's telecom giant Huawei has established an Indian presence, it continues to face cyber security concerns in India, as indeed in many other countries.[29] Other Chinese companies like Lenovo and Haier have had a better record of investment in India. While the joint venture (JV) route has traditionally been the preferred option for new foreign entrants into India, anecdotal evidence suggests that Indian firms are still wary of entering into JVs with Chinese counterparts. One reason offered is that Chinese counterparts do not share technology, and indeed may even steal technology.[30]

The sectors where Chinese FDI would be welcomed into India are industries like steel and infrastructure, especially construction. The roads and the real estate sectors are expected to attract massive Chinese investment.[31] The challenge going forward for both China and India is to convert the trade relationship into an investment relationship, so that capital flows from China to India can help reduce the trade deficit. However, even this route can be a challenging one if there is a lack of trust between Indian and Chinese counterparts.

Trade deficit and trust deficit

Given these trends and concerns, where are India-China trade relations headed, and how can the problem of the trade deficit be tackled? First, it is important to recognise that the trade deficit has become political mainly on account of persisting concerns about lack of transparency in China's domestic policies and the larger problem of a trust deficit between the two countries. Absence of credible data enables critics to speculate about intentions, including charges that China is out to 'subvert' India's manufacturing sector.[32] In fact, both China and India have levelled anti-dumping charges against each other. According to the Indian Ministry of Commerce, out of a total of 290 anti-dumping investigations initiated by the Directorate General of Anti-Dumping and Allied Duties between 1992, when the WTO system came into being, and 2013, as many as 159 cases involved imports from China.[33] Hence, China must address the issue at a political and administrative level to gain India's trust. Establishing trust is the first major challenge.

Second, Indian exporters must do more to win brand recognition and the trust of Chinese consumers. India's overall image has to improve before ordinary consumer resistance can be overcome. China has been trying to overcome such consumer resistance around the world, including in India. If a select number of Indian brands emulate Lenovo's strategy in India, they may be able to overcome consumer resistance and widen the market for Indian goods in China.[34]

Finally, China will have to graduate from exporting products to India to making India a part of its global supply chain and manufacturing some of these products in India. This is the only way in which the problem of the trade deficit can be tackled.

Managing competition and cooperation

Prime Minister Manmohan Singh best captured the reality of the China–India bilateral economic relationship when he said that it would be defined both by 'competition' and 'cooperation'. On the eve of his visit to Tokyo in December 2006, Prime Minister Singh told the Japanese newspaper *Yomiuri Shimbun*:

> My own view is that the world is large enough to accommodate the development ambitions of both countries (China and India). And, therefore, there is immense scope for us to cooperate with one another. There will be certain fields where we will also be competing, as is inevitable, so there is a policy of competition as well as of cooperation.[35]

In order for both countries to manage their larger bilateral relationship, it would be useful for them to identify and manage these elements so that the natural 'competition' between two 'emerging economies' and 'rising powers' – for markets, for resources, and for investment opportunities – does not result in 'conflict', and the avenues available for 'cooperation' can build trust and confidence. China and

India will compete for market access in countries around the world. They will compete for access to resources including oil and gas, minerals, and food. They will compete for investment opportunities in third countries. It would be short-sighted not to recognise the potential for competition between the two economies.

However, both countries will also have opportunities to cooperate in building a global order that would be conducive to and supportive of their individual growth ambitions. Thus, they have a shared interest in creating a multilateral trading and financial regime that is supportive of their individual growth as well as the growth of other developing economies, just as they have a shared agenda with respect to the emergent regime to deal with the threat of global warming and climate change. New Delhi and Beijing would seek to ensure that the developed industrial economies eschew protectionism and continue to offer market access.

In short, in their attempt to avoid conflict on bilateral economic issues pertaining to market access, and in order to manage the competition they would engage in to secure access to third markets and resources, China and India will have to identify areas of cooperation at the regional and global level.

It would seem that has been the approach of the two governments. Their cooperation on climate change and global economic governance are obvious examples. In trade, while Indian companies have serious complaints about 'unfair trade' practices on the part of Chinese exporters, India and China have sought to work together in the WTO and have also decided to pursue a new regional trading initiative in the Indo-Pacific region, namely, the Regional Comprehensive Economic Partnership (RCEP) launched in 2012.

Opportunities for regional cooperation

The dynamics of regional economic integration in the 'Indo-Pacific' region have been complex and changing. Early initiatives towards regional integration were in fact taken by the smaller economies of the region, the members of the Association of Southeast Asian Nations (ASEAN). Japan, China, and India remained outside this process until Malaysia, with Japan's blessing, proposed the idea of an East Asian Economic Caucus/ Group (EAEC/EAEG) in the early 1990s. However, this proposal did not find favour in the ASEAN region and even with the US.[36] Malaysian Prime Minister Mahathir's EAEG was then resurrected as ASEAN's 'ASEAN+3' (China, Japan and South Korea) group in the aftermath of the Asian financial crisis in 1997–98.[37] ASEAN took the lead to bring together China, Japan, South Korea, India, Australia, and New Zealand into an ASEAN+3 and later an ASEAN+6 grouping. China reluctantly went along with the ASEAN+6 initiative, even though its main interest was in making the ASEAN+3 group the fulcrum of East Asian regionalism. On the other hand, China quickly endorsed the RCEP idea.[38]

India also responded with alacrity to the RCEP initiative. Finding itself excluded from earlier attempts at regional cooperation like the Asia Pacific Economic Cooperation (APEC) and the ASEAN+3 (China, Japan, and South Korea) initiatives, India has been careful not to exclude itself from any new initiatives for regional economic integration in the Asia-Pacific region. Even though the RCEP is viewed as an ASEAN–China response to the US-inspired Trans-Pacific Partnership (TPP), India signed on to RCEP on the side-lines of the 2012 East Asia Summit (EAS) in Cambodia in November 2012. Welcoming this initiative and explaining India's decision, Prime Minister Singh said: "Concerted effort and collective action on the part of the countries gathered in this room can strengthen mutual understanding and help us address shared challenges. For this, it would be necessary to develop a common set of principles, establish cooperative mechanisms and deepen regional economic integration".[39]

India viewed China's initial diplomacy in the Asian community building process as aimed at keeping India out of the region, while Chinese commentators have viewed India's 'Look East Policy' as aimed at 'encircling China'.[40] However, given ASEAN's enthusiastic endorsement of India's participation in the 'ASEAN plus' processes, China has had to relent and modify its stance on India's desire to seek greater economic integration with Southeast and East Asia.[41] An important factor driving China and India closer on the issue of the regional economic, if not security, architecture in Asia is the US decision to follow up its 'Asian pivot', which India welcomes, with the TPP initiative.

The exclusion of both China and India from the TPP, it would seem, imparted momentum to ASEAN's RCEP initiative.[42] More important, China and India's shared concerns about the TPP's objectives, given its attempt to go beyond existing WTO 'rules of the game' in multilateral trade, may encourage China and India to cooperate in making RCEP a success.[43]

The trend towards regionalism in global trade, however, benefits neither China nor India, nor indeed the global economy. As an emerging and developing economy, India would be hurt by the regionalisation of trade. This concern is heightened by the fact that apart from RCEP, India is not a member of any other major regional trade arrangements and was even kept out of APEC. The new process of economic regionalisation is fraught with problems not just for India but also for all developing economies, especially if one consequence is a weakening of the multilateral trading system under the aegis of the WTO.

As the biggest developing economies, China and India have a stake in revitalising the multilateral trading regime and reversing the current process of regionalisation of free trade arrangements. They therefore have the opportunity to work together and with other like-minded countries to revitalise the WTO rather than allow new regional blocs to marginalise the WTO. It remains to be seen if the European Union (EU) will also drift away from the WTO process and join hands with the US in promoting the regionalisation of trade regimes by signing up to the proposed Transatlantic Trade and Investment Partnership (T-TIP).

The multilateral system

China and India recognise that the regionalisation of trade arrangements and a weakening of the multilateral system are as hurtful to their future growth as the attempt by the developed industrial economies to relate free trade to a variety of social, environmental, and other factors. Greater transparency in domestic policy will, of course, go a long way in bolstering their case. Given that the regionalisation of trade and financial systems over the past decade is not necessarily in the interests of China or India, nor indeed of developed industrial economies, rule-based access to markets around the world is a goal that both China and India should pursue. It ought to be acknowledged that the mushrooming of regional, preferential, and plurilateral trade agreements in Asia, Europe, and the Americas is not a healthy trend. The WTO Ministerial Conference in Bali, Indonesia, held in December 2013, offered an opportunity to revitalise the multilateral system.

While India has vigorously pursued FTAs with ASEAN, Japan, South Korea, and other countries to ensure market access in response to the regionalisation of trade around the world, it is in India's strategic interest that the multilateral regime is strengthened, albeit in keeping with the principles enshrined in the WTO of providing developing countries adequate space for development. The Doha Round was in fact named the Doha Development Round with a view to preserving these principles.

Both China and India are concerned that the US and the EU, seeking to overcome the consequences of the trans-Atlantic financial crisis and economic slowdown, may be walking away from the post-Cold War multilateral trading system established under the WTO in favour of regional and plurilateral arrangements. China and India may be able to work together, and with the US, EU, Japan, Brazil, and other major trading economies, to revive the multilateral process and contain the current wave of regionalism. This would be a good shared agenda for cooperation between the two countries that can have positive externalities for the global economy.

Given the size of their markets, if China and India join forces on strengthening the multilateral trading regime under the aegis of the WTO, rather than allow themselves to be overtaken by the dynamic of TPP/T-TIP, they have the potential to modify the behaviour of the US and EU given the size of their markets. In other words, a coming together of emerging economies, especially China and India, in favour of multilateralism and against regionalism can help preserve the gains of the WTO process and thwart the threat of trade regionalisation through the TPP/T-TIP route.

China and India should also work with the US, EU, Russia, and other emerging economies to strengthen the G20 as an institution and as a process. The emerging tensions between the G7 and the BRICS within the G20 should not be allowed to grow and disrupt the G20. Both the G7 countries and the BRICS countries have a stake in the successful management of global economic challenges by the G20. Unfortunately, Russia, a member of the G-8 and of BRICS, could have but has not yet been able to play a bridging role between these two blocs.[44] Global political developments in the run up to the G20 Summit in Russia in September 2013, including the conflict in Syria and growing US–Russia tensions, as well as Moscow's belligerence during the on-going Ukraine crisis, have only further reduced the prospect of Moscow playing this bridging role. Perhaps China and India can play that role by working together with the US. A US–China–India trilateral partnership may help stabilise the global economy and address other global challenges, including those of climate change and energy security.

Finally, historically India has always been supportive of China's proper representation in international institutions. Thus, India supported China's membership of the UN Security Council, multilateral financial institutions, and the World Trade Organisation. China should reciprocate by supporting India's proper representation in all such international and multilateral institutions.

Conclusion

While it is true that, as Indian Prime Minister Manmohan Singh put it, "the world has enough space for the growth ambitions of both countries",[45] the jury is still out on Dr Singh's other hopeful assertion – that of positive externalities flowing from the rise of China and India for the rest of the world, from the new opportunities for development they would offer to the international community, especially other developing countries. If the two Asian neighbours can translate their own rise into new opportunities for others, resolving their differences in the process, then then their individual growth and bilateral cooperation will have global benefits. Both countries seem to recognise this challenge.

President Xi Jinping has outlined 'five principles' for bilateral China–India relations, under which the two countries should:

> harness each other's comparative strengths and expand win-win cooperation in infrastructure, mutual investment and other areas . . . strengthen cultural ties and increase mutual understanding and friendship between our peoples . . . expand coordination and collaboration in multilateral affairs to jointly safeguard the legitimate rights and interests of developing countries and tackle global challenges.[46]

These principles have also been echoed by Prime Minister Singh in his own way.[47] If these principles are honoured, then the two would be able to address global challenges and provide both regional and global leadership. If not, their bilateral differences will keep them tied down and restrain and constrain them, individually and collectively.

Acknowledgment

I am grateful to Suvi Dogra, Nagaraja Naidu and Abhishek Shukla for assistance in writing this paper and to the editors of this volume for their comments on an earlier draft.

Notes

1 "China emerges as India's top trading partner: Study", *The Times of India*, 2 March 2014, http://timesofindia.indiatimes.com/business/india-business/China-emerges-as-Indias-top-trading-partner-Study/articleshow/31268526.cms.
2 "Is World Big Enough for India, China?" *The China Post*, 10 April 2013, http://www.chinapost.com.tw/commentary/the-china-post/frank-ching/2013/04/10/375571/Is-world.htm.

3 Angus Maddison, *The World Economy: A Millennial Perspective*, Paris: Organisation for Economic Co-operation and Development (OECD), 2001; Angus Maddison, *Chinese Economic Performance in the Long Run, 960–2030 AD*, Paris: OECD, 2007.
4 Fernand Braudel, Civilization and Capitalism, 15th–18th Century: Volume II. The Wheels of Commerce, London: Fontana Press, 1985.
5 Fernand Braudel, Civilization and Capitalism, 15th–18th Century: Volume III. The Perspective of the World, Chapter 5, London: Fontana Press, 1984, p. 484.
6 Ibid., pp. 484–535.
7 Ibid., p. 484.
8 Ashin Das Gupta, *The World of the Indian Ocean Merchant, 1500–1800*, New Delhi: Oxford University Press, 2001, p. 61.
9 Ibid.
10 Surjit Mansingh, "India-China Relations in the Post-Cold War Era", *Asian Survey*, 34/3, March 1994, pp. 285–300.
11 John W. Garver, *Protracted Contest: Sino-Indian Rivalry in the Twentieth Century*, New Delhi: Oxford University Press, 2001.
12 Arvind Panagariya, *India and China: Trade and Foreign Investment*, Working paper 302, Stanford: Stanford Center for International Development, November 2006, http://www.stanford.edu/group/siepr/cgi-bin/siepr/?q=system/files/shared/pubs/papers/pdf/SCID302.pdf.
13 Sanjaya Baru, *Strategic Consequences of India's Economic Performance*, Chapter 38, New Delhi: Academic Foundation, 2006, p. 337.
14 For an early critique of Chinese trade policy, see Surjit Bhalla, *Chinese Mercantilism: Currency Wars and How the East was Lost*. Working Paper 45, New Delhi: Indian Council for Research on International Economic Relations, July 1998, http://www.icrier.org/pdf/SurjeetB.pdf.
15 T.P. Bhat, Atulan Guha and Mahua Paul, *India and China in WTO: Building Complementarities and Competitiveness in the External Trade Sector*, New Delhi: Institute for Studies in Industrial Development, April, 2006, http://planningcommission.nic.in/reports/sereport/ser/stdy_indch.pdf.
16 Ibid., p. xvii.
17 Quoted in Aqueil Ahmad, "India and China: Conflict, Competition and Cooperation in the Age of Globalization", *Share the World's Resources (STWR)*, 21 February 2008, www.stwr.org/india-china-asia/india-and-china-conflict-competition-and-cooperation-in-the-age-of-globalization.html.
18 "In January 2004, the government of the Shenzhen Special Economic Zone signed an agreement with an Indian software company, Zensar Technologies Ltd, to train 1000 Chinese software managers in India. Besides, a large software training company, NIIT, has set up 106 learning centres in China, training more than 25,000 Chinese software students". Quoted in Bhat, Guha and Paul, *India and China in WTO*, p. 234.
19 For a review of the rapid growth of China–India trade relations, see T.N. Srinivasan, *China, India and the World Economy*, Working Paper 286, Stanford: Stanford Centre for International Development, July 2006, www.stanford.edu/group/siepr/cgi-bin/siepr/?q=system/files/shared/pubs/papers/pdf/SCID286.pdf; Arvind Panagariya, *India and China: Past Trade Liberalization and Future Challenges*, 4 February 2007, http://www.nomurafoundation.or.jp/app_list/hdd/2006120607_Arvind_Panagariya.pdf.
20 Ministry of External Affairs, Government of India, *India–China Relations*, http://www.mea.gov.in/Portal/ForeignRelation/India-China_Relations.pdf.
21 Ibid.

22 Embassy of India, Beijing, "Trade and Commercial Relations", http://www.indianembassy.org.cn/DynamicContent.aspx?MenuId=3&SubMenuId=0.
23 Ibid.
24 As India's ambassador in Beijing recently put it: "If overall there is a diversity of views on our ties with China, trade is perhaps the sector that is most polarized. While there is no denying that sourcing from China has created efficiencies and lowered costs in many sectors, advantages Chinese companies enjoy at home have also hurt many of their competitors in India. Reconciling the costs and benefits of our expanding trade with China is a real challenge that continues to be hotly debated. Discussions are focused around the growing trade imbalance, market access challenges faced by Indian companies in China, trade investigations, and occasionally, even national security concerns. While the Indian economy has been largely open to goods from China, our companies exporting to that country find themselves hampered by duty structures, non-tariff barriers, quotas, local production requirements, closed vendor loops and restricted Government buying". Quoted in S. Jaishankar, "India and China: Perceptions and Reality", Distinguished Alumni Lecture, Jawaharlal Nehru University, New Delhi, 14 March 2013.
25 "India cannot be an exporter of raw materials and commodities to China all the time", says Nirupama Rao, the Indian Ambassador to China, flagging the rising concern over a situation she says is "unsustainable in the long run". The ambassador adds that a "deficit [with China] is tolerable only for a finite period, beyond which we risk seeing a 'positive' of the relationship assuming negative tones". Quoted in Pallavi Aiyar, "Sino-Indian Trade: Growing Concern", *The Hindu*, 28 August 2007, http://www.hindu.com/2007/08/28/stories/2007082855521000.htm.

In 2008, India's Commerce Minister Kamal Nath raised the issue in Beijing: "Commerce Minister Kamal Nath talked tough at his meeting with the newly appointed Chinese Commerce Minister Chen Deming, a day ahead of Prime Minister Manmohan Singh's visit to Beijing". "I told the [Chinese] Minister that we [India and China] have substantial trade but that this is sustainable only if there is no large deficit". Quoted in Pallavi Aiyar, "Kamal Nath Asks China to Address Trade Deficit", *The Hindu*, 13 January 2008, http://www.hindu.com/2008/01/13/stories/2008011359630800.htm.
26 Elizabeth Roche, "India, China Discuss Reducing Trade Gap, Peace Along Borders", *Live Mint,* 20 August 2013, http://www.livemint.com/Politics/JZZDDEinFFSAVpiEZoIxTM/India-China-discuss-reducing-trade-gap-peace-along-borders.html.
27 Muneesh Kapur and Rakesh Mohan, *India's Recent Macroeconomic Performance: An Assessment and Way Forward*, IMF Working Papers 14/68, 2014, p. 26.
28 "India Invites Chinese Foreign Direct Investment", *The Economic Times*, 27 February 2013, http://articles.economictimes.indiatimes.com/2013-02-27/news/37331014_1_chinese-companies-china-s-jaishankar-mutual-investment.
29 "Huawei Deal: We are not Compromising India's Security, says Kapil Sibal", *DNA India*, 30 June 2011, http://www.dnaindia.com/india/1560793/report-huawei-deal-we-are-not-compromising-india-s-security-says-kapil-sibal; Ellyn Phneah, "Huawei, ZTE under Probe by Indian Government," *ZDNet*, 10 May 2013, http://www.zdnet.com/in/huawei-zte-under-probe-by-indian-government-7000015185/.
30 This complaint was made to this writer by two prominent Indian business leaders, who wish to remain anonymous, who tried the JV route with Chinese companies and ended the relationship deeply unhappy with the experience.
31 Ronojoy Banerjee, "Government Looks to Attract FDI in Roads from China; Seeks MoU", *Moneycontrol.com*, 26 August 2013, http://www.moneycontrol.com/news/

cnbc-tv18-comments/govt-looks-to-attract-fdiroadschina-seeks-mou_940906.html; "Anil Ambani Teams up with China's Wanda", *The Times of India*, 14 December 2012, http://timesofindia.indiatimes.com/business/india-business/Anil-Ambani-teams-up-with-Chinas-Wanda/articleshow/17606754.cms.

32 Arup Chaudhury, "China Posing Threat to India's Manufacturing Sector", *Machinst360*, 5 February 2010, http://www.machinist360.com/article/48/20100205201002051043 44777757f22c6/China-posing-threat-to-India%E2%80%99s-manufacturing-sector.html.

33 "India Initiated 159 Anti-dumping Cases against China", *The Economic Times*, 12 August 2013, http://articles.economictimes.indiatimes.com/2013-08-12/news/41332741_1_anti-dumping-probe-trade-deficit-product-and-country.

34 "Lenovo Remains Bullish on its India Business", *Lenovo*, 30 January 2013, http://www.lenovo.com/news/in/en/2013/01/press-note.html.

35 "Enough Room for India and China – India PM Singh", *China Daily*, 5 December 2006, http://www.chinadaily.com.cn/china/2006-12/05/content_751323.htm.

36 Tadahiro Yoshida, East Asian Regionalism and Japan, Working Paper 03/04, 9, IDE APEC Study Center, March 2004, http://www.ide.go.jp/English/Publish/Download/Apec/pdf/2003_09.pdf.

37 Ibid., p. 7

38 Zhong Sheng, "Asean Plus Three Cooperation is the Driving Force for East Asia", *People's Daily Online*, 16 August 2011, http://english.peopledaily.com.cn/90780/91343/7571027.html.

39 Press Information Bureau, Government of India, "Statement by the Prime Minister at Plenary Session of 7th East Asia Summit", 20 November 2012, http://pib.nic.in/newsite/erelease.aspx?relid=89132.

40 "India's Look East Policy Shouldn't Mean 'Encircle China': People's Daily", *The Times of India*, 28 October 2010, http://articles.timesofindia.indiatimes.com/2010-10-28/china/28237805_1_largest-trade-partner-east-china-sea-wen-jiabao.

41 Pei Yuanying, "India's 'Look East Policy'", *People's Daily Online*, 6 April 2012, http://english.peopledaily.com.cn/90780/91343/7778951.html.

42 Sanchita Basu Das "RCEP and TPP: Comparisons and Concerns" ISEAS Perspective #02, Singapore: Institute of South East Asian Studies, 7 January 2013, http://www.iseas.edu.sg/documents/publication/ISEAS%20Perspective%202013_2.pdf.

43 Basu Das, RCEP and TPP; Suvi Dogra and Jun Jie Woo, "Where Does India Stand Amid Changing Asia-Pacific Trade Dynamics?" The Financial Express, *4 April 2013*, http://www.financialexpress.com/news/where-does-india-stand-amid-changing-asia pacific-trade-dynamics-/1097246/0.

44 Sanjaya Baru and Samuel Charap, "Russia and the G20", Conference Papers: Prospects for the Russian Chairmanship of the G20, New York: Council on Foreign Relations, December 2012, pp. 28–31.

45 "World has Enough Space for India and China to Grow: PM", *The Indian Express*, 27 October 2010, http://archive.indianexpress.com/news/world-has-enough-space-for-india-and-china-to-grow-pm/703293/; Sanjaya Baru, "India's Five Thoughts on China", *Project Syndicate*, 24 March 2013, http://www.project-syndicate.org/commentary/india-and-china-at-the-brics-summit-by-sanjaya-baru.

46 Ministry of Foreign Affairs of the People's Republic of China, "President Xi Jinping Gives Joint Interview To Media from BRICS Countries" 19 March 2013, http://www.fmprc.gov.cn/mfa_eng/wjdt_665385/zyjh_665391/t1023070.shtml

47 Baru, "India's Five Thoughts on China".

4 Competitive cooperation in trade

A Chinese perspective

Hu Shisheng

This chapter reviews the outstanding features and the prospects of trade relations between China and India. It argues that the trade imbalance and one-way complementarity, the two outstanding features of Sino-India trade relations, result from different economic development modalities. India's trade deficit with China is mainly an endogenous problem of India, related to its poor performance in the manufacturing sector. If transformations in economic and even social developments are carried forward in both countries, the bilateral trade pattern and composition will undergo changes, which will make bilateral trade more complementary and more balanced. With the two most populated countries interacting more economically, Sino-India trade will concomitantly have an impact upon the existing global trade regime, which is still dominated by the developed economies.

The self-liberalisation by China since 1978 and India since 1991, combined with China's entrance into the WTO (India being a founding member) in 2001, have not only successfully integrated the two economies into the global economy, but have also substantially interrelated the two economies with each other, notwithstanding their disparity in economic size, contrasting international specialisations, and different political-cum-economic systems.

In 2001, China further reformed the import control regime that was implemented as part of its WTO accession, and India abolished its licensing on consumer goods. Such export-friendly policies and import liberalisation politics have triggered a phenomenal bilateral trade increase, by leaps and bounds, especially after 2001. Bilateral trade volume increased from US$ 339 million in 1992 to nearly US$ 5 billion in 2002 and then to around US$ 74 billion in 2011.[1] Between 2000 and 2008, the average annual growth rate in bilateral trade was 43 per cent.[2] Trade fell only twice during the past decade: once in 2009 and the other in 2012, with respective decreases of 16.5 per cent and 9.4 per cent, because of the impact of the global financial crisis and concomitant world economic recession and due to the readjustments of development policies in both countries.[3] At any rate, since 2008, China has become one of India's top two trading partners, and as of 2012, India was the 15th largest trade partner for China.[4]

The rapid increase of bilateral trade and other economic interactions have affected perceptions toward the other country from within and without, especially dampening their mutual conflicts. Flourishing bilateral trade has now become a powerful engine in driving bilateral relations forward in a sustainable and steady way. At the same time, with the rapid development of bilateral trade – some disturbances, like the trade imbalance, one-way complementarity, and protectionism – have begun to worry both governments.

This chapter evaluates the logics contributing to bilateral trade, complementarity, imbalance, and protectionism, and looks ahead to future trends. China and India's their different development modalities have contributed to the current trade pattern and composition. With more efforts by the two governments in deepening their economic and social reforms in the coming years, bilateral trade will probably become more balanced and hence will have a greater impact on the world trade regime.

Trade complementarity

The bilateral complementarity in trade has occurred in line with comparative and late-development advantages and market operations between the two countries. In terms of respective comparative advantages, India's strengths are concentrated both in the traditional sectors, especially in textiles fibres and their wastes; cotton, where the value added is proportionally low, and in the knowledge-intensive sectors, including IT-enabled services, pharmaceuticals, customised services, and auto-parts manufacturing. China has a comparative advantage in many areas including machinery, transport equipment, and miscellaneous manufactured articles.

There are two outstanding features in the bilateral trade in commodities. On the one hand, the items traded between the two countries have been limited to a few items (see Tables 4.1 and 4.2).

Tables 4.1 and 4.2 show that the top five commodities have a total share above 60 per cent, even over 70 per cent. For example, in the 2000s, the share of the top five commodities in Chinese exports to India occupied between 61.9 per cent and 67.5 per cent; the share was 71 per cent in 2010; and in 2011 the share was 67.2 per cent. The pattern of Indian exports to China is similar: The share of the top five commodities in India's exports to China constituted between 66.3 per cent in 2002, 70.6 per cent in 2009, 77.9 per cent in 2010 and 68.5 per cent in 2011.

At the same time, complementarity is very asymmetric. China's exports mainly meet India's high demands for ready-made and value-added equipment, machinery products, and iron and steel, while India's exports to China mainly meet China's demand for raw materials (see Tables 4.3 and 4.4). The composition of the commodity trade has not shown much change in the past ten years. The items exported by India to China, mainly raw materials and primary products, are not India's strengths. India's export strengths are in its IT-enabled services, pharmaceuticals, and textiles and related products. However, China's exported items to India, mainly manufactured goods, are China's strengths. China is well-known for its manufacturing scale and capacity, which has earned it the title of the world's factory.

Table 4.1 Top five commodities' share (%) in Chinese exports to India

Items	2001	2002	2003	2004	2005	2006	2007	2008	2009	2010	2011	2012
Electric, electronic equipment	13.19	21.13	19.68	24.26	20.14	24.96	29.16	26.52	29.59	23.82	21.28	21.04
Organic chemicals	19.93	20.34	19.06	13.54	13.30	11.73	10.00	9.64	10.00	9.98	9.15	9.97
Silk	9.55	8.22	7.16	6.04	4.76							
Machinery, nuclear reactors, boilers, etc.	8.29	7.47	8.09	12.82	17.27	18.66	17.60	22.03	25.05	23.68	24.41	23.30
Mineral fuels, oils, distillation products, etc.	13.94	7.08	7.05	7.71	5.70							
Articles of iron or steel						4.91	4.92	3.81	3.91		4.28	3.76
Iron and steel						4.18	6.08	5.49	2.00	4.96		
Fertilizers										4.72	7.01	6.22
Total	64.90	64.24	61.03	64.38	61.17	64.44	67.76	67.48	70.55	67.16	66.12	64.28

Source: UN Comtrade, "United Nations Commodity Trade Statistics Database", http://comtrade.un.org/db/.

Table 4.2 Top five commodities' share (%) in Indian exports to China

Items	2001	2002	2003	2004	2005	2006	2007	2008	2009	2010	2011	2012
Ores, slag and ash	27.07	25.46	22.47	44.18	55.08	46.17	51.72	57.75	45.48	36.40	25.69	
Plastics and articles thereof	12.39	9.48	7.82	9.25	4.71	5.13	6.44	4.52	4.40			
Organic chemicals	10.84	10.33	7.53	7.57	6.06	6.62				4.35	5.15	
Fish, crustaceans, molluscs, aquatic invertebrates	9.89	6.99	3.42									
Cotton	8.07					9.00	9.86	7.72	5.96	12.08	16.75	
Iron and steel		14.01	28.92	10.86	10.18	5.17	3.59		4.06	4.24		
Inorganic chemicals, precious metals compound, isotopes				4.37	4.23							
Copper and articles thereof							5.13			20.81	11.19	
Slat, earth, stone, plaster, sulphur, lime and cement								2.91				
Commodities								2.66				
Total	68.26	66.27	70.17	76.22	80.26	72.09	76.73	75.56	59.90	77.88	58.78	

Source: UN Comtrade, "United Nations Commodity Trade Statistics Database", http://comtrade.un.org/db/.

Table 4.3 Indian imports from China and the world (shares by commodity in % share of total all products)

Imports	2000 China	2000 World	2005 China	2005 World	2007 China	2007 World	2010 China	2010 World
Food and live animals	0.51	2.12	0.51	1.93	0.42	1.72	0.59	1.66
Beverages and tobacco	0.01	0.08	0.01	0.1	0.01	0.07	0.01	0.04
Crude materials, inedible	3.6	6.9	3.6	6.61	1.71	5.83	1.51	4.7
Lubricants, mineral fuels and related materials	7.07	17.64	7.07	12.48	3.16	29.48	2.9	32.68
Vegetable oils, animal and, fats and waxes	0.02	3.83	0.02	2.31	0.01	1.53	0.03	1.93
Chemicals and related products	18.1	11.37	18.1	12.04	17.64	9.26	17.55	9.47
Manufactured goods	22.82	21.57	22.82	22.85	23.11	15.59	20.96	14.71
Machinery and transport equipment	41.51	23.41	41.51	27.26	48.04	24.91	50.55	20.64
Miscellaneous manufactured articles	5.88	5.19	5.88	5.14	4.97	3.79	5.83	3.34
Commodities and transactions	0.45	7.89	0.45	9.29	0.93	7.83	0.07	10.83

Source: United Nations Conference on Trade and Development (UNCTAD), "Statistics", http://unctad.org/en/pages/Statistics.aspx.

This asymmetric complementarity is a one-way trade complementarity, similar to China's trade with the developed manufacturing powers. That is to say, China's export pattern matches the import needs of India, but not vice versa. India imports manufactured goods made of the raw materials imported by China from India and other countries, while India exports its manufactured goods, produced by the machines and equipment imported from China, mainly to countries other than China. China is able to import raw materials at good rates from other countries, but India would find it difficult to import machines or other manufactured items at comparable rates from countries other than China. Table 4.5 shows that the share of Indian exports of 'crude materials (inedible)' are mainly to China, while the value-added products that India manufactures are mainly exported to countries other than China.

The logic behind this can be explained in two ways. One explanation is based on the different development patterns of these two giant economies, with China's

Table 4.4 Indian exports to China and the world (shares by commodity in % share of total all products)

Exports	2000 China	2000 World	2005 China	2005 World	2007 China	2007 World	2010 China	2010 World
Food and live animals	16.73	11.25	3	7.99	3.32	8.12	3.66	8.68
Beverages and tobacco	0.01	0.46	0.01	0.34	0.02	0.35	0.03	0.39
Crude materials, inedible	28.10	3.76	65.15	7.47	67.37	7.47	62.87	7.94
Mineral fuels, lubricants and related materials	0.12	3.41	0.34	10.46	1.05	16.19	0.93	15.73
Animal and vegetable oils, fats and waxes	3.12	0.56	0.6	0.34	0.7	0.3	1.27	0.39
Chemicals and related products	25.45	10.25	12.45	11.39	11.18	11.22	9.87	11.04
Manufactured goods	17.85	39.94	14.50	33.61	10.95	29.56	14.23	27.59
Machinery and transport equipment	5.35	7.31	2.52	10.53	3.67	11.29	4.37	13.62
Miscellaneous manufactured articles	3.11	21.08	1.2	16.75	1.58	14.34	2.76	14.52
Commodities and transactions	0.15	1.99	0.25	1.13	0.18	1.16		0.09

Source: United Nations Conference on Trade and Development (UNCTAD), "Statistics", http://unctad.org/en/pages/Statistics.aspx.

economy mainly driven by the development of the manufacturing sector and export-oriented policies, while India's economic growth had been fuelled by the services sector and domestic consumption. The second explanation is based on the gap in development, with the performance of China's economy being far better than that of India, partly because India undertook its economic liberalisation 12 years later than China.

In terms of commodity trade, this kind of one-way complementarity will not change unless India successfully transforms and upgrades its manufacturing sector and unless China's advantage and strength in the manufacturing sector is replaced by other developing countries or even by developed ones, like Japan, the US, and Germany. There is one outstanding exception to the asymmetry: in the pharmaceutical and chemical sectors, there is a balanced two-way complementary trade between China and India (see Table 4.6).

Table 4.5 Indian exports to China and the world (shares by commodity in % share of total all products)

Exports	2000 China	2000 World	2005 China	2005 World	2007 China	2007 World	2010 China	2010 World
Crude materials, inedible	28.10	3.76	65.15	7.47	67.37	7.47	62.87	7.94
Mineral fuels, lubricants and related materials	0.12	3.41	0.34	10.46	1.05	16.19	0.93	15.73
Chemicals and related products	25.45	10.25	12.45	11.39	11.18	11.22	9.87	11.04
Manufactured goods	17.85	39.94	14.50	33.61	10.95	29.56	14.23	27.59
Machinery and transport equipment	5.35	7.31	2.52	10.53	3.67	11.29	4.37	13.62
Miscellaneous manufactured articles	3.11	21.08	1.2	16.75	1.58	14.34	2.76	14.52

Source: United Nations Conference on Trade and Development (UNCTAD), "Statistics", http://unctad.org/en/pages/Statistics.aspx.

In the chemicals sector, India imports raw materials from China and exports finished products. Over the past half century or more, India has developed skills in chemicals as well as finished plastic and pharmaceutical products that are exported to China. Indian pharmaceutical companies rely on China as one of their primary suppliers of pharmaceutical ingredients.

Trade imbalance

With the rapid and continuing increase of bilateral trade volumes, the trade imbalance has also been become more alarming. Especially in recent years, for every USD worth of exports to China, India imports almost three USDs worth of

Table 4.6 India's trade with China (shares of commodity in % to shares of total all products)

	2000 China	2005 China	2007 China	2010 China
Imports from				
Chemicals and related products	18.1	18.1	17.64	17.55
Exports to				
Chemicals and related products	25.45	12.45	11.18	9.87

Source: United Nations Conference on Trade and Development (UNCTAD), "Statistics", http://unctad.org/en/pages/Statistics.aspx.

Table 4.7 Bilateral trade (in billions USD)

	Trade in goods		Export		Import	
	Volume	Growth %	Volume	Growth %	Volume	Growth %
2012	66.47	−10.10	47.67	−5.70	18.80	66.47
2011	73.92	19.70	50.54	23.50	23.37	73.92
2010	61.78	42.20	40.92	38.00	20.84	61.78
2009	43.38	−16.30	29.67	−6.10	13.71	43.38
2008	51.78	34.00	31.49	23.00	20.29	51.78
2007	38.65	55.50	24.02	64.70	14.63	38.65
2006	24.86	32.92	14.58	63.21	10.28	24.86
2005	18.70	37.50	8.94	50.80	9.77	18.70
2004	13.64	79.10	5.93	77.30	7.68	13.64
2003	7.60	53.56	3.34	25.15	4.25	7.60
2002	4.95	37.50	2.67	40.85	2.27	4.95
2001	3.60	23.44	1.90	21.52	1.70	3.60
2000	2.91	46.58	1.56	34.34	1.35	2.91
1999	1.99	3.43	1.16	14.26	0.83	1.99
1998	1.92	4.97	1.02	8.89	0.91	1.92
1997	1.83	30.14	0.93	35.76	0.90	1.83
1996	1.41	20.98	0.69	−10.07	0.72	1.41
1995	1.16	29.94	0.77	33.51	0.40	1.16
1994	0.90	32.40	0.57	122.09	0.32	0.90
1993	66.47	−10.10	47.67	−5.70	18.80	66.47
1992	73.92	19.70	50.54	23.50	23.37	73.92

Source: Ministry of Commerce, People's Republic of China, "Statistics", http://english.mofcom.gov.cn/article/statistic/; China Commerce Yearbook; China Statistical Yearbook, http://www.yearbookchina.com/.

good from China (see Table 4.7). In 2012, China accounted for one fifth of India's overall trade deficit with the world, or more than half if oil imports are excluded.[5]

This imbalance has mainly been a result of the one-way complementary trade, mentioned above. India's exports cannot meet the requirements of the Chinese market (both household consumption and government consumption), due to India's weak capacity in manufacturing. The share of manufacturing is about 15 per cent (see Table 4.8) in India, compared with an average of 26 per cent for other low-middle income countries.[6]

From Table 4.8, we can see furthermore that the share of manufacturing has actually declined in the past decade in India. China has a much better performance in the export of manufacturing goods. During 1995–2008, China's manufactured exports grew by 26.7 per cent, almost twice as fast as India's growth (at 15.4 per cent). China not only exports manufactured goods to India but also to the whole world. China's share of the world's manufacturing exports increased from 0.5 per cent in 1995 to 10.8 per cent in 2008, while India's share increased from 0.5 per cent to just 1.3 per cent during the same period.[7]

Table 4.8 The structures of the Indian economy (% of GDP)

Five-Year Plan	Agriculture	Manufacture	Services
6th (1980–84)	41.0	14.6	37.1
7th (1985–89)	36.6	15.9	40.1
8th (1992–96)	32.3	17.1	43.1
9th (1997–2001)	27.5	17.1	47.9
10th (2002–06)	19.36	15.5	52.9
11th (2007–10)	18.1	15.1	54.2

Source: Manmohan Agarwal, *Comparing India and China's Economic Performance since 1991*, Occasional Paper, New Delhi: Institute of Chinese Studies, February 2013, p. 7.

The record shows that in 1995 the export capacity in manufactured goods for both countries was nearly at the same level. But, over the past 20 years, China has developed skills in consumer electronics, telecommunications, and other consumer durables. After specialising in unskilled labour-intensive sectors such as toys, footwear, and light manufactures in the 1990s, China has made remarkable progress in electrical and electronic equipment, home appliances, and office machinery as a result of differences in sector-specific skills.

The prolonged imbalance of trade in commodities between India and the world had existed even before 2001, when both India and China eased barriers in manufactured goods. This fact itself indicates that India's performance in manufacturing has been lacklustre not only in comparison to China. Hence, in terms of trade (in commodities), India's imbalance is not China-specific.

Even when India enjoyed a trade surplus with China at times prior to 2006 (see Table 4.7), India faced the problem of a trade deficit in goods with the world (see Table 4.9). The only difference now is that the deficit has shifted from being with the world (other than China) to being primarily with China.

It is worthwhile pointing out that, at present, there are 15 countries with which India either has a Free Trade Agreement (FTA) (or regional arrangement) or is negotiating one. India runs a trade surplus with five of these countries and a trade deficit with the other ten (see Table 4.10).

Table 4.9 Trade balances (% of GDP)

Five-Year Plans	Goods	Non-factor services	Net income	Private transfers	Current account balance
6th (1980–84)	–3.4	0.6	–0.1	1.3	–1.5
7th (1985–89)	–3.0	0.3	–0.6	0.9	–2.2
8th (1992–96)	–2.0	0.2	–1.1	2.3	–1.1
9th (1997–2001)	–3.2	0.6	–0.9	2.8	–0.9
10th (2002–06)	–4.4	2.1	–0.7	3.2	0.2
11th (2007–10)	–8.3	3.2	–0.5	3.5	–2.2

Source: Manmohan Agarwal, *Comparing India and China's Economic Performance since 1991*, Occasional Paper, New Delhi: Institute of Chinese Studies, February 2013, p. 9.

Table 4.10 India's trade balance with some of India's top trade partners in 2009–10 (Rs'000 Crore)

	Exports	Imports	Trade balance
EU	159.21	173.19	−13.99
UAE	113.35	91.80	21.55
China	54.71	146.05	−91.33
Singapore	35.95	30.62	5.32
Saudi Arabia	18.55	80.66	−62.11
Japan	17.14	31.89	−14.75
Korea Republic (South)	16.13	40.55	−24.42
Indonesia	14.60	41.01	−26.40
Malaysia	13.50	24.49	−10.99
Bangladesh	11.50	1.21	10.30
Brazil	11.36	16.26	−4.90
Sri Lanka	10.29	1.85	8.44
South Africa	9.75	26.90	−17.15
Vietnam	8.67	2.46	6.21
Thailand	8.23	13.89	−5.66
All	502.95	722.84	−219.88

Source: Government of India, Department of Commerce, "Export Import Databank", http://www.commerce.nic.in/eidb/. These are countries with which India already has RTAs or is negotiating RTAs. This list is drawn from the top 20 export markets of India in 2009-10. Refer to India Trades database by CMIE and Ministry of commerce website on India's Trade Agreements. See Department of Commerce, Government of India, "Export Import Databank," http://www.commerce.nic.in/eidb/.

As a matter of fact, India's tariffs are relatively higher than the tariffs of its FTA partners and/or major trade partners. Take the comparison between China and India. The tariff rate for China is generally lower than India's (see Figure 4.1). In terms of the simple average tariff, China is at 9.6 per cent for all products, 15.6 per cent for agriculture, and 8.7 per cent for non-agriculture, while India is at 12.9 per cent, 31.8 per cent, and 10.1 per cent, respectively. In terms of the trade-weighted average tariff, China is at 4.3 per cent for all products, 10.3 per cent and 4 per cent respectively for agriculture and non-agriculture; for India, the figures are 6 per cent, 13.7 per cent, and 5.85 per cent.[8] This strongly demonstrates that the root cause of India's trade deficit is not market access, but rather the capacity to export what its trading partners really want.

By comparing the trade deficits of India with China and with the world (see Table 4.11), we can see that the fluctuation in the India-China trade deficit bears little relation to India's trade deficit with the rest of the world.

The devaluation of the Indian rupee in the last several years has not been of much help in reducing the deficit. Since 2010, the Indian rupee has depreciated by 43 per cent. Between July 2011 and July 2012, the rupee depreciated by 20 per cent. In intra-day trading on August 6, 2013, the Indian rupee depreciated

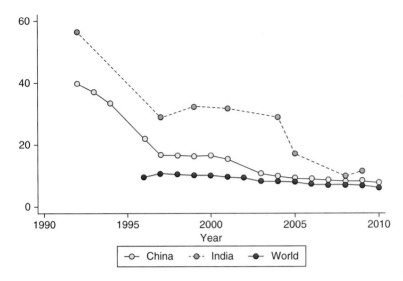

Figure 4.1 Simple average of tariff rates for China, India and the world (for goods), 1992–2010.

Source: Kaliappa Kalirajan et al., "China and India: A Comparative Analysis of Trade and Investment Performance", 2013, p. 4, http://mjyu.ccer.edu.cn/EABER_Routledge%20chapter_2.pdf.

to a historic low of 61.80. The Indian rupee has fallen over 12 per cent against the USD in the fiscal year from April 2013 to March 2014.[9] However, due to the lack of strong capacity in manufacturing, the depreciation did not help much in improving India's exports of goods, while it drove up import costs. India cannot reduce its imports from China (which it needs to meet its requirements in addressing its infrastructural and manufacturing deficit), while China has had to reduce the import of raw materials with iron ore, in particular from India, in recent years.[10] The Indian rupee's depreciation has therefore further increased, not decreased, India's trade deficit with China.[11]

Given that India's market share in global merchandise trade is only 1.3 per cent,[12] demand-side factors are really not the major constraint in India's export growth. In fact, the supply side, not the demand side, really matters in the weak export capacity

Table 4.11 India's trade deficit (as % of Indian GDP) with China and with the rest of the world

	2005	2006	2007	2008	2009	2010
India–China trade deficit	7.56	0.98	1.23	1.86	1.56	1.23
India–rest of the world trade deficit	4.84	6.02	6.03	10.43	6.62	5.97

Source: Author.

of India. That is to say, the supply-side inefficiencies are the major constraining factors for India's export growth and hence the major contributors to the trade deficit. In general, India's trade deficit is mainly an endogenous problem related to its poor performance in the manufacturing sector.

The reason behind the stagnancy of India's manufactures is due to the lack of liquidity in three flows: labour flows (blocked by rigid labour laws, the caste system, and a high illiteracy rate),[13] materials and goods flows (blocked or delayed by poor infrastructure and rampant red tape),[14] and capital flows (discouraged by the slack flows of labour, materials, and goods).

If we look closely, we will see that the major factors really constraining India's commodity exports include major infrastructural backwardness, such as the severe lack of facilities in power, ports, roads, and railways; a low-technology manufacturing sector; insufficient R&D; poor literacy and technical education levels; unimpressive productivity; high transaction and information costs; high lending costs; bureaucratic and legal delays; and massive corruption.

That is to say, India lacks a favourable business environment for the manufacturing industry. This can be easily seen in the striking differences in terms of FDI inflows into China and India. The accumulated FDI inflows into China during 1978–2010 stood at US$ 1582.1 billion, while India received US$ 199.9 billion.[15] FDI inflows have greatly improved the infrastructure in China and empowered China's labour-intensive and capital-intensive manufacturing capacity.[16] According to statistics issued by the US Department of Commerce and China's General Administration of Customs, China has replaced the US as the biggest trader in commodities. In 2012, the total export and import volume of the US was US$ 3.82 trillion, while that of China was US$ 3.87 trillion.[17] In 2012, China had a trade surplus (of about US$ 8 billion) with ASEAN for the first time.[18]

If the trade imbalance is conducive to economic and social development, then some degree of imbalance should be tolerated. The import of power equipment from China is instructive in this regard. According to news reports in *The Indian Express* on August 4, 2012, Chinese companies could account for almost half of the 100,000 MW target stipulated by the Five-Year Plan starting from 2012. Despite the Indian government's efforts to restrict Chinese investments within the power sector, the involvement of Chinese companies, particularly in the construction of Indian power plants, is only growing. Andrew Brandler, CEO of CLP Holdings, rightly points out that:

> Dongfang, Harbin Electric and Shanghai Electric, China's three big makers, can provide equipment to the Haryana plant at almost half the price of either Indian or international manufacturers, even taking into account the cost of transportation and any tariffs on imports. Moreover, when the Chinese bid for supply contracts, they offer fixed prices, whereas Indian groups offer quotes on a cost-plus basis, leaving their potential customers with the kind of uncertainty they hate. Speed is also a factor. The Chinese can deliver the turbines for the Haryana plant, a 1,320 MW behemoth, in 36 months, whereas the Indians will take 60 months.[19]

Protectionism

For understandable reasons, India is more aggressive in trade protection against imported commodities from China than vice versa. India has taken various protective measures and discriminated against Chinese imports, such as launching anti-dumping and anti-subsidy censoring cases, carrying forward investigations on Special Safeguard Measures, and implementing some restrictions via tariff and non-tariff barriers, amongst others. According to statistics submitted to the Indian Parliament by the Directorate General of Anti-Dumping and Allied Duties (DGAD), since 1992, India has launched 149 anti-dumping cases against Chinese goods, which accounted for over half of the total anti-dumping investigations initiated by India against foreign countries.[20]

Especially in the years around the global financial crisis, India increased anti-dumping and anti-subsidy censoring cases against Chinese products. Even those produced in third countries were not spared. The reason from the Indian side for taking such protectionist measures against Chinese imports is the complaint of "lack of transparency in pricing". India refuses to grant Market Economy Status to China (but China will automatically obtain that status in 2016 in line with the WTO Protocol). India would like to re-fix the values or the prices of imported Chinese items by referring to a third country's domestic pricing regime or price. This practice has artificially increased the price of Chinese commodities, hence reducing the competitiveness of imported Chinese goods in the Indian market. Of course, some practices of the Chinese government at various levels in subsiding external trade have entailed complaints and hence retaliation by India.

In some years, India has taken measures to exclude Chinese companies from exporting their items to the Indian market in the name of national security. For example, in May 2009, the Indian Intelligence Bureau and the Ministry of Defence jointly opposed the National Telecommunication Department's decision to install telecommunication equipment manufactured by two Chinese companies and Huawei's bidding for a US$ 6 billion telecommunication network project. The investigation led to the Bharat Sanchar Nigam Limited (BSNL), India's state-owned telecommunications company, tearing up three big deals with Huawei.[21] In December 2011, India's National Security Council Secretariat even hinted that the trade deficit with China may pose security concerns.[22] In June 2012, the Indian government approved a levy of 21 per cent against all imported power-generating equipment (this levy will be implemented in 2017). Due to the fact that 40 per cent of India's imported electric equipment and machineries comes from China, Chinese companies will be more affected than any others once this levy is implemented.[23]

The stronghold for such trade protectionism mainly includes the Confederation of Indian Industry (CII), the Federation of Indian Chambers of Commerce and Industry (FICCI) and the Associated Chambers of Commerce and Industry of India (ASSOCHAM), as well as the Commerce Ministry. T.S. Vishwanath, head of the international trade policy division of CII, stated, "The pricing mechanism in China is not very transparent and hence we do not understand it. Until then, it should not be granted market economy status. The CII is working with its Chinese counterparts in this regard".[24] A FICCI study also found that cheap imports from China had made deep inroads into sectors like machinery items, electronic goods, and auto components.[25] FICCI, being mainly a conglomeration of Indian medium and small enterprises, is the most vocal on trade protectionism. As early as 2008, FICCI advised against a Regional Trading Agreement (RTA) with China, highlighting India's continued over-reliance on Chinese imports. FICCI feels that the majority of Indian small and medium enterprises are not yet ready to compete with Chinese goods.[26]

It will be a big challenge for Indian enterprises and their conglomerates to continue the current protectionism against Chinese imports after China automatically obtains Market Economic Status in 2016. In any case, with the rising cost of Chinese labour, and with the elevation of Chinese companies' positions in various value chains, most of the protectionism from the Indian side (concentrated in the areas of labour-intensive and low-value added industries) may soon disappear.

Indian businessmen also have complaints about access to Chinese markets, especially in the areas of IT and IT-enabled services, pharmaceutical products, and fruits and farming products. However, this could be the result of market needs. For example, Chinese markets need more Chinese-language IT products and enabled services, which are not the strength of Indian IT companies.

In the pharmaceutical industry, the performance of Chinese companies is at least as good as their Indian counterparts. Moreover, due to the chaotic pharmaceutical market in China, it is not easy for Indian pharmaceutical giants to gain access, until the Chinese government implements reforms in areas like establishing the credit system of the pharmaceutical market, separating dispensing from prescription, and separating accounting and management for medical and pharmaceutical income, among other things.

As for the import of more Indian fruits and agro-products by China, the situation has been difficult due to the differences in quarantine criteria and Chinese requirements regarding the storage and transportation of fruits prone to decay. Thus, China has only imported three kinds of fruit from India, although China agreed to open its market to as many as seventeen Indian fruits upon its entrance into the WTO in 2001. It is true that protectionism on the Chinese side has prevented Indian tobacco products from entering Chinese markets, as liquor and tobacco have long been the top contributors to Chinese national and local revenues.

During Chinese Prime Minister Li Keqiang's May 2013 visit to India, the two sides signed memoranda of understanding (MOUs) on buffalo meat, pharmaceuticals, and fisheries as well as an agreement on feed and its ingredients, to deal with the severe trade imbalance between the two countries. An agreement was also signed between the Export Inspection Council of India (EIC) and China's General Administration of Quality Supervision, Inspection and Quarantine (AQSIQ) on trade and safety of feed and feed ingredients.[27]

During President Xi Jinping's visit to India in September 2014, several agreements pledging greater Chinese investment into India's infrastructure sectors as well as agreements to give greater access to Indian exports to China, particularly pharmaceuticals and agricultural products, were signed.[28]

Institutional efforts at trade promotion

Bilateral trade-promoting institutions have played a bigger role in promoting bilateral trade relations. The China–India Joint Economic Group (JEG) on Economic Relations and Trade, Science and Technology was established in 1988. After Prime Minister Vajpayee's visit to China in 2003, a Joint Study Group to study the setting up of a Free Trade Agreement (FTA), and a Joint Task Force to study the feasibility of a China–India Regional Trade Agreement (RTA), were initiated.

The most important trade-promoting mechanism is the Strategic Economic Dialogue (SED), which was established during Prime Minister Wen Jiabao's visit in December 2010. Two more rounds of SED dialogues have been held already. The bilateral SED mechanism is commissioned to deepen and elevate current levels of economic interactions. The SED has functioned as a forum for both sides to undertake macro-economic coordination, to share their respective practices in handling various challenges, and to identify specific fields for enhancing and enlarging cooperation. With the SED, the two sides have set up five working groups on policy coordination, infrastructure, energy, environment protection, and high technology.[29] These groups, under the umbrella of SED, have been tasked to diversify bilateral economic interactions, including mutual trade promotion, investment, R&D, and so on.

For example, in the second round of the SED dialogue, the two sides signed four government-to-government and seven business MOUs, with about US$ 4.8 billion of mutual investment. Other avenues of cooperation included improvement of energy efficiency; greater environmental protection; infrastructure development, particularly within India's railway sector; and water conservation and development of clean water technologies.[30]

After two rounds of dialogues, the SED has already become one of the most significant platforms to explore new areas and approaches to address the two countries' respective concerns, such as how to deal with Indian concerns over its severe trade deficit with China and market access for Indian companies in China, especially in sectors such as pharmaceuticals and IT, and how to address China's concerns about the obstacles that Chinese companies face in the expansion of their operations in India and the protectionist measures taken by the Indian side against Chinese goods.

China has only two similar dialogues, including the China–US Strategic and Economic Dialogue, established in April 2009. This shows that China attaches the highest importance to economic interactions with India.

After the May 2013 visit of Chinese Prime Minister Li Keqiang, the two sides also agreed to consult two other parties with the purpose to establishing a Joint Study Group on "strengthening connectivity in the BCIM (Bangladesh, China, India and Myanmar) region for closer economic, trade, and people-to-people linkages and to initiating the development of a BCIM Economic Corridor".[31] India's Planning

Commission and China's State Development and Reform Commission, who are also the coordinators of the SED mechanism, will monitor the progress of the BCIM Economic Corridor.

Powerful engine for bilateral relations

Although there exist 'developmental competitions', 'strategic suspicions, 'territorial disputes', 'historical legacies', and 'political otherness' between China and India, the general stability of bilateral relations has not been disturbed much since the end of the 1980s. One of the key reasons has been the outstanding constructive role played by the economic interactions between these two countries.

Sino-India relations could well be described as dual-engined, with political and economic interactions being equally important. Compared to China's relations with other major powers, this phenomenon is unique. Politically, the top leaders of both countries have met frequently. President Hu Jintao and Prime Minster Wen Jiabao, in their ten years in power, met Indian Prime Minister Manmohan Singh as many as 26 times. They also set up the prime ministers' hotline. It is safe to say that Sino-India relations have been guided and managed by the top leadership on both sides.

At the same time, bilateral trade relations have undergone a dramatic increase. In 2002, bilateral trade was only about US$ 4.9 billion; in 2011, this figure had rocketed to US$ 73.9 billion.[32] In 2012, bilateral trade had decreased to US$ 66.5 billion due to the impact of the global economic recession,[33] but the economic complementarities between the two countries could, in the long run, be the most powerful driving force of their economic interactions. China has been India's biggest trade partner several times since 2007. This, to a larger extent, has modified mutual perceptions. Thus, the Joint Statement, issued during Li Keqiang's 2013 visit, declared that "both countries view each other as partners for mutual benefit and not as rivals or competitors".[34]

One outstanding contribution to bilateral relations via their blossoming economic interactions was the resumption of border trade at Nathu La Pass in July 2006, which had been closed after the 1962 border war.[35] The resumption of the Nathu La border trade was accompanied by China's acceptance of Sikkim as part of India and India's acceptance of Tibet as part of China.

Future trends

The current bilateral trade pattern between China and India will continue for some years. The trade imbalance will be addressed by both sides. In line with the Joint Statement issued on May 20, 2013, the two countries agreed to take steps to address the issue of the trade imbalance, including "cooperation on pharmaceutical supervision including registration, stronger links between Chinese enterprises and Indian IT industry, and completion of phytosanitary negotiations on agro-products".[36] Looking ahead, there are three things China and India need to do on economic matters.

First, the two countries need to be attentive to the dynamics in their economics and to be open to opportunities. Due to the improvement of India's infrastructure and manufacturing industry, and the upgrading of China's position in the world manufacturing industry value chain, Sino-Indian bilateral trade could be more complementary. In both countries, the agrarian transformation, urbanisation, the emergence of a middle class, and the creation of a modern economy could lay the foundations of even greater levels of bilateral trade.

On the one hand, in order to maintain its advantage in the manufacturing sector, China has made unremitting efforts in upgrading its position in the manufacturing value-chain. Ever since China's entrance into the WTO, China's exports of manufactured goods have encompassed an increasing proportion of hi-tech goods, and it has become the world's biggest exporter of hi-tech products, having overtaken the US in 2004.[37] Most of China's hi-tech exports are in household electronic goods, made from imported hi-tech parts and components. China's dependence on foreign technology is illustrated by its ranking third in the world for net payment of royalties.[38] One more important development in this regard is that, although IT-tech exports are still dominated by foreign companies, "Chinese firms have been enlarging their position in the domestic market, taking advantage of the presence of foreign suppliers producing parts and components".[39]

More important, China has ambitious plans to tap the huge potential of domestic consumption, based on the build-up of a comprehensive social welfare network and safeguard system, on rapid urbanisation (from 52.6 per cent in 2012 to an estimated 70 per cent in 2030 with an additional 400 million people moving to the cities), and on the reform of the income distribution system (with the elimination of 80 million people living under the poverty line and with minimum salary increased by 40 per cent by 2015).[40] These kinds of efforts could provide enormous opportunities for India to balance its trade deficit and enrich its trade composition with China. For example, the high demand for more urban-related and IT-enabled customised services in China could provide a golden opening for Indian IT giants.

Take another example. India's pharmaceutical industry could find a huge potential market in China as the Chinese government's efforts to construct a national medical and health care network progresses. The Indian pharmaceutical industry has seen rapid development especially after the abolition of product patent protection for pharmaceuticals in 1972. India emerged as an impressive and significant player in the global pharmaceutical sector, regarded worldwide as a low-cost producer of high-quality pharmaceuticals. India supplies medicines not only to developed countries such as the US, but also to other developing countries. The cooperation and bilateral trade between India and China in this area has just started. During Li Keqiang's visit in India in May 2013, the two sides signed an MOU between the Pharmaceuticals Export Promotion Council of India (Pharmexcil) and the China Chamber of Commerce for Import and Export of Medicines and Health Products.

In the past, India has complained about the difficulties in expanding its trade with China in the pharmaceutical sector. The signing of the MOU is expected to facilitate access to the Chinese market. In China, the cost of drugs accounts for about 40 per cent of treatment compared with 20–30 per cent in OECD countries.[41] India's low-cost drugs could help reduce the financial burden on the Chinese governments at different levels. With China expanding the coverage of its healthcare system, Chinese officials have become more conscious of the need to reduce the costs of drugs. Between 2008 and 2013, China imported around US$ 4332.37 million worth of pharmaceutical products; imports from India amounted to US$ 692.44 million.[42] On the other hand, the annual exports and imports of drugs and formulations by India have been respectively around US$ 5 billion and US$ 1 billion in recent years.[43] The potential in this area is huge.

On the other hand, the Indian government is becoming more ambitious about increasing India's manufacturing capacity. In 2011, New Delhi published its "National Manufacturing Policy", planning to build up special manufacturing zones where infrastructure is better and regulations fewer in the coming ten years. Since then, Prime Minister Modi has initiated the "Make in India" programme. The Indian government will make efforts to attract as much as US$ 1 trillion into infrastructure construction during the Twelfth Five-Year Plan (2012–2017). In this regard, China's abundant capital and cheap-but-good machines and equipment could make substantial contributions to India's efforts.

More important, with the development of 3D printing, big data and cloud-based technologies, smart product manufacturing, intelligent cities, the current restrictions on India's manufacturing might become less significant, and the gap between China and India in manufacturing industries could be narrowed. Indian manufacturing, by taking advantage of its strength in customised production and IT-enabled services, would enhance its capacity in meeting the requirements of smart and customised products and services, domestically and externally. By then, the trade patterns and composition between China and India might have been transformed dramatically. The enormous number of engineers and post-graduates would be powerful driving forces in transforming the countries' industries and hence their bilateral trade.

There are already some positive developments in this regard. About seven large Chinese banks are serviced by Tata Consultancy Services (TCS), including the Bank of China, Huaxia Bank, and Guangdong Rural Credit Cooperative, among others. Shanghai's Foreign Exchange Center uses a TCS-designed trading system. According to Kalirajan et al., further opportunities for TCS also exist in "building IT architecture and applications platforms for newly developed 'intelligent cities'".[44] On August 8, 2011, TCS said it would set up iCity Lab in association with the Singapore Management University (SMU) and will initially invest 6 million Singapore dollars directly in the lab over the next three years.[45]

During Xi Jinping's visit to India in September 2014, the two sides agreed that China would invest US$ 20 billion in India and India would open industrial parks for Chinese businesses.

Secondly, China and India should have a greater say in the international trading regime. In the past several decades, although China and India are big traders, they have been mainly observers, even passive observers, of the rules and regulations formulated by the Western developed countries. They have little say and voting rights in reforming the current trade regime.

However, with China's and India's growing expertise in knowledge and technology-intensive industries, the world trade map could change. Both China and India would become innovators and producers of new knowledge and technologies. The much-advocated concept of 'Chindia' technologies and innovations could contribute tangibly to the on-going global shift in production, trade, and employment in many areas.[46] At the very least, the importance of traditional exports, such as textiles and clothing, will diminish as both countries develop new export sectors.

Take Information and Communications Technology (ICT) for example. The new sectors in ICT are already outward-oriented, and their contribution to exports far exceeds their shares of GDP in both countries. India has focused on specific technological niches and has become an advanced centre for ICT services, which means that the real weight of India's exports is not reflected by trade data. China also has progressively become a fast-growing exporter of ICT products, and it now accounts for around one fifth of world exports of such products.[47] In the last few years, China has overtaken the US in exports of ICT and high-technology goods.[48] The biotech sector is expected to follow a similar path in the future.[49]

When the two most populated economies get comprehensively involved with each other in trade the world will become much more dependent upon these two giants' markets, and this will influence world trade arrangements and will give them a greater say in the reform of international trade rules and practices.

China and India have to cooperate to meet the challenges ahead. For example, both countries will face pressure from the emerging trading regimes like the US-led Trans-Pacific Partnership (TPP) and Transatlantic Trade and Investment Partnership (T-TIP) currently under negotiation. TTP and T-TIP would go well beyond the WTO rules and would be very likely to impose higher levels of restrictions on the developing economies, China and India in particular. These agreements will also force countries to adopt more rigid measures in areas such as investment, state-owned units, intellectual property rights, and government purchases, among other things, which could negatively affect China and India.

One of the best ways for China and India to address this emerging challenge would be to have regional trade arrangements or an FTA. The potential of a combined market of nearly three billion people cannot easily be neglected. The Bangladesh–China–India–Myanmar (BCIM) Economic Corridor and the Regional Comprehensive Economic Partnership (RCEP) (between ASEAN and its partners) are two areas that China and India should pay more attention to. At the very least, China and India should cooperate in enhancing their influence in regional trade regimes.

Thirdly, China and India should enhance bilateral trade cooperation aiming at third markets. Jointly sharpening the Chindia technological and competitive edge is a promising area for the two countries to explore, with an eye on third markets in which they could sell their products.[50] The two countries can take full advantage of the cost efficiency of their huge, cheap, and skilled human resources.[51]

They can also make full use of their technological progress, especially in the areas of biology, pharmaceuticals, farming, automobiles, aerospace, new materials, and new energy. Companies from both countries should use their late-development advantage, comparative advantage, and the mutual complementarities between them to create world-famous brands and manufacture more value-added and technology-innovative products to "reshape their future".[52] China and India have the markets to cultivate, develop, and sharpen the Chindia technology edge, innovate products, and even set up Chindia criteria, pricing regimes, and market rules.

In this regard, there are already some successful examples. India's Mahindra & Mahindra has jointly, with Chinese partners, manufactured tractors that have not only been sold in China and India but have also been exported to third markets.

In the Joint Statement on the State Visit of Chinese Premier Li Keqiang to India, issued on May 20, 2013, the two sides agreed "to consider collaborating on development projects of common interest in third countries".[53] During the visit, the two governments expressed willingness to cooperate "on establishing industrial zones so as to provide platforms for cluster-type development of enterprises".[54] These industrial zones will not only manufacture commodities for their own markets, but also for third markets.

Conclusion

This chapter has evaluated the outstanding features of Sino-India trade from the normalisation of relations in 1988 onwards. Bilateral trade has witnessed a dramatic increase in the past 20 years due to the huge economic complementarity that exists between the two economies. In the past ten years, the trade imbalance, which has been in favour of China, has worsened, to the point of being regarded by the Indian side as a national threat. The growing trade imbalance has made India very reluctant to enter into far-reaching trade agreements such as an FTA or RTA with China. However, this chapter concludes that the imbalance is mainly an endogenous problem related to the poor performance in the Indian manufacturing sector.

The current trade pattern and composition will continue in the foreseeable future. Even in the coming years, India's demand for electric, electronic, machinery products, and equipment will remain high as India transforms its economic structure by enhancing infrastructural facilities and manufacturing capacities. Although the trade imbalance will be further enlarged, trade with China is serving the long-term development interest of India. This is the developmental phase which India cannot bypass, if India wants to be a global power.

Notes

1 National Bureau of Statistics of China, *China Statistical Yearbook 2012*, Beijing: China Statistics Press, 2012.
2 Amitendu Palit, *China–India Economics: Challenges, Competition and Collaboration*, Oxford: Routledge, 2012, p. 73.

3 Embassy of India, Beijing, China, "Trade and Commercial Relations", http://www.indianembassy.org.cn/DynamicContent.aspx?MenuId=3&SubMenuId=0.
4 Embassy of India, Beijing, "Trade and Commercial Relations", http://www.indianembassy.org.cn/DynamicContent.aspx?MenuId=3&SubMenuId=0.
5 R. S. Kalha, *Sino-Indian Relations: Are Trade Issues Likely To Cause Even More Problems?* IDSA Comment, New Delhi: Institute of Defence Studies and Analyses, 24 December 2012, http://idsa.in/idsacomments/SinoIndianRelations_RSKalha_241212.
6 Manmohan Agarwal, *Comparing India and China's Economic Performance since 1991*, Occasional Paper, New Delhi: Institute of Chinese Studies, February 2013, http://www.icsin.org/publications/comparing-india-and-chinas-economic-performance-since-1991.
7 Ibid., p. 8.
8 Parthapratim Pal, "India and RTAs: Getting Tangled in the Noodle Bowl", *Economic and Political Weekly*, XLVI/15, 9 April 2011, p. 17, http://www.epw.in/commentary/india-and-rtas-getting-tangled-noodle-bowl.html.
9 "Economy Faces Challenges, Government has to do More on Rupee: FM", *The Economic Times*, 12 August 2013, http://articles.economictimes.indiatimes.com/2013-08-12/news/41332707_1_current-account-deficit-oil-imports-forex-reserves.
10 In order to meet China's efforts in solving its overcapacity problem, for example, there is about 900 million cubic tons of iron and steel in storage. See Chuin-Wei Yap, "China Raises Steel Capacity Closure Targets", *The Wall Street Journal*, 8 May 2014, http://online.wsj.com/news/articles/SB10001424052702304655304579549130649982174.
11 The effect on bilateral trade is vividly demonstrated by Table 4.7. In 2012, China's imports from India decreased by 19.6 per cent, with the trade deficit increasing by 6.3 per cent to US$ 28.87 billion.
12 Parthapratim Pal, "India and RTAs: Getting Tangled in the Noodle Bowl".
13 In line with Paper No.1 of the Census of 2011, not only are a quarter of all Indians and one-third of women still illiterate, the literacy figures are in severe short of the 85 per cent mark set by the Planning Commission for 2011–12. Refer to "The People of India", *Economic and Political Weekly*, XLVI/16, 16 April 2011, p. 8, http://www.epw.in/editorials/people-india.html.
14 India's infrastructure shaves off about two percentage points from its gross domestic product growth annually. See Santanu Choudhury, Romit Guha and Saurabh Chaturvedi, "After Blackout, India Seeks to Restore Faith", *The Wall Street Journal*, 1 August 2012, http://online.wsj.com/article/SB10000872396390443687504577563001658535464.html.
15 The World Bank, "Databank", http://databank.worldbank.org/.
16 There was an absolute decline of 3.7 million in total manufacturing employment in India between 2004–05 and 2009–10. Of the 86.5 million new non-agricultural jobs created in India between 1993–94 and 2009–10, just 9.2 million were in the manufacturing sector. India's manufacturing sector employed a total of 52 million workers in 2009–10, including both organised and unorganised sector workers. The employment in India's factory sector, generally representing the organised manufacturing sector, numbered only 11.8 million in the same year. In China, it was the steady expansion of the manufacturing sector that first provided an impressive and appealing exit out of agriculture for the vast majority of the population. In 2005, the Chinese manufacturing sector employed 104 million 'regular' workers, making it almost double the size of India's manufacturing sector in that year. Refer to Barry Naughton, *The Chinese Economy: Transitions and Growth*, Cambridge: MIT Press, 2007, pp. 274–275.

17 "China Eclipses U.S. as Biggest Trading Nation", *Bloomberg*, 11 February 2013, http://www.bloomberg.com/news/2013-02-09/china-passes-u-s-to-become-the-world-s-biggest-trading-nation.html.
18 "China–ASEAN Trade to hit 500 bln USD", *People's Daily*, 23 July 2013, http://english.people.com.cn/90778/8338447.html.
19 Henny Sender, "Lead Over India Widens as China's Industry Powers Ahead", *The Financial Times*, 12 June 2012, http://www.ftchinese.com/story/001045066/en.
20 "149 Anti-dumping Cases against China Highest among Foreign Nations: Govt", *The Economic Times*, 21 December 2011, http://articles.economictimes.indiatimes.com/2011-12-21/news/30542669_1_anti-dumping-measures-dgad-anti-dumping-probes.
21 Wang Zhao Bin, "Who Are Encircling Huawei?" Article in Chinese, *China Economy & Information*, 8 December 2010, http://www.bianews.com/news/20/n-329220.html.
22 Anil K. Gupta and Haiyan Wang, "Let China Supply India's Public-Works Boom", *The Wall Street Journal*, 23 August 2012, http://online.wsj.com/article/SB10000872396390444358404577604593624357120.html.
23 Gupta and Wang, "Let China Supply India's Public-Works Boom".
24 Rupesh Janve and Rituparna Bhuyan, "Commerce Ministry Opposes China FTA," *Business Standard*, 9 February 2008, http://www.business-standard.com/article/economy-policy/commerce-ministry-opposes-china-fta-108020901016_1.html.
25 Ibid.
26 "Imports from China rising fast: FICCI", *The Economic Times*, 13 January 2008, http://articles.economictimes.indiatimes.com/2008-01-13/news/28389441_1_total-imports-trading-partners-regional-trade-agreement.
27 "India, China Take Steps to Reduce Trade Gap", *The Hindu*, 20 May 2013, http://www.thehindu.com/business/Economy/india-china-take-steps-to-reduce-trade-gap/article4733147.ece?ref=relatedNews.
28 "China's Xi Jinping Signs Landmark Deals on India Visit", *BBC News*, 18 September 2014, http://www.bbc.com/news/world-asia-india-29249268.
29 Embassy of India, Beijing, China, "Trade and Commercial Relations", http://www.indianembassy.org.cn/DynamicContent.aspx?MenuId=3&SubMenuId=0.
30 Ministry of External Affairs, Government of India, "Agreed Minutes of the 1st India-China Strategic Economic Dialogues", 26 September 2011, http://mea.gov.in/bilateral-documents.htm?dtl/5100/Agreed+Minutes+of+the+1st+IndiaChina+Strategic+Economic+Dialogue.
31 Ministry of External Affairs, Government of India, "Joint Statement on the State Visit of Chinese Premier Li Keqiang to India", 20 May 2013, http://mea.gov.in/bilateral-documents.htm?dtl/21723/Joint+Statement+on+the+State+Visit+of+Chinese++Li+Keqiang+to+India.
32 UN Comtrade Database, "Trade Statistics", http://comtrade.un.org/data/.
33 Ibid.
34 Ministry of External Affairs, "Joint Statement on the State Visit of Chinese Premier Li Keqiang to India".
35 Pallavi Aiyar, "Future of trade through Nathula Pass bright", *The Hindu*, 20 June 2006, http://www.thehindu.com/todays-paper/tp-national/future-of-trade-through-nathula-pass-bright/article3121846.ece.
36 "India, China Agree to Take Steps to Address Trade Imbalance", *The Economic Times*, 20 May 2013, http://articles.economictimes.indiatimes.com/2013-05-20/news/39392909_1_trade-imbalance-cooperation-trade-deficit.

37 James Kynge, "China leads EM surge in high tech exports", *Financial Times*, 18 March 2014.
38 Isabelle Bensidoun, Francoise Lemoine and Deniz Unal, "The Integration of China and India into the World Economy: A Comparison", *The European Journal of Comparative Economics*, 6/1, 2009, p. 145.
39 Ibid.
40 The Central People's Government of the People's Republic of China, "Official Gazette", Website in Chinese, http://www.gov.cn/zwgk/2013-02/05/content_2327531.htm.
41 Andrew Jack, "China Steps Up its Scrutiny of Western Drugs Prices", *Financial Times*, 11 August 2013.
42 "India, China Sign MoUs to Address Concerns on Trade Deficit", *Press Information Bureau*, 20 May 2013, http://pib.nic.in/newsite/PrintRelease.aspx?relid=96098.
43 Sudip Chaudhuri, "Multinationals and Monopolies", *Economic and Political Weekly*, XLVII/12, 24 March 2012, p. 49, http://www.epw.in/special-articles/multinationals-and-monopolies.html.
44 Kaliappa Kalirajan et al., "China and India: A Comparative Analysis of Trade and Investment Performance", 2013, p. 4, http://mjyu.ccer.edu.cn/EABER_Routledge%20chapter_2.pdf.
45 See "From Pupil to Master", *The Economist*, 1 December 2012, http://www.economist.com/news/21567390-ratan-tatas-successor-cyrus-mistry-has-some-dirty-work-do-pupil-master.
46 Chindia is a portmanteau word that refers to China and India together in general. The credit of coining the term goes to Jairam Ramesh, who is an Indian economist and parliament member and has held several portfolios in the central government. See Jairam Ramesh, *Making Sense of Chindia: Reflections on China and India*, New Delhi: India Research Press, 2005.
47 United Nations Conference on Trade and Development (UNCTAD), "UNCTAD Statistics Show China Now the World's Largest Exporter and Importer of ICT Products", 29 March 2012, http://unctad.org/en/pages/PressRelease.aspx?OriginalVersionID=72.
48 Ibid.
49 Benjamin Shobert, "Could China Achieve In Biotech What It Did in Clean-Tech?" *Forbes*, 21 October 2013, http://www.forbes.com/sites/benjaminshobert/2013/10/21/could-china-achieve-in-biotech-what-it-did-in-clean-tech/.
50 On India's patent applications, see C. Niranjan Rao, "Long-term Trends in Patent Applications in India, 1948–2010", *Economic and Political Weekly*, XLVII/41, 13 October 2012, pp. 69–73, http://www.epw.in/notes/long-term-trends-patent-applications-india-1948-2010.html. On China, see World Intellectual Property Organization (WIPO), *2012: WIPO IP Facts and Figures*, Geneva: WIPO, 2012, http://www.wipo.int/edocs/pubdocs/en/statistics/943/wipo_pub_943_2012.pdf.
51 A 2012 study by the British Council, entitled "The Shape of Things to Come: Higher Education Global Trends and Emerging Opportunities to 2020", indicates that China and India will remain in the first and second places, with 37 and 28 million enrolments, respectively. China produces 30,000 engineers with PhD degrees each year; the corresponding number in India is around 4,500. China has been aggressive in encouraging publication and patents. According to the preliminary findings of the International Benchmarking Study (2012), with about 25,000 articles (in English) on engineering published in 2011, China ranked very high, while only about 5,000 were published in India. See Jandhyala B.G. Tilak, "Higher Education in the BRIC Member-Countries:

Comparative Patterns and Policies", *Economic and Politics Weekly*, XLVII/14, 6 April 2013, pp. 42–45, http://www.epw.in/special-articles/higher-education-bric-member-countries.html.
52 Tarun Khanna, *Billions of Entrepreneurs: How China and India Are Reshaping Their Futures and Yours*, Cambridge: Harvard Business School Press, 2008.
53 Ministry of External Affairs, Government of India, "Joint Statement on the State Visit of Chinese Premier Li Keqiang to India".
54 Ibid.

Part II
Environment and energy

5 Working together towards an ecologically civilised world
A Chinese perspective

Pan Jiahua

China and India are late-comers in the process of industrialisation and urbanisation. In a world in which industrialism has already shaped a civilizational view, China and India will undoubtedly compete for finite natural resources to accomplish their process of industrialisation and urbanisation and become rivals for regional and global leadership or dominance. If the civilizational views are transformed from industrialism into ecologicalism, however, the two Asian giants will be able to lead the world into stability and sustainability.

Industrialisation, urbanisation, and energy use

Historical experiences and modern practices prove that industrialisation and urbanisation are highly material and energy intensive. The current definition of being a developed society is characterised by high levels of urbanisation and post-industrialisation such that people can enjoy a high quality of life that is represented by large amounts of material consumption, supply of social services such as transport, education, and medical care, and high levels of energy consumption and emissions.

As colonial powers and early industrialising nations, the developed countries in their process of urbanisation and industrialisation were faced with a frontier economy in which they could explore and take over natural resources by force with low or zero cost. Latecomers are therefore inspired to industrialise and urbanise. As the most populous countries in the world, industrialisation and urbanisation levels in China and India are relatively low as compared to the developed nations. In terms of the aggregate demand for natural resources and waste generation, as illustrated in Table 5.1 for energy consumption, both countries are among the highest in the world and are expected to grow further.

Currently, China looks more advanced than India. In terms of industrialisation, China's industrial capacity is greater – steel production in China is nearly ten times that of India, for instance. Per capita energy consumption and per capita greenhouse gas emissions in China are some three times or more than in India. In 2012, official figures indicated that China's population was 52.6 per cent urban.[1] But this number has been considered an exaggeration as nearly one third of these

Table 5.1 Primary energy consumption for selected economies (Mtoe)

	2001	2004	2008	2011	2011 % world
US	2,259.7	2,348.8	2,320.2	2,269.3	18.5
China	1,041.4	1,512.5	2,041.7	2,613.2	21.3
India	297.4	345.8	445.9	559.1	4.6
Japan	512.8	522.4	515.3	477.6	3.9
Germany	338.8	337.3	326.7	306.4	2.5
OECD	5,407.4	5,621.8	5,660.9	5,527.7	45.0
World	9,343.0	10,449.6	11,492.8	12,274.6	100.0

Source: British Petroleum, *BP Statistical Review of World Energy,* June 2012, bp.com/statisticalreview.

urban residents are called rural migrants who are not entitled to enjoy the same urban social services as those who have official urban household registration.[2]

If we take the urbanisation level as 52.6 per cent, there will be some 300 million – nearly the total population in the United States – more people to be added to the urban population in order to reach the level compatible with the stage of a developed society. If the rural migrants are counted as non-urban, the total number to be urbanised would be more than the EU. China has a long way to go for it to be an advanced, industrialised, and urbanised country.

Colonialism is no longer a viable means to access low-price labour and natural resources. And the global economy is no longer a frontier economy, as we all must live within the finite boundary of spaceship earth. What China buys has become expensive, and the price for what China sells is decreasing. The price of iron is now six times higher than it was a decade ago. In the 1970s, the price of oil was about US$ 10 a barrel. In recent years, the price for crude oil has averaged above US$ 100 a barrel, although prices have sharply declined since late 2014.[3]

Even so, China has been described by some as neo-colonialist given the country's operations in Africa, Brazil, and other places. Water shortage is on the increase year by year. Dependence on energy imports has been increasing at an alarming rate. Nearly 60 per cent of oil consumption is imported now as compared to 1993, when China was a net exporter.[4] China is said to have plenty of coal, but the ratio of reserves to production is only 35 years (see Table 5.2). Car ownership is at 69.9 per 1,000 people, only one tenth that in Western Europe and one twelfth that in the US, giving China significant potential for expansion.[5] Greenhouse gas (GHG) emissions per capita are 25 per cent higher than the world average.[6] Smog is unprecedented in terms of scale and severity. Water is polluted and the soil poisoned.

Internationally, both China and India are under increasing pressure to reduce GHG emissions (Figure 5.1). Emissions in the developed economies have been stabilised at the aggregate level and decreasing at per capita levels while the emerging economies, in particular China and India, are increasing both in per capita and aggregate terms.[7] Domestically, there is an increasing consensus in China on reducing emissions, to ensure environmental improvement and sustainability at home. There has been agreement inside China that the

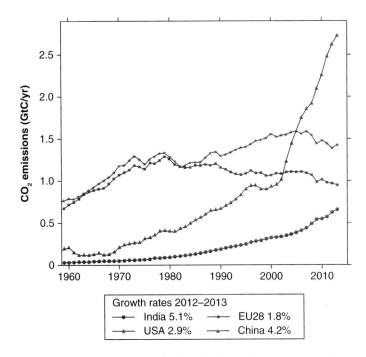

Figure 5.1 Territorial CO_2 emissions for the top three country emitters and the EU.

Source: CDIAC (2013) and Global Carbon Project (2015).

conventional approach to industrialisation and urbanisation cannot be sustained. There is an urgency to move to an ecologically civilised way of production and consumption.

If industrialisation is to be copied in both China and India, how much energy demand can we imagine? Resource endowments in both China and India are poor as compared to the world average (Table 5.2). According to BP estimates, oil reserves in China could be fully extracted in less than ten years; in the case of coal the reserves-to-production ratio is only 33 years (see Table 5.2). The number for India looks slightly better. But this does not mean that India is rich in fossil fuel energy reserves. If India's energy production level reaches the Chinese level, India will deplete her resources even faster than China.

Even if fossil fuel energy supplies were unlimited, increased GHG emissions would put the entire world at high risk. There is only one earth. Getting rid of poverty and increasing the quality of living does not have to follow the conventional path. If China and India work together, the world can be reshaped into a liveable and sustainable homeland. For the sake of the world and the sake of China and India, we need to find an alternative path. Otherwise the two Asian giants are destined to be rivals for the natural resources that are required for their processes of urbanisation and industrialisation.

Table 5.2 Fossil fuel production (Mtoe) reserves-to-production (R/P) ratios (years) for selected economies at end of 2011

		China	India	OECD	World
oil	production	203.6	40.4	866.7	3,995.6
	R/P	9.9	18.2	34.7	54.2
coal	production	1,956.0	222.4	1,004.4	3,955.5
	R/P	33	103	182	112

Source: British Petroleum, *BP Statistical Review of World Energy*, June 2012, bp.com/statisticalreview.

China, India and an ecological civilisation

The current world economy leads to unsustainability and therefore conflict and instability. The production process is linear, from raw material to products and wastes. The dominant mode of living encourages overconsumption and waste, as demonstrated by the greedy ownership of material wealth, luxurious consumption such as large houses and SUVs, and excessive heating and air conditioning.

China and India are seemingly constrained to follow the path of the developed countries. We have to find a new approach: that is, ecological civilisation (EC). Elements of ecological civilisation have been part of human development and culture, but their role and importance were ignored or neglected under industrialism. For more than 5,000 years, the key ethical value and worldview of Chinese civilisation has been man in harmony with nature. The continuity of Chinese civilisation indicates the value of ecological civilisation for sustainability.

EC as understood and practiced in China is in contrast to industrial civilisation (IC). The ethical foundation for IC is utilitarianism. So long as there is positive utility, efforts must be made to find and consume more natural resources. With the help of technological progress, human beings are able to conquer nature and to destroy natural systems. Market competition and profit maximisation are the principles for commercial operation. The outcome is of course natural degradation and resource depletion, which lead to unsustainability and social instability due to resource competition.

In a world where there is no such a thing as a frontier economy any longer, we have to respect limits. The ethical foundation of EC as developed in China lies in a man-nature harmony advocated by Lao Dan, the ancient philosopher of 2,500 years ago. Human beings are born to respect nature, adapt to nature, and conserve nature. Man and nature are one. Production has to be circular to reduce its negative impact on nature, and consumption has to be green and sustainable. However, EC is not a simple denial of IC. Technological innovation and legal institutions are certainly consistent with and desired in EC.

In China, practices consistent with ecological civilisation have been advocated and successful. One example is ecological agriculture. Animal excreta from pig farms are put into bio-digesters to produce methane for cooking, heating, and electricity generation. Bio-digested wastes are organic fertilisers that replace chemical fertilisers. Crop wastes are used as feedstuff. Technological improvement has made the process highly efficient and effective. In the southern part of China, hundreds of millions of rural households use bio-digesters to produce energy for residential uses and organic fertilisers. Medium and large scale bio-digesters are constructed in large livestock farms such as pig farms and poultry farms for power generation. Hydropower may have some socially and ecologically negative impacts, but these impacts can be minimised without reducing clean power production. Solar water-heaters are everywhere in China without subsidy, and the subsidy for solar photovoltaics (PV) has been reduced substantially.

A fee is levied for resource extraction, not only for resource saving but more for resource protection. Coal mining is required to reclaim the land. Public transport is encouraged in the more developed areas. Apartment buildings are constructed as shelters instead of land-consuming houses. Slope-land is returned to forest-land and lowland to wetlands. China's pursuit of ecological civilisation may take some time, but a departure from conventional industrialism is certainly good for sustainability within China and in the world.

If China and India work together for a revision and modification of industrialism using ecologicalism, material consumption and natural degradation will be brought under control and the ecological footprint can be made compatible with the capacity of ecological systems. In the meantime, the human quality of life will be improved and a decent – though not luxurious and wasteful – existence will be ensured.

In a world of absolute physical limits, it is impossible for the developing countries to follow the conventional way of industrialisation and urbanisation. Similarly, the production and consumption lifestyle in the industrialised nations is not sustainable. If China and India can demonstrate to the other developing countries that there is a different approach to development, they would not go the conventional way. Also, the developed countries are very likely to change their way of production and consumption to be more ecologically sustainable.

International climate change cooperation

Amongst the greatest ecological and development challenges is climate change as characterised by global warming. There is global recognition that the conventional development mode of industrialisation and urbanisation is contributing to environmental degradation in several ways, including likely irreversible long-term global warming. In 1994, the United Nations adopted the United Nations Framework Convention on Climate Change (UNFCCC), which was ratified by nearly all the member countries. The Convention's stated objective is "to stabilize greenhouse gas concentrations", thereby minimising man-made effects on climate change. According to the UNFCCC, this goal could only be achieved in the long run by enabling "economic development to proceed in a sustainable manner".[8] The Kyoto Protocol, enforced in 2005 in accordance with the UNFCCC, obligates the already industrialised states, mainly in the West, to adhere to internationally binding carbon emission reduction targets, due to their contribution to GHG emissions and climate change "as a result of more than 150 years of industrial activity".[9]

Developing countries, including China and India, were excluded from legally binding emissions reduction targets owing to their lower level of development and per capita emissions levels; they were encouraged to voluntarily reduce emissions and to slowly shift towards cleaner modes of energy generation.

Both China and India have, per the UNFCCC, voluntarily agreed to take appropriate nationally determined actions to reduce their GHG emissions and adapt to climate change, while emphasising that economic and industrial development remains the priority. In 2009, ahead of the Copenhagen climate change summit, China and India stated voluntary targets of 40 to 45 per cent and 24 per cent reduction in carbon intensity by 2020 as compared to 2005 levels, respectively.[10] Both countries drafted action plans by which they could domestically, mitigate climate change through low carbon development. In 2007, China became the first developing country to adopt a National Action Plan on Climate Change, while India released its own action plan on climate change in 2008. The need to move away from fossil-fuel based energy sources towards clean renewable energy sources form a common theme in both action plans.[11] China and India continue to invest extensively into developing their rapidly growing wind and solar energy generation capacities.

The rapid economic and industrial growth of China and India over the past two decades has, however, resulted in a substantial increase in the countries' share of carbon dioxide emissions. In 1990, the US carbon dioxide emissions came to 5 billion tonnes, compared to China at 2.5 billion tonnes and India at 0.7 billion tonnes. In the same year, the per capita carbon dioxide emissions for the United States stood at 19.6 tonnes, while China was at 2.1 tonnes per capita and India was at 0.8 tonnes per capita. In 2013, however, US carbon dioxide emissions were 5.3 billion tonnes, while China's were 10.3 billion tonnes and India's were 2.1 billion tonnes. Per capita emissions in 2013 stood at 16.6 tonnes for the US, 7.4 tonnes for China and 1.7 tonnes for India.[12] As can be seen in Table 5.3, between 1990 and 2013, China and India's contributions to carbon emissions have significantly grown both in total and per capita terms, while those from the EU and the US have grown more slowly or declined. China is currently the world's largest carbon emitter, though it still lags far behind the US in terms of emissions per capita.[13] These results are not surprising as the developed countries have reached a saturation level of energy use while the developing countries' efforts to satisfy basic needs for large segments of the population require substantial increases in energy use. As China is ahead of India in the industrialisation process, its future emissions increases in aggregate and per capita terms will be lower than India.

Both China and India have held to principle of 'common but differentiated responsibilities' as articulated in the Convention on Climate Change, which requires that developed countries take the lead and demonstrate low and zero carbon development pathways. In this regard, China and India have often successfully cooperated in international climate change forums, putting up a joint stance against assumption of greater responsibility in emissions reductions for developing countries.[14]

Table 5.3 Carbon emissions in 1990 and 2013

	1990		2013	
	Carbon emissions (billion tonnes)	Emissions per capita (tonnes)	Carbon emissions (billion tonnes)	Emissions per capita (tonnes)
US	5	19.6	5.3	16.6
EU-28	4.3	9.2	3.7	7.3
China	2.5	2.1	10.3	7.4
India	0.7	0.8	2.1	1.7

Source: PBL Netherlands Environmental Assessment Agency and European Commission Joint Research Centre, *Trends in Global CO2 Emissions*, The Hague, 2014, pp. 22, 49.

Note: These numbers are not based on national communications to the UNFCCC and may be substantially different from the latest official statistics. They are given here for illustrating the different growth rates between the developed and developing countries, owing to their different stages of development.

During US President Barack Obama's visit to Beijing in November 2014, an agreement was signed with President Xi Jinping whereby China, for the first time, agreed to a timeframe for emissions peaking. While the US pledged to cut carbon emissions by as much as 28 per cent below 2005 levels by 2025, China pledged to peak its carbon emissions by 2030, if not sooner, and to "increase the non-fossil fuel share of all energy to around 20 per cent by 2030".[15] To this end, the US and China agreed to cooperate on various aspects of carbon emissions reductions, including through joint clean energy research, through the inception of a US–China Clean Energy Research Center, and through the launch of the Climate-Smart/ Low-Carbon Cities Initiative, which aspires to reduce the carbon footprint of large cities in both countries.[16] The US hoped to repeat this success with India during President Obama's visit to New Delhi in January 2015. In his speech in New Delhi, President Obama said, "even if countries like the United States curb our emissions, if countries that are growing rapidly, like India, with soaring energy needs don't also embrace cleaner fuels, then we don't stand a chance against climate change".[17] Unlike Beijing, New Delhi did not accede to an emissions cap, arguing that its carbon emissions were not in the same league as China's and thus a cap was not warranted.[18]

This agreement between China and the US seems to signal China's determination for low carbon development and its move towards assuming greater responsibility within the international climate change framework. It also seems to herald an era of greater cooperation between China and the US in the development of clean energy capacity within China. India's refusal to enter into an agreement with the US suggests a different position from China, considering its national circumstances.

During President Xi Jinping's visit to New Delhi in May 2015, however, a joint statement between China and India called for greater international cooperation towards sustainable development as the primary means of climate change mitigation. Crucially, the statement also affirmed that "bilateral partnership on climate change is mutually beneficial" and pledged to strengthen cooperation "in the areas of clean energy technologies, energy conservation, energy efficiency, renewable energy, sustainable transportation including electric vehicles, low-carbon urbanization and adaptation".[19] Another crucial point is the reaffirmation of the idea of 'common but differentiated responsibilities' between the developing countries, including China and India, and the developed countries.

This joint statement once again points to the importance of cooperation between China and India in international climate change forums as well as in their own efforts in moving towards low-carbon energy generation. It also points to the fact that China and India, while far from being developed themselves, cannot strictly be classified along with other developing countries, as they are rapidly growing economies with a substantial share of global carbon emissions and appear to be willing to assume more responsibilities than in the past for emissions reductions and cooperative efforts to address climate change at the global level.

The main obstacles preventing the two giants from working together

Clearly, there is a need and urgency for China and India to work together on a range of environmental challenges including climate change. However, there are a number of obstacles that are politically, economically, technologically, and environmentally rooted. Geopolitical and bilateral conflicts of interest cannot be easily removed. South Asia geographically covers the Indian subcontinent. Any attempts by China to work together with smaller subcontinental countries cause suspicion in India. As imports of raw materials and exports from China have to go through the Indian Ocean, China watches India's diplomatic and military moves in the region with some concern. The territorial dispute between the two countries will take time to settle. The hosting of Tibetan separatists and the Dalai Lama government-in-exile is certainly not welcomed by China. And of course, there are ideological differences between China and India.

Although statistics suggest that China is more economically advanced than India, India is confident that it can do better than China.[20] Half a century ago, China and India began the process of development from roughly the same level. Cooperation is usually seen as being win-win, but current trade patterns – most notably, India's large trade deficit with China – may suggest that one wins at the expense of the other. Each country has its own comparative advantages – India does better in information technology and China's high-speed train technologies can help India to improve her railway systems for a faster and more comfortable public transport system – but trade between the two, while increasing, is less than might have been expected.

Neither side seems to take the initiative. Extension of the Beijing–Tibetan railway to New Delhi would be mutually beneficial, but the project may face opposition. Overall, the benefits for bilateral cooperation are discounted dramatically by the lack of political trust and the feeling of psychological competition.

Technologically, China and India's status as latecomers to industrialisation allows them to enjoy technological spill overs for resource saving and emissions control. At the same time, intentionally or unintentionally, both countries have become places for relocating labour, capital, energy, and resource and emissions-intensive manufacturing facilities. As these technologies are mainly from the developed countries and there is a lack of capacity for indigenous innovation and production of advanced technologies, many production facilities are locked in with existing or out-dated technologies.

As the scales of building and production have been so large due to rapid expansion through a simple duplication of technologies, turning away from this pattern would prove a huge challenge for both countries. Take steel as an example. According to the World Steel Association (Table 5.4), China and India together produced more than half of the raw steel in the world in 2014. In terms of value added and technologies used, however, steel production in these two countries is at the lower end. Technological cooperation may prove productive, but competition is a possibility that cannot be discounted.

Both countries have large populations, and so the security of supply of natural resources is a shared challenge. However, neither country appears to be keen on environmental cooperation, in particular on joint efforts. For example, both China and India are dependent on oil imports. If the two would work together, they could join hands to secure oil transportation in the Indian Ocean. Cross-border rivers are very rich in hydropower potential. When China dammed the Yarlung Tsangpo (the upper section of the Brahmaputra) for electricity, the Indian media were alarmed and critical. Hydropower generation does not actually consume water, but there is a problem of water security and a division of benefits from hydropower. If China and India could work together on renewables, both countries would have access to cleaner energy and enjoy a better environment.

Table 5.4 World steel production (2014)

	Megatonnes (Mt)	Share of world (%)
China	822.7	50.2
India	86.5	5.3
EU-28	169.3	10.3
Japan	110.7	6.7
USA	88.2	5.4
Russia	71.5	4.4
South Korea	71.5	4.4
Brazil	33.9	2.1
Turkey	34.0	2.1
Ukraine	27.2	1.7
Rest of world	124.9	7.6

Source: World Steel Association, "Crude Steel Production 2014–2015", http://www.worldsteel.org/statistics/crude-steel-production.html. The 65 countries included here accounted for 98 percent of total world crude steel production in 2014.

India's information technology would help China improve its service industry with less negative environmental effects.

Cooperation between China and India is a typical case of the prisoners' dilemma. A move by one side may cause the other to be either suspicious or to act in an oppositional way. As a result, neither takes the initiative, and many win-win possibilities cannot be realised.

What are the scenarios for working together?

The two giants can work together. After the Cold War, global geopolitics has been reshaped and the world economy is now different from decades earlier. In 2010, both China and India were among the top ten economies in the world. Some estimates suggest that by 2050 China and India would be among top three economies in the world.[21] The dominance by the developed OECD countries is not as strong as it was decades earlier. Economic and environmental cooperation would be of benefit to both countries. Both countries are expected to take on more responsibilities in the world arena for international affairs. There are many areas with substantial cooperation potential.

With respect to global governance, the geopolitical map has already brought the two countries together. Currently, China and India are both members of the G20, BRICS (Brazil, Russia, India, China, and South Africa), BASIC (Brazil, South Africa, India and China) and G77+China. Within the G20, China and India represent the developing world, and there is no doubt that the two are on the same side in many cases. The BASIC bloc, which brings together Brazil, South Africa, India and China, was formulated at Copenhagen in 2009 to strengthen the bargaining power of the developing world. BRICS is a more economically oriented bloc of emerging economies. In the past, the G7 was able to determine world economic norms and practices without consulting the developing countries, and the interests of the emerging powers were largely ignored. But these emerging economies as a bloc would like to have a larger voice to protect their interests and the interests of the less-developed countries. Despite the opportunities for cooperation, a 'Chindia' will be as unlikely as 'Chinamerica' or a 'G2'. If the two large economies cooperated, the role they could play would be significant. On the other hand, if the two choose rivalry, their role would have less of an impact. In areas of global governance, geopolitics, economics, and natural resources, there are a number of scenarios for the two to consider:

1   Chindia: The two move to be close partners for global governance. They formulate a strategic partnership in all areas, and either they take the initiative together as leaders in global governance or they at least adopt similar positions within the G20, BRICS, or BASIC.
2   Strategic partnership: The two cooperate and support each other on key strategic issues, but do not take joint leadership in global affairs. They would cooperate strategically, but might compete on less important issues. This would be similar to the situation between the two countries in the 1950s.

3 Economic cooperation but political rivalry: This would be similar to the case between China and the US or China and Japan, to a certain extent. Economically, the countries would be highly integrated and dependent on one another, but politically, mistrust and rivalry would shadow relations.
4 Strategic competition: In this scenario, geopolitical interests do not overlap between the two giants, and each tries to compete for regional influence and a global role. Political mistrust prevents the two from closer economic ties. To a degree, this describes current relations between the two countries. There is much potential for economic cooperation, but the level of economic integration does not match the size of their economies.
5 Complete rivalry: A war was fought between the two neighbours in 1962. Competing territorial claims and the treatment of Tibetan separatists are the elements for a potential clash between the two.

Of course, which way China and India would go does not depend upon their choices alone; other elements will also determine their moves. Among the external factors are the position and actions of other big players, in particular the United States, Russia, and the EU. These powers would not like to see either the formation of a Chindia or a complete rivalry, as these two extremes would not be in the interest of world stability and global prosperity. Neither China nor India wishes to admit to the possibility of or accept these two extreme cases.

However, the most important factors are domestic politics, economic development, social stability, and the demand for natural resources. If the development gap widens between the two countries (although this is rather unlikely), complete rivalry can probably not be avoided. If social instability takes place in either country, the level and capacity for bilateral cooperation would be limited. If their growth paths follow a material and energy intensive one, competition for natural resources is a likely scenario. As China and India try to avoid economic slowdown and recession, both would try to accelerate industrialisation and urbanisation. Both countries have suffered from social instability, and the price for such instability would be too high to be acceptable. The peoples of both countries would insist on social stability.

This social stability would generate a demand for a better quality of life and this in turn would speed up industrialisation and urbanisation. Urban infrastructure and buildings would require substantial energy-intensive products. Industrialism and materialism would drive up consumerism. As indicated earlier, large populations and high levels of consumption must be supported by a massive supply of natural resources, such as energy, forests, water, iron ore, and the like. That is why the two Asian giants have to work together for an ecologically harmonised world.

Conclusion: the way forward

Among the five scenarios, scenario four (strategic competition) does not help for a joint push to ecological civilisation. Scenario three (economic cooperation but political rivalry) would provide a window for joint efforts, but the basis would be too fragile. Given that Chindia is unlikely, scenario two (strategic partnership) would be the best choice for the two countries aiming for an ecologically-harmonised world.

How can the two countries move towards such a strategic partnership? First of all, political mistrust must be removed. Cooperation is in the interest of both countries, and there is no need to be narrow minded. The territorial dispute will be an obstacle, but it can be contained. Tibetan separatists are unlikely to succeed, and India is unlikely to shelter them in the long run. Joint efforts on this would be a win-win. Differences in ideological approaches may exist but could be bridged for environmental sustainability. With these understandings, political rivalry will have no firm basis.

Then the issue becomes how to make the push and how to speed up the process. To resolve a technical issue, one has to be practical. First, the two countries must leverage the benefits by identifying and making use of economic complementarities. China can learn from India in market operations, information technology, and grassroots participation in governance. Chinese technologies in hydropower generation, fast rail, and solar energy utilisation can be of use to Indians. Cotton and other textiles in India will soon have a comparative advantage over China. Many manufactured goods from China can be competitive in the Indian market. Economic cooperation can improve both countries' welfare and their global standing.

Second, technological cooperation has substantial potential. As Table 5.5 shows, renewable energy production (power generation) in China and India was largely negligible at the beginning of this century. But the rate of growth has been significant, particularly in comparison with the developed nations. Energy security and employment are major challenges for the emerging economies; they have no choice but to accelerate the development and deployment of renewable technologies. As the developed countries are somewhat locked in with fossil fuel technologies, it is easier for the late-comers to change their paths. Domestic market demand constitutes a potent driver for further advancement of renewable technologies. This indicates that cooperation on new technologies will benefit both countries where the biggest markets exist and energy security is of great concern.

Table 5.5 Energy generation from renewable sources (wind, solar, geothermal, biomass and wastes), (Mtoe)

	2001	2004	2008	2011	2011 % world
US	16.8	19.6	29.5	45.3	23.2
China	0.7	0.9	3.6	17.7	9.1
India	0.9	1.9	4.8	9.2	4.7
OECD	43.0	60.7	98.6	138.0	76.0
World	54.0	75.1	122.7	194.8	100.0

Source: British Petroleum, *BP Statistical Review of World Energy,* June 2012, bp.com/statisticalreview.

Third, China and India must opt for joint development of resources in the border regions between the two countries. There is, for instance, a huge potential for tourism. If the Beijing-Tibet railway is extended to India, economic ties will be strengthened, as will cultural ties, as tourism will deepen mutual understanding. Hydropower from the river that runs from China into India can deliver huge amounts of clean energy, which would enhance energy security and reduce greenhouse gas emissions.

Fourth, technological cooperation in the development of renewable energy, in particular solar, wind, biomass and geothermal, would substantially increase the countries energy security and employment and thereby contribute to economic development and improved quality of life. Such cooperation would also have spill-over benefits for other developing countries for resource security and economic development.

In order for such practical measures to work, China and India will need a cooperative global environment and governance structure. In this regard, cooperation between the two under existing architectures must be further strengthened, including through BASIC, BRICS, and the G20. In addition, continuous and deepening direct dialogue between the two Asian giants is vital.

Acknowledgements

The author would like to thank Huang Jing and Kesava Chandra Varigonda for their help on part of the text related to climate change issues; any errors are the responsibility of the author. The author is also appreciates the editorial work provided by the Lee Kuan Yew School of Public Policy.

Notes

1 National Bureau of Statistics of China, *China Statistical Yearbook*, Beijing: China Statistics Press, 2013.
2 The official number (using the criterion that the resident lives in an urban area for a period of half a year or longer) is considered an over-estimation of the actual urbanisation level; if the criterion for an urban citizen is "urban household registration", the level is 35.3 per cent. This means that 17.3 per cent of urban residents are only half urbanised (with limited entitlements to urban social services) or temporally urbanised (and will return to their village). In accordance with the newly announced National Plan for New Type of Urbanisation 2014–2020, the urbanisation level will reach 60 per cent from 52.6 per cent and the rate of completely urbanised residents would increase from 35.3 per cent in 2012 to around 45 per cent in 2020. See "China Unveils Landmark Urbanization Plan", *People's Daily*, 17 March 2014, http://english.people daily.com.cn/90785/8567957.html.
3 BP, *Statistical Review of World Energy June 2014*, http://www.bp.com/content/dam/ bp/pdf/Energy-economics/statistical-review-2014/BP-statistical-review-of-world-energy-2014-full-report.pdf.
4 In 1990, China imported 7.6 Mt of oil while it exported 31.1 Mt, with net exports amounting to 23.5 Mt. In 1995, imports and exports were 36.6 Mt and 24.6 Mt, respectively, with net imports of 12 Mt. See National Bureau of Statistics of *China, China Statistical*

Yearbook, Beijing: China Statistics Press, 1994. In 2013, China imported 281.9 Mt of raw oil and 39.6 Mt of refined oil, with virtually zero exports of oil. See National Bureau of Statistics of China, "Statistical Communique of the People's Republic of China on the 2013 National Economic and Social Development," 24 February 2014, http://www.stats.gov.cn/english/PressRelease/201402/t20140224_515103.html.
5 See Stacy Davis, Susan Diegel and Robert Boundy, *Transportation Energy Data Book: Edition 32*, Tennessee: Oak Ridge National Laboratory, July 2013, p. 3–9.
6 International Energy Agency (IEA), *World Energy Outlook 2012*, Paris: OECD/IEA, 2012.
7 CDIAC (2013) and Global Carbon Project (2015): CDIAC (T. Boden, G. Marland, and R. Andres), "Global, Regional, and National Fossil-Fuel CO2 Emissions in Trends", Carbon Dioxide Information Analysis Center (CDIAC), 2013, http://cdiac.ornl.gov/trends/emis/meth_reg.html; Global Carbon Project (Le Quéré, C., Moriarty, R., Andrew, R. M., Peters, G. P., Ciais, P., Friedlingstein, P., Jones, S. D., Sitch, S., Tans, P., Arneth, A., Boden, T. A., Bopp, L., Bozec, Y., Canadell, J. G., Chini, L. P., Chevallier, F., Cosca, C. E., Harris, I., Hoppema, M., Houghton, R. A., House, J. I., Jain, A. K., Johannessen, T., Kato, E., Keeling, R. F., Kitidis, V., Klein Goldewijk, K., Koven, C., Landa, C. S., Landschützer, P., Lenton, A., Lima, I. D., Marland, G., Mathis, J. T., Metzl, N., Nojiri, Y., Olsen, A., Ono, T., Peng, S., Peters, W., Pfeil, B., Poulter, B., Raupach, M. R., Regnier, P., Rödenbeck, C., Saito, S., Salisbury, J. E., Schuster, U., Schwinger, J., Séférian, R., Segschneider, J., Steinhoff, T., Stocker, B. D., Sutton, A. J., Takahashi, T., Tilbrook, B., van der Werf, G. R., Viovy, N., Wang, Y.-P., Wanninkhof, R., Wiltshire, A., and Zeng, N.), "Global Carbon Budget 2014," *Earth Syst. Sci. Data*, 7, pp. 47–85, 2015, http://www.earth-syst-sci-data.net/7/47/2015/essd-7-47-2015.html.
8 United Nations Framework Convention on Climate Change (UNFCCC), "First Steps to a Safer Future: Introducing the United Nations Framework Convention on Climate Change", http://unfccc.int/essential_background/convention/items/6036.php.
9 United Nations Framework Convention on Climate Change (UNFCCC), "Kyoto Protocol", http://unfccc.int/kyoto_protocol/items/2830.php.
10 Randeep Ramesh, "India Reveals Carbon Emission Targets", *The Guardian*, 2 December 2009, http://www.theguardian.com/environment/2009/dec/02/india-reveal-carbon-emission-target; Jonathan Watts, "China Sets First Targets to Curb World's Largest Carbon Footprint", The Guardian, 26 November 2009, http://www.theguardian.com/environment/2009/nov/26/china-targets-cut-carbon-footprint.
11 Prime Minister's Council on Climate Change, Government of India, *National Action Plan on Climate Change*, 2008, http://www.moef.nic.in/sites/default/files/Pg01-52_2.pdf; "China's National Climate Change Program", *Xinhua*, 4 June 2007, http://news.xinhuanet.com/english/2007-06/04/content_6197309.htm.
12 PBL Netherlands Environmental Assessment Agency and European Commission Joint Research Centre, *Trends in Global CO2 Emissions*, The Hague, 2014, pp. 22, 49, http://edgar.jrc.ec.europa.eu/news_docs/jrc-2014-trends-in-global-co2-emissions-2014-report-93171.pdf.
13 John Vidal and David Adam, "China Overtakes US as World's Biggest CO2 emitter," *The Guardian*, 19 June 2007, http://www.theguardian.com/environment/2007/jun/19/china.usnews.
14 For detailed information on China–India cooperation in international climate change forums, see Fuzuo Wu, "Sino-Indian Climate Cooperation: Implications for the International Climate Change Regime", *Journal of Contemporary China*, 21/77, 2012, pp. 827–843.

15 The White House, "Fact Sheet: U.S.-China Joint Announcement on Climate Change and Clean Energy Cooperation", 11 November 2014, https://www.whitehouse.gov/the-press-office/2014/11/11/fact-sheet-us-china-joint-announcement-climate-change-and-clean-energy-c.
16 Ibid.
17 Peter Baker and Ellen Barry, "As Visit Ends, Obama Presses India on Human Rights and Climate Change", *The New York Times*, 27 January 2015, http://www.nytimes.com/2015/01/28/world/asia/obama-ends-visit-with-challenge-to-india-on-climate-change.html.
18 Navin Singh Khadka, "No US-India Deal on Climate Change", *BBC*, 27 January 2015, http://www.bbc.com/news/world-south-asia-31008165.
19 Press Information Bureau, Government of India, "Joint Statement on Climate Change between India and China during Prime Minister's Visit to China", 15 May 2015, http://pib.nic.in/newsite/PrintRelease.aspx?relid=121754.
20 In 2015, both the World Bank and the IMF released projections that India's economic growth will surpass China's. See International Monetary Fund, *World Economic Outlook*, April 2015, http://www.imf.org/external/pubs/ft/weo/2015/01/ and World Bank, *Global Economic Prospects*, January 2015, http://www.worldbank.org/content/dam/Worldbank/GEP/GEP2015a/pdfs/GEP15a_web_full.pdf.
21 In 2010, the top ten economies included the US, Japan, China, Germany, UK, France, Italy, India, Brazil and Canada. By 2050, the order of the top ten is projected as follows: China, US, India, Japan, Germany, UK, Brazil, Mexico, France, and Canada. However, China and India are among the top three world economies on a purchasing power parity basis. See Raymond J. Ahearn, *Rising Economic Powers and U.S. Trade Policy*, Congressional Research Service, Library of Congress, 3 December 2012, http://www.fas.org/sgp/crs/row/R42864.pdf.

6 Cooperation on climate change mitigation
An Indian perspective

Arabinda Mishra and Neha Pahuja

Developing country participation in mitigating climate change has always been a contentious issue in climate negotiations, given the historic responsibility of rich industrialised nations in causing climate change and the weak national capability of the developing world in addressing the impact of climate change.[1] The 2007 Bali Action Plan (BAP) gave scope to enhance the participation of developing countries in climate change mitigation when it launched a two-year negotiating process to conclude at the 15th Conference of Parties (COP) to the UN Framework Convention on Climate Change in Copenhagen in 2009. The outcome – the Copenhagen Accord – was a weak and contested political agreement. Many developing countries, including India and China, had voluntarily put forth their mitigation pledges in Copenhagen in a bid to motivate the developed countries to be more ambitious.[2] While India pledged "to reduce the emissions intensity of its GDP by 20–25 per cent by 2020 in comparison to the 2005 level",[3] China's pledge was to lower its carbon emissions intensity of GDP by 40–45 per cent by 2020 in comparison to the 2005 level, as well as to "increase the share of non-fossil fuels in primary energy consumption to around 15 per cent by 2020 and increase forest coverage by 40 million hectares and forest stock volume by 1.3 billion cubic meters by 2020 from the 2005 levels".[4] Both India and China had already announced their respective national action plans on climate change.[5]

The outcomes of the climate negotiations that followed (especially at Durban in 2011 and Doha in 2012) are being interpreted by commentators as the beginning of another round of multilateral negotiations that will end in 2015.[6] The process ahead is likely to substantially change the principles of the global climate regime, in particular the substance of the principle of "common but differentiated responsibility" and respective capability.[7] At Doha, the Ad Hoc Working Group on the Durban Platform for Enhanced Action (ADP) decided "to identify and to explore in 2013 options for a range of actions that can close the pre-2020 ambition gap" and to "consider elements for a draft negotiating text for 2020" by 2015, for which negotiations will take place under two workstreams.[8] Further, the outcome at the 19th COP in Warsaw decided that all Parties should "initiate or intensify domestic preparations for their intended nationally determined contributions, and communicate them ... by the first quarter of 2015".[9] The implications for India and China, along with other major developing economies, are serious. The multifaceted nature of global climate policy is bound to influence the way that development is perceived and pursued. Besides being watchful and protective of possible negative impacts on national development, India and China can lead through active engagement with a view to influence the outcome of negotiations so as to safeguard national interests and create a space for the transformation of political and economic relations between countries.

While India and China have emerged as key actors in international climate negotiations, there is growing pressure on both countries, in their capacity as major emerging economies, to contribute to the emissions mitigation effort in a more stringent manner. Studies have established the inadequacy of the Copenhagen pledges with respect to the 2 degree Celsius goal.[10] The focus is therefore on the mitigation efforts of India and China, since their rapid economic growth has led to an increased share in global emissions (Table 6.1). This is especially the case for China, which surpassed the US and the EU in 2006 to become the world's largest contributor to emissions flows.

As compared with China, India has a much smaller share in global emissions (Table 6.1) as well as lower per capita emissions (Figure 6.1). Further, it is argued that while mitigation efforts by both countries are crucial to meet ambitious global climate targets, India possibly has more time to peak its emissions compared to China.[11] There is also a parallel discussion on whether India is being fairly treated as a major greenhouse gas (GHG) emitter or is a "disadvantaged newcomer", given its "unfinished" developmental agenda.[12] According to Srivastava:

Table 6.1 Top ten emitters

1950	1990	1997	2005	2006
US (42.3)	US (23.3)	US (24.2)	US (21.3)	**China (21.8)**
EU-27 (30.1)	EU-27 (19.8)	EU-27 (17.5)	**China (20.3)**	US (20.3)
Germany (8.7)	**China (11.0)**	**China (14.6)**	EU-27 (14.9)	EU-27 (14.5)
UK (8.5)	Russia Fed (10.5)	Russia Fed (6.4)	Russia Fed (5.6)	Russia Fed (5.7)
Russia Fed (7.1)	Japan (5.3)	Japan (5.3)	Japan (4.6)	**India (4.7)**
France (3.4)	Germany (4.6)	**India (4)**	**India (4.5)**	Japan (4.4)
Canada (2.6)	Ukraine (3.3)	Germany (3.9)	Germany (3)	Germany (3)
Ukraine (2.0)	**India (3)**	UK (2.3)	Canada (2)	Canada (1.9)
Poland (1.9)	UK (2.7)	Canada (2.2)	UK (2)	UK (1.9)
Japan (1.7)	Canada (2.1)	S. Korea (2)	S. Korea (1.8)	S. Korea (1.8)

Source: World Resources Institute (WRI), "Climate Analysis Indicators Tool (CAIT) Version 2.0," Washington, DC: WRI, 2010. The table is adapted from Srivastava and Pahuja 2009. The figures in brackets indicate the percentage share of the country in global emissions. Non Annex I Countries are indicated in bold.

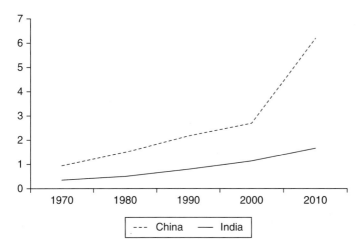

Figure 6.1 CO$_2$ emissions in China and India (metric tons per capita).
Source: The World Bank, "DataBank", http://data.worldbank.org/.

India still falls in the category of low-income countries – largely because of disparities in income within its population. When countries such as the United States make demands for India to participate in future emissions reductions initiatives they are looking at the top 10 percent of India's population and demanding equivalence.[13]

Given the above context, this chapter looks into a key question: will India and China, who have come together at the international level to present a shared position in climate negotiations, be able to scale up bilateral cooperation on domestic climate action? Some related questions that follow from this are: What may be the national circumstances that would encourage such bilateral cooperation? What constraints would need to be overcome in both countries to translate promise into practice? What is the general framework in which such bilateral engagement happens in a durable and progressive manner?

The chapter is organised as follows: the second section presents a brief description of India–China cooperation on climate change and the scholarly perspectives on this; sections 3 and 4 respectively discuss the national circumstances in each country leading to emissions growth and vulnerability to future climate change impacts; section 5 describes the policy response in both countries to mitigate emissions; as a related issue, section 6 focuses on the countries' contrasting experiences with the Kyoto Protocol's Clean Development Mechanism (CDM); section 7 introduces the South-South framework for cooperation; sections 8 and 9 discuss specific opportunities in mitigation and adaptation for India–China cooperation in this framework; and the last section concludes.

India–China cooperation on climate change: the journey so far

In international climate negotiations under the UN Framework Convention, the positions of India and China have always adhered to the principle of 'common but differentiated responsibility' and have supported the right of developing countries to act on achieving their developmental goals without the hard constraint of binding emissions reduction obligations. In October 2009, just before the Copenhagen COP, India and China came together in New Delhi to sign an agreement on cooperation in addressing climate change.[14] The agreement established the India–China Partnership on Combating Climate Change and the India–China Working Group on Climate Change – two specific bilateral mechanisms for strengthening dialogue, exchange of views, and practical cooperation on both mitigation and adaptation actions. Jairam Ramesh, then Minister of Environment and Forest for Government of India, confirmed that both India and China aimed to collaborate to ensure a fair and equitable outcome at Copenhagen and that there "is virtually no difference in Indian and Chinese negotiating positions".[15] From the Chinese side, Minister Xie Zhenhua echoed the cooperative sentiment and expressed confidence that both countries "will make a positive contribution to Copenhagen".[16]

As already mentioned, both India and China came up with voluntary pledges at Copenhagen. Since then, in the subsequent COPs, both countries have displayed the same solidarity in presenting a shared negotiating position on key climate change issues, especially those related to equity, technology transfer, and finance. At the Durban COP in December 2011, the developing countries, led by India and China, were successful in operationalising to a significant extent the Bali Road Map by setting up the Green Climate Fund, the Technology Mechanism, and the Adaptation Framework. Moreover, India and China are a crucial part of the BASIC (Brazil, South Africa, India, and China) group which came together to form common positions on issue of climate change. An expert group has met regularly, and this has resulted in joint submissions on 'shared vision' in 2011 and 'equity' in 2010.

The growing engagement between India and China in a multilateral context is not limited to climate change. Swaran Singh, in fact, finds evidence that suggests a shift in the 'centre of gravity' in India–China relations "from purely bilateral to multilateral interactions and that these two parallel streams are often merging and influencing each other, the result of which has been, on balance, positive".[17] The growing rapport between the two countries at the multilateral level does seem to have influenced some important bilateral initiatives. During the visit of Chinese Premier Wen Jiabao to New Delhi in December 2010, India and China signed six agreements covering cultural exchange, media exchange, and sharing of hydrological data, along with cooperation in the areas of banking and green technologies. During the same visit, a bilateral trade target of US$ 100 billion was set to be reached by 2015; a Strategic Economic Dialogue (SED) and a CEO Forum were established; and 2011 was declared as 'Year of India–China exchange'.[18] The first India–China SED took place in Beijing in September 2011 and policies on energy conservation and environmental protection were among the issues discussed.

There is, however, a contrary viewpoint that sees the India–China relationship as "intrinsically competitive",[19] especially when it comes to energy and natural resource requirements. Geopolitics is a major driver of this economic competition, with a significant potential for generating conflict between the two countries. From this perspective, India–China solidarity on climate change in the multilateral context is a paradox, and has little relevance to the more immediate determinants of mutual trust and reciprocity that are so vital for a healthy and enduring bilateral relationship.

National circumstances: energy, emissions and development in India and China

India and China together account for about 36 per cent of the world's population and are responsible for about 22 per cent of the global demand for primary energy.[20] The economic growth projections for both countries present impressive trajectories through the 2050s, which obviously has major implications for their energy demand (Figures 6.2 and 6.3). It is anticipated that the two countries together will account for about 50 per cent of the world's incremental energy demand over the next 20 years.[21]

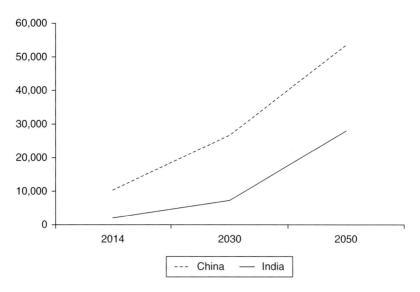

Figure 6.2 GDP projections for China and India at market exchange rates (2014 US$ billions).

Source: PricewaterhouseCoopers, The World in 2050: Will the Shift in Global Economic Power Continue?, 2015, p. 40, http://www.pwc.com/gx/en/issues/the-economy/assets/world-in-2050-february-2015.pdf.

Cooperation on climate change mitigation 113

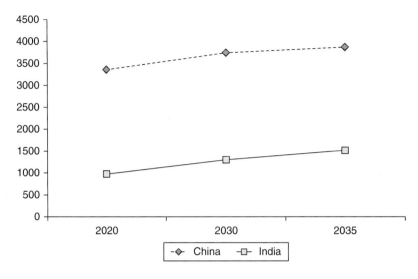

Figure 6.3 Primary energy demand projections for China and India (Mtoe).
Source: International Energy Agency (IEA), *World Energy Outlook 2012*, Paris: OECD/IEA, 2012, p. 58.

The focus on high and rapid economic growth is tied to the major development and poverty alleviation challenges faced by both countries (Table 6.2). In India, for instance, in addition to meeting the growing energy demand, a major challenge is to provide equitable access to "modern" energy services across all segments of its society. Roughly one-third of India's population, mainly rural, does not have access to electricity. China, on the other hand, has achieved almost complete rural electrification; its urbanisation process is, however, throwing up acute concerns related to environmental quality and equitable provisioning of urban services.

With their burgeoning energy demand, India and China are becoming increasingly dependent on energy imports. It is projected that India's and China's oil dependence will increase to 94 per cent and 75 per cent, respectively, by 2030. China will also become increasingly dependent on imported coal for electricity generation.[22] High levels of energy import dependency exacerbate concerns

Table 6.2 Key development indicators: a comparison

Indicators	China		India	
	2005	2009	2005	2010
Poverty gap at $2 a day (PPP) (%)	12.5	9.1	29.5	24.5
GDP per capita, PPP (constant 2005 international $)	4,114.6	6,206.8	2,233.9	3,121.6
Energy use (kg of oil equivalent per capita)	1,342.4	1,689.6	478.4	574.5

Source: The World Bank, "DataBank", http://data.worldbank.org/.

regarding security of energy supply, and this has major implications for a country's mitigation response to climate change.

A comparison between the rapid growth of India and China shows different patterns of structural changes, energy use, and GHG emissions (Figures 6.4 and 6.5). While China's economic growth in recent years has mostly been driven by the manufacturing sector, in the case of India it is the services sector that is increasingly taking over agriculture to be the dominant source of growth. India's informal economy is also much larger and structurally different than that of China.[23] These structural differences make emissions reduction scenarios difficult to compare for both countries.

According to the Intergovernmental Panel on Climate Change (IPCC), globally, about two-thirds of anthropogenic (human activity-related) greenhouse gas

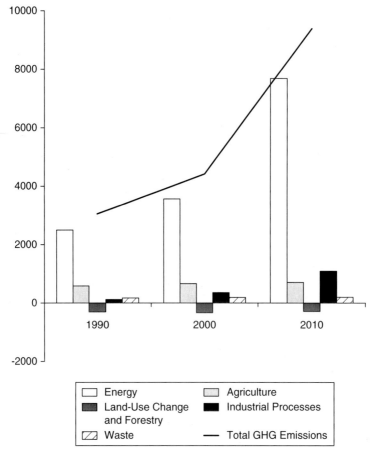

Figure 6.4 GHG emissions by source in China (MtCO$_2$e).

Source: World Resources Institute, "CAIT 2.0", http://cait2.wri.org.

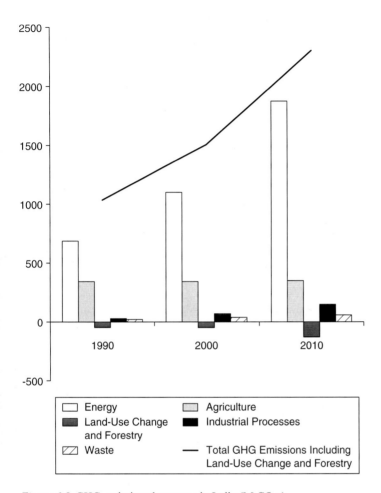

Figure 6.5 GHG emissions by source in India (MtCO$_2$e).

Source: World Resources Institute, "CAIT 2.0", http://cait2.wri.org.

emissions are from the combustion of fossil fuels, 26 per cent are related to energy supply, 19 per cent to industry, 14 per cent to transport, and 8 per cent to buildings. With India and China's high levels of dependence on fossil fuels, particularly on coal and oil, both countries have high carbon dioxide (CO$_2$) emission levels, and these are also growing at high rates (3 to 6 per cent annually).[24]

Vulnerability to climate change impacts: the adaptation challenge

Both India and China are highly vulnerable to risks arising out of future climate change, and there is growing scientific evidence on the likely impact in specific sectors. About 39.6 per cent of the population in China is dependent on agriculture, while in India the figure stands at 58.4 per cent, as of 2010. The agriculture sector makes up about 11 per cent of China's GDP and 18 per cent of India's GDP as of 2007. Water availability per capita, however, declined by as much as 15 per cent between 1997 and 2007 in China and by as much as 9 per cent between 2001 and 2007 in India.[25] Agriculture and water resources are therefore likely to be the two sectors in which the adaptation challenge would be the greatest in both countries.

Both China and India possess extensive coastlines; as such, a rise in sea level can have a considerably adverse impact in both countries. About 8.1 per cent of China's population and 3.8 per cent of India's total population is living at an elevation below five metres.[26] At the trans-national scale, a shared resource system, such as the Brahmaputra river basin, is a potential hot spot of climate change-induced conflict in the absence of appropriate mechanisms for prior consultation and information exchange. In a similar manner, adaptation action on global commons such as Himalayan glaciers would need to be framed as a 'regional public good' calling for greater cooperation among all the Himalayan countries.

Domestic policy responses in India and China for emissions mitigation

India's National Action Plan on Climate Change (NAPCC) – adopted in 2008 – states that India's policy response to climate change will primarily address "the urgent and critical concerns of the country" with "co-benefits for addressing climate change" through "a directional shift in the development pathway".[27] China's National Climate Change Program (NCCP) was approved in 2007 and includes measures to strengthen the energy-related regulatory framework. In the recent 12th Five-Year Plan, China has set a carbon-intensity reduction target of 17 per cent and intends to achieve it by 2015.[28] Similarly, the Government of India, ahead of drawing up its 12th Five-Year Plan, has recognised the importance of low-carbon development and inclusive growth.[29]

A study by The Energy and Resources Institute (TERI) on 'Low Carbon Development in India and China' contrasts the approach to public policy on low carbon development in both countries.[30] In India, the Planning Commission-constituted "Expert Group on Low Carbon Strategies for Inclusive Growth" has described a low-carbon strategy as a means to identify policy interventions to overcome adoption barriers of mitigation strategies.[31] In China, on the other hand, the National Development and Reform Commission (NDRC) describes low-carbon development as "the development of a socio-economic system that can realize low-carbon emissions".[32]

For the Indian economy, the 2011 interim report by the Expert Group on Low Carbon Strategies provides a menu of options to reduce GHG emission intensity in critical sectors such as power, transport, industry, buildings, and forestry, and is premised on the fact that a GDP growth rate of 8–9 per cent by 2020 is required to achieve India's developmental objectives.[33] The report identifies two scenarios of emissions intensity reduction by 2020, namely, (a) A 'Determined Effort Scenario' under which the country could achieve 23 to 25 per cent emissions intensity reduction through the vigorous pursuit of policies (current or planned) with a continuous up-gradation of technology and finance from both public and private sources, and (b) an 'Aggressive Effort Scenario' under which the country could achieve 33 to 35 per cent emissions intensity reduction through additional and scaled-up efforts that will require adequate international support in terms of technology and finance.[34]

India's NAPCC has eight core national missions, four of which have an explicit focus on mitigating climate change through, among other things, a huge scale-up of solar power generation (the National Solar Mission), a market-based scheme on tradable energy saving certificates (the National Mission for Enhanced Energy Efficiency), a nationwide effort to increase forest cover and density (the National Green Mission), and a sustainable habitat approach to urban planning and management (the National Mission on Sustainable Habitat).[35] Of particular note is the Perform, Achieve and Trade (PAT) scheme that allows for trading of energy saving certificates among the country's most energy-intensive industries and is expected to unlock a multi-billion market for energy efficiency.[36] The interim report of the Expert Group on Low Carbon Strategies presents an estimate that the scheme, once fully implemented, has the potential to result in an overall energy savings of about 24 million tons oil equivalent by 2020.[37] The first cycle of the scheme ran from 2012 to 2015; thereafter energy saving certificates will be traded on energy exchanges like Power Exchange India Limited (PXIL) and India Energy Exchange (IEL).[38] The Renewable Energy Certificate (REC) is another market-based instrument introduced under the NAPCC, which aims at achieving a 15 per cent share for renewable energy in the energy mix of India in the next 10 years.[39] The renewable energy certificate registry of India is now fully functional with more than 150 million RECs issued already.[40]

China's NCCP has identified sector-specific mitigation and adaptation actions that encompass science and technology development, public awareness, institutions and mechanisms, and international cooperation.[41] So far the implementation of the actions has predominantly been through administrative measures. Thus, for instance, the country's top 1,000 state-owned enterprises (SOEs) have signed contracts with the central government to meet energy efficiency targets.[42] This was expected to help the country realise its 20 per cent energy intensity reduction target during the 2006–2010 period.[43] While China reportedly fell short of achieving this target (it managed to attain about 19.1 per cent reduction), the government's 12th Five-Year Plan aimed for a further 16 per cent reduction of energy intensity during the 2011–2015 period.[44] However, it is well acknowledged that administrative measures can turn out to be very expensive, especially when the country is on a fast growth trajectory of domestic energy consumption.

To supplement the administrative measures with cost-effective market-based mechanisms, China has launched seven pilot carbon trading schemes at the city level – in Beijing, Tianjin, Shanghai, Chongqing, Guangdong, Hubei and Shenzhen (each of these locations already has its own carbon emissions exchange) – and has initiated the process to have carbon trading schemes at the provincial and national levels over the next decade.[45] Regional carbon trading schemes are already operational in Beijing and Shanghai.[46] There are plans to have a cap on energy consumption that can later (possibly in 2016–20) be converted into a national emissions target; this in turn is expected to pave the way for provincial carbon budgets and a national carbon trading system in 2021–25.[47] However, it remains to be seen what approach the Chinese authorities will adopt for the design of these market-based mechanisms, and the degree to which government oversight will control the functioning of the carbon markets.

Experience with CDM

It is clear from the previous section that both India and China are in the early stages of the development of domestic policy instruments for emissions mitigation, especially with regard to market-based mechanisms. India has already launched the PAT and REC schemes, while China is in the process of rolling out its city and province-level pilot emissions trading schemes. The design of these market mechanisms has been influenced by the carbon currency and the market created as a result of the Clean Development Mechanisms (CDMs) and Emissions Trading Schemes elsewhere (largely EU-ETS). Interestingly, the presently low certified emissions reductions (CER) prices have not hindered the rapid developments in conceptualisation and creation of market mechanisms and ETSs across the globe, nor the interest expressed by countries in initiatives like the World Bank's Partnership for Market Readiness (PMR). These developments are being cited as an indicator of a paradigm shift from centralised CDM-type approaches for mitigation to a variegated future landscape of multiple schemes and instruments that will need to be interlinked at some stage.[48]

Moreover, these developments form an interesting avenue for intellectual enquiry and research collaboration on a number of issues, such as exploring the possibility of harmonisation and potential future integration between the trading schemes and markets being created in emerging economies like India and China; the potential of these carbon (or pseudo-carbon) currencies to be fungible, deciphering early lessons from the respective domestic instruments, and the possibility of linkages with regional and international efforts. International examples exist on the possibility of such linkages, for instance between California and Quebec ETSs under the Western Climate Initiative,[49] and the European Union and Australia ETSs.[50] However, no such linkages exist between the developing or soon-to-be-developed schemes in developing nations.

There is no doubt that the possibility of a harmonised evolution of carbon markets in India and China is an exciting scenario, but it is constrained by the severely contrasting approaches to carbon governance in both countries. The experience with the CDM has brought up interesting insights in this regard.

India and China between themselves accounted for 68 per cent of the total registered CDM projects in June 2015.[51] Interestingly, a large part of project development in both India and China has taken place in the energy efficiency

Cooperation on climate change mitigation 119

and renewable energy sectors, which is indicative of the huge GHG abatement potential in both countries in the industrial and residential sectors. Chinese CDM projects are on an average larger than projects from the rest of the world.[52] In the Indian case, the number of methodologies developed for CDM projects has been the highest.[53] Thus, the Indian project developers have moved away from low hanging fruit and are exploring and implementing new and diverse project opportunities and engaging new sets of project developers. However, only a limited number of the Indian CDM projects have involved cooperation with foreign participants, particularly those from developed countries, which is indicative of limited technology transfer and foreign investment in Indian projects.[54]

India seems to have created an institutional advantage in relation to the CDM, going by the following observations: (i) that the number of methodologies developed for CDM projects has been the highest in India; (ii) that there is greater diversity among the Indian CDM projects and an ample pool of CDM consultants and developers; and (iii) that the government appraisal of project sustainability is quicker in the case of India. In fact, CDM governance in India has come under strong criticism as a "case of market-dominated carbon governance".[55]

In China, on the other hand, the CDM market is characterised by hard steering and an overall "state capture of the market".[56] In contrast to the market-dominated approach on the Indian side, the approving authorities in China keep control of the market and foreign actors (CDM projects can only be set up in companies with at least 51 per cent equity held by Chinese entities); in addition, there is a focus on technology transfer, foreign investment, and the development of energy infrastructure.[57]

A South-South framework for enhanced cooperation

A review of policy responses in India and China suggest that a paradigm shift is currently underway that favours low-carbon development while retaining the strategic emphasis on energy security and poverty alleviation (through rapid economic growth). Both countries appear to have embraced the idea of 'leapfrogging' from carbon-intensive technologies to low-carbon technologies in select energy-intensive sectors through enhanced access to international technology and climate finance.[58] At the same time, it is recognised that there are common barriers in the form of limited access to technology, economic and financial constraints, weak legal and regulatory frameworks, irrational pricing and subsidy policies, information sharing bottlenecks, institutional limitations, and poor governance.

To illustrate the paradigm shift, especially in the case of China, one may consider the 2014 study by the Pew Charitable Trusts on G20 members and clean energy investment, which indicates that China leads this group in clean energy finance and investment with US$ 54.2 billion in 2013.[59]

Despite the common pursuit of low-carbon development, bilateral engagement between India and China on this front is conspicuous by its lack of 'depth' – interactions have mainly remained confined to either official channels or to the side-lines of forums such as the G20 and multilateral processes such as

Table 6.3 Top ten G20 countries in clean energy investment (2013)

China	$54.2 billion
United States	$36.7 billion
Japan	$28.6 billion
United Kingdom	$12.4 billion
Rest of EU-28	$11.5 billion
Germany	$10.1 billion
Canada	$6.5 billion
India	$6.0 billion
South Africa	$4.9 billion
Australia	$4.4 billion
India	$2.3 billion

Source: The Pew Charitable Trusts, *Who's Winning the Clean Energy Race?* Philadelphia: The Pew Charitable Trusts, 2014.

the Conference of Parties (COP). The promise of a South-South framework of cooperation, on the other hand, is immensely exciting not only for the two Asian giants but also for the Asia-Pacific region as a whole.

What would be the key elements of such a framework? The motivational goal, undoubtedly, is the possibility of India and China coming together for a joint effort for the transition of Asia into an 'innovation hub' in the area of low-carbon energy technologies. Technology-based cooperation is an essential pre-requisite to building technological capacity that causes technological change at the level of the firm, country, region, and so on.[60] Further, indigenous innovations are believed to be realised through cross-country collaborative initiatives, involving key actors and organisations from the public sector, private sector, and academia.[61] Public-private partnerships cutting across both countries can focus on capacity development, demonstration, and deployment of clean energy technology at the regional scale.

Given such a framework, it is instructive to take a look at the way clean technology development has actually happened in both countries. The development of renewable energy in China, and the solar and wind power industries in particular, relied heavily on foreign technologies imported and licensed from advanced countries like Europe and the US. The foreign companies, it seems, did not bother much about the alleged weak intellectual property rights (IPR) regime in China, largely because they could make large profits by transferring the technologies and designs with their IPRs to Chinese companies. Similarly, in India, development in these sectors has depended largely on imported technologies. In the case of wind power both countries have been able to get the latest and broad-based technologies; in the case of solar power, China has been successful but India has not. India's solar industry has largely operated on technologies that are mostly in the public domain with expired IPRs.

While Chinese companies worked very closely with their foreign partners and understood the technology that they received, Indian companies always maintained a distance from their foreign partners and the technology received has remained a black box, particularly in the wind power industry. This has meant the technologies remained more or less the same as they were received. Chinese companies, on the other hand, made significant efforts in assimilating, adapting, and upgrading the technologies – as can be confirmed from the fact that Chinese companies have obtained large numbers of patents compared to Indian companies who have hardly made a mark in this regard. Another feature of the Chinese experience is that the domestic research institutes at universities and at public sectors and industrial firms have cooperated to assimilate, adapt, and upgrade the imported technologies, something missing in India. As a result, despite an earlier start, India has lagged behind China.

Bilateral cooperation: the promise in low-carbon development

The agreed minutes of the Bilateral China–India Strategic Economic Dialogue held in Beijing on September 26, 2011, state, "the two sides agreed to strengthen cooperation on energy efficiency and conservation as well as on environmental protection and actively develop cooperation in energy matters including in the renewable energy sector in order to promote sustainable development. Enhanced exchanges in these spheres would be the new engine for greater cooperation between the two sides".[62]

Both India and China have taken initiatives relevant to low-carbon development and a significant commonality is the emphasis on accelerated renewable energy development. The policy framework in this respect is largely similar in the two countries. Regulatory policies include a feed-in tariff for electricity generators, an obligation to maintain a prescribed quota for renewables-based electricity for electric utilities, and an obligation to maintain a prescribed quota for biofuels for retailers of transportation fuels.[63] In addition, as already mentioned, India has introduced tradable renewable energy certificates.[64]

Renewable energy-based decentralised energy systems have been widely chosen as a cost-effective mode of electrification for remote and far flung regions in both China and India, and there exists great scope for bilateral cooperation in this field. Both countries have spent substantial resources in designing, developing, demonstrating, and disseminating various decentralised energy systems. For instance, while China has the largest biogas and improved stove programme, and a very strong solar water heater system programme, India takes pride in having a robust decentralised solar energy programme.[65] Efforts have been made in the past to enhance cooperation in the field of renewable energy in general (e.g. the MoU signed in 2003 between India's Ministry of New and Renewable Energy and China's Ministry of Water Resources), but nothing meaningful has been achieved so far. Possible areas of collaboration include technology transfer, sharing of knowledge about policy and institutional innovations, joint research and development activities, exchange of technical know-how, and building information networking. For instance, while India could support China in developing its biomass energy technology programme, China could supplement the efforts of India in tapping solar energy for decentralised applications. Outcomes of this cooperation could be commercialised, and sustainable market development could be promoted.

The scale at which renewables can contribute to a low-carbon transition in India and China is brought out in some important scenario-based studies. Mallet (2010) cites the study by Wang and Watson (2009), in which the authors explore four different scenarios, or pathways, which China can pursue, based on previous medium-term modelling exercises to 2020.[66] Differences in the scenarios examined include how China's overall carbon emissions were allocated (on a per capita or per unit of GDP basis), treatment of concurrent priorities for the government (poverty alleviation and innovation), and year of emissions peak (2020 or 2030). These scenarios determined that continuous improvements are needed in energy efficiency and that renewables have the potential to substitute fossil fuels on a large scale, which the authors suggest can account for more than 60 per cent of power generation and 40 per cent of China's total energy demand in 2050.[67]

A 2009 TERI study on India's energy future discusses four scenarios in which the country may aspire to achieve energy security while addressing, in a complementary manner, the goals of reduced import dependence, equitable energy access, and a low carbon economy.[68] In every 2031 scenario alternative to the business as usual reference, there is a significantly increased uptake of renewables for power generation and improved efficiency in energy generation and use.[69] Such transitions obviously come with high upfront costs, the magnitudes of which are indicative of the scale at which change may need to be considered when the external constraints become too stringent.

Adaptation as a 'regional public good' and the case for cooperation on food security

Country-specific policy responses on adaptation to climate change impacts can generate significant spill-over transnational benefits. An example is national disaster preparedness efforts that may reduce cross-country migration. Another example would be budgetary support to R&D in bio-technology applications in the agriculture sector, which have the potential to contribute to food security at the larger regional scale. Since the impacts of climate change will vary by region depending on the region's exposure, sensitivity, and adaptive capacity, adaptation to the impact of climate change can be viewed as a scale-dependent regional public good – one that can have non-rival and non-excludable benefits in a specific region rather than the whole world.[70] These public and trans-boundary benefits can make the provision of adaptation "a classic collective action dilemma", where no single participant has the incentive to provide the public good.[71] This usually necessitates an agreement or institutional framework that encourages international cooperation for the provision of the regional public good.

With their large populations, both India and China have reason to worry about the likely impacts of climate change on food security. Most studies on the impact of climate change on agriculture conclude that climate change will reduce crop yields in the tropical areas. Further, an increase in the frequency and patterns of extreme weather events is very likely to affect the stability of, as well as access to, food supplies. The impact of climate change on the behaviour of pests and diseases still remains largely unclear, while their economic implications are being increasingly felt.

Even without the challenge of climate change, food security is an issue in tropical areas considering that almost 800 million people in the developing world are already suffering from hunger. Although India ranks third globally in terms of agricultural produce, the country is still home to more than 230 million undernourished people.[72] In China, industrial development in the water-rich south has made the country more dependent on food production in the relatively dry north, leading to extensive overexploitation of groundwater resources in that region; in addition, China may be self-sufficient in wheat, rice, and corn, but buys more than half the world's soybean exports, according to figures from the United States Department of Agriculture.[73]

Cooperation between India and China on food systems and related technology can be a potential game-changer for the entire Asia-Pacific region. In fact, there is scope to structure such cooperation around the complete food-water-energy nexus and under comparable agro-ecological circumstances in both countries.

Conclusion

Both India and China have their own strengths and weaknesses, their own unique cultural traditions, and their own political histories. Both countries have still some way to go towards becoming advanced industrial societies, and they face serious social and environmental challenges to their development aspirations. There is both overt and covert competition between the two countries for world markets and resources. Geopolitical tensions have coloured public perceptions in both countries about the nature and process of relationship building. Given this context, BASIC's evolution from a forum for negotiation coordination to a forum for cooperative actions on mitigation and adaptation, including exchange of information and collaboration in matters relating to climate science and climate-related technologies, has been a hugely enabling process towards greater South–South cooperation around an India–China axis.

This chapter presents an approach to future India–China cooperation on climate change that draws insights from the contradictory perspectives presented in section 2. Both countries have already demonstrated their willingness to come together and provide leadership in multilateral climate negotiations. A key factor underlying their solidarity is the shared understanding on equity and its implication for a country's "potential for growth and sustainable development".[74] The latter consideration is certain to keep the two countries together in the multilateral process to define a post-2015 climate regime. At the same time, it is equally certain that there will be increasing pressure on both countries, and particularly on China, to scale up mitigation efforts.

While both India and China have rolled out ambitious domestic actions in this regard, there are significant synergies to be reaped if there is a pooling of the appropriate technology and skills. Low-carbon and climate resilient strategies taken by countries such as China and India can serve as examples for less developed countries to pursue at later stages of their development. In the process, it is quite possible that the barrier presented by the current situation of a trust deficit (mostly because of other geopolitical reasons) will be successfully overcome. Much more is required from the political leadership in both countries to provide incentives as well as to institutionalise greater public and business participation in this process. The time seems to be ripe for such initiatives given the new political leadership in both countries.

Notes

1 The UN Convention on Climate Change sets a Framework for action where Parties have to achieve its goal on the basis of equity and in accordance with their common but differentiated responsibilities and respective capabilities wherein the developed country Parties should take the lead (Article 3.1, FCCC). Accordingly, developed countries have commitments under the Convention in relation to mitigation, finance, technology transfer and capacity building as specified in its Article 4. The primary concern raised by the developed country Parties is to emphasise 'meaningful' participation of developing countries, especially large developing economies such as China and India, by undertaking certain obligations under the Convention. The developing country Parties have always reiterated that the extent of such participation cannot or should not challenge their developmental process.
2 Navroz K. Dubash, *Toward a Progressive Indian and Global Climate Politics*, Working Paper 1, Centre for Policy Research Climate Initiative: 2009, http://www.cprindia.org/sites/default/files/1253785461-CPR%20WP%202009-1_Dubash.pdf.
3 Ministry of Environment and Forests, Government of India, Letter to United Nations Framework Convention on Climate Change, 30 January 2010, http://unfccc.int/files/meetings/cop_15/copenhagen_accord/application/pdf/indiacphaccord_app2.pdf.
4 Department of Climate Change, National Development and Reform Commission of China, Letter to United Nations Framework Convention on Climate Change, 28 January 2010, http://unfccc.int/files/meetings/cop_15/copenhagen_accord/application/pdf/chinacphaccord_app2.pdf.
5 According to Bodansky (2010), the Copenhagen pledges were an 'internationalization' of the countries' national climate change policies. This was also an attempt of the BASIC group (Brazil, South Africa, India, and China) to come together to forge a common position. For details, see Daniel Bodansky, "The Copenhagen Climate Change Conference: A Postmortem", *The American Journal of International Law*, 104/2, April 2010, pp. 230–240.
6 Daniel Bodansky, *The Durban Platform Negotiations: Goals and Options*, Policy Brief, Belfer Center Programs or Projects: 2012, http://belfercenter.hks.harvard.edu/files/bodansky_durban2_vp.pdf; Michael Grubb, "Doha's Dawn", *Climate Policy*, 13/3, 2013, pp. 281–284.
7 Many observers already perceive a blurring of the principles of common but differentiated responsibility and respective capability since 2009 through the Copenhagen Accord, Cancun Agreements and Durban Platform.

Cooperation on climate change mitigation 125

8   Report of the Conference of the Parties on its eighteenth session, held in Doha from 26 November to 8 December 2012, Decision 2/CP.18: Advancing the Durban Platform, 28 February 2013, http://unfccc.int/resource/docs/2012/cop18/eng/08a01.pdf#page=19, pp. 19–20. Work-stream 1 will explore the scope, structure, and design of the 2015 agreement, ensuring application of the principles of the Convention to the ADP, and suggest ways to define and reflect undertakings by the Parties; work-stream 2 focuses on the enhancement of mitigation ambitions while ensuring application of the principle of the Convention.
9   Report of the Conference of the Parties on its nineteenth session, held in Warsaw from 11 to 23 November 2013, Addendum, p. 4. http://unfccc.int/resource/docs/2013/cop19/eng/10a01.pdf.
10 The 2 degree Celsius goal has been reiterated in many meetings, including with the WEF and G20 as well as in the Cancun Agreements. For a detailed analysis of pledges, see United Nations Environment Programme (UNEP), *The Emissions Gap Report: Are the Copenhagen Accord Pledges Sufficient to Limit Global Warming to 2°C or 1.5°C?* UNEP: November 2010, http://www.unep.org/publications/ebooks/emissionsgapreport; Sivan Kartha and Peter Erickson, *Comparison of Annex 1 and Non-Annex 1 Pledges under the Cancun Agreements*, Working Paper, Stockholm Environment Institute, June 2011, http://sei-us.org/Publications_PDF/SEI-WorkingPaperUS-1107.pdf.
11 B.J. van Ruijven et al., "Emission allowances and mitigation costs of China and India resulting from different effort-sharing approaches", *Energy Policy*, 46, July 2012, p. 126.
12 Navroz Dubash, "Climate Politics in India: How Can the Industrialized World Bridge the Trust Deficit?" In David Michel, Amit Pandya, eds., *Indian Climate Policy: Choices and Challenges*, Washington, D.C.: The Henry L. Stimson Center, 2009, pp. 49–57.
13 Leena Srivastava, "Climate Protection for Sustainable Development or Sustainable Development for Climate Protection? A Case Study from India", *Global Environmental Change*, 16/2, 2006, pp. 122.
14 The agreement aimed to intensify collaboration, particularly in the areas of energy efficiency, renewable energy, clean energy technologies, sustainable agriculture and afforestation along with climate negotiations. See Ministry of Environment and Forests, Government of India, "Agreement on Cooperation on Addressing Climate Change Between the Government of the Republic of India and the Government of the People's Republic of China", http://envfor.nic.in/sites/default/files/India-China%20Agreement%20on%20Climate%20Change.pdf.
15 As reported in various news articles. For details see: Gaurav Singh and John Duce, "China, India Sign Climate Change Cooperation Accord", *Bloomberg,* 21 October 2009, http://www.bloomberg.com/apps/news?pid=newsarchive&sid=aFyFHkF6C3Fs; "India and China signs Agreement on Cooperation on Addressing Climate Change," *Press Information Bureau*, 21 October 2009, http://www.pib.nic.in/newsite/erelease.aspx?relid=53317.
16 Gaurav Singh and John Duce, "China, India Sign Climate Change Cooperation Accord".
17 Swaran Singh, "Paradigm Shift in India–China Relations: From Bilateralism to Multilateralism", *Journal of International Affairs*, 64/2, Spring/Summer 2011, pp. 155–168.
18 Further information on the details of the visit, see Ministry of External Affairs, Government of India, *India–China Bilateral Relations*, http://meaindia.nic.in/meaxpsite/foreignrelation/china.pdf.
19 Yasheng Huang, "The Myth of Economic Complementarity in Sino-Indian Relations", *Journal of International Affairs*, 64/2, Spring/Summer 2011, pp. 111–124.

20 International Energy Agency (IEA), *World Energy Outlook 2012*, Paris: Organisation of Economic Co-operation and Development, 2012, p. 667.
21 Ibid.
22 The Energy and Resources Institute (TERI), *National Energy Map for India: Technology Vision 2030*, New Delhi: TERI Press, 2006, p. 184, http://www.teriin.org/div/psa-fullreport.pdf.
23 Kankesu Jayanthakumaran, Reetu Verma and Ying Liu, "CO2 Emissions, Energy Consumption, Trade and Income: A Comparative Analysis of China and India", *Energy Policy*, 42, 2012, pp. 450–460.
24 Chinese Academy for Environmental Planning (CAEP) and The Energy and Resources Institute (TERI), *Environment and Development: China and India*, New Delhi: TERI Press, 2011.
25 Chinese Academy for Environmental Planning (CAEP) and The Energy and Resources Institute (TERI), *Environment and Development: China and India*, New Delhi: TERI Press, 2011.
26 Ibid.
27 Prime Minister's Council on Climate Change, Government of India, *National Action Plan on Climate Change,* June 2008, http://www.moef.nic.in/downloads/home/Pg01-52.pdf.
28 Jun Li and Xin Wang, "Energy and Climate Policy in China's Twelfth Five Year Plan: A Paradigm Shift", *Energy Policy,* 41, 2012, pp. 519–528.
29 An expert group on Low Carbon Strategies for Inclusive Growth was set up by planning commission in this context. See "Prime Minister Releases Green National Accounts in India a Framework – Report of the Expert Group," *Press Information Bureau,* 5 April 2013, http://pib.nic.in/newsite/erelease.aspx?relid=94488.
30 For details see TERI, "Low Carbon Development in India and China", http://www.teriin.org/projects/locci/.
31 Planning Commission, Government of India, *Interim Report of the Expert Group on Low Carbon Strategies for Inclusive Growth*, May 2011, http://www.moef.nic.in/downloads/public-information/Interim%20Report%20of%20the%20Expert%20Group.pdf.
32 Gao Yinan, "China and India low carbon pursuits central to south-south cooperation", *People's Daily*, 19 March 2014, http://english.peopledaily.com.cn/98649/8570877.html.
33 Planning Commission, Government of India, Interim Report of the Expert Group on Low Carbon Strategies for Inclusive Growth.
34 Ibid.
35 Prime Minister's Council on Climate Change, Government of India, *National Action Plan on Climate Change,* June 2008, http://www.moef.nic.in/downloads/home/Pg01–52.pdf.
36 More information on the PAT scheme can be found at the Bureau of Energy Efficiency, Government of India, http://www.beeindia.in/schemes/schemes.php?id=9. The reports on the launch of the PAT scheme can be found at "Make Energy Conservation a Mass Movement: Sushilkumar Shinde," *Press Information Bureau,* 14 December 2009, http://www.pib.nic.in/newsite/erelease.aspx?relid=55875.
37 Planning Commission, Government of India, *Interim Report of the Expert Group*, p. 35.
38 N.K. Janardhanan and M.K. Shrivastava, "MRV Challenges of Integrating National Initiatives into International Mechanisms: A Case of Perform, Achieve and Trade Mechanism in India", *IGES Working Paper*, November 2012, http://pub.iges.or.jp/modules/envirolib/upload/4170/attach/IGES_Working_Paper_CC-2012-03.pdf.

Cooperation on climate change mitigation 127

39 Renewable Energy and Energy Efficiency Partnership (REEP), *Roadmap for implementation of Renewable Energy Certificate Mechanism in India: Report 1*, December 2009, http://toolkits.reeep.org/file_upload/107010543_1.pdf.
40 For more details, see Renewable Energy Certificate Registry of India, https://www.recregistryindia.nic.in.
41 National Development and Reform Commission (NDRC), People's Republic of China, *China's National Climate Change Programme*, June 2007, http://en.ndrc.gov.cn/newsrelease/200706/P020070604561191006823.pdf.
42 Lynn Price, Xuejun Wang and Jiang Yun, China's Top-1000 Energy-Consuming Enterprises Program: *Reducing Energy Consumption of the 1000 Largest Industrial Enterprises in China*, Ernest Orlando Lawrence Berkley National Laboratory: 2008, http://china.lbl.gov/sites/all/files/lbl-519e-top1000-programjune-2008.pdf; "The East is grey", The Economist, 10 August 2013, http://www.economist.com/news/briefing/21583245-china-worlds-worst-polluter-largest-investor-green-energy-its-rise-will-have.
43 NDRC, *China's National Climate Change Programme*.
44 Joanna Lewis, "Energy and Climate Goals of China's 12th Five-Year Plan", *Center for Climate and Energy Solutions*, March 2011, p.1, http://www.c2es.org/docUploads/energy-climate-goals-china-twelfth-five-year-plan.pdf.
45 Da Zhang, Valerie Karplus, Cyril Cassisa, and Xiliang Zhang, "Emissions Trading in China: Progress and Prospects," *Energy Policy*, 75, 2014, pp. 9–16.
46 Ibid.
47 "The East is grey", *The Economist*, 10 August 2013.
48 CDM Policy Dialogue, *Climate Change, Carbon Markets and the CDM: A Call to Action*, Luxembourg: 2012, http://www.cdmpolicydialogue.org/report/rpt110912.pdf.
49 Marc Lifsher, "Cap-and-trade Programs in California and Quebec to Merge", *Los Angeles Times*, 22 April 2013, http://www.latimes.com/business/la-fi-capitol-businessbeat-20130422,0,1672943.story.
50 European Commission for Climate Action, "Linking EU ETS with Australia: Commission Recommends Opening Formal Negotiations", 21 January 2013, http://ec.europa.eu/clima/news/articles/news_2013012401_en.htm.
51 For more on CDM projects, see United Nations Environment Programme (UNEP) DTU, "CDM/JI Pipeline Analysis and Database", including the full pipeline data, at http://cdmpipeline.org/.
52 Authors' analysis of data from United Nations Environment Programme (UNEP) DTU, "CDM/JI Pipeline Analysis and Database", http://cdmpipeline.org/.
53 Ibid.
54 Fuhr and Lederer, "Varieties of Carbon Governance in Newly Industrializing Countries", *The Journal of Environment and Development*, 18/4, 2009, pp. 327–345.
55 Gudrun Benecke, "Varieties of Carbon Governance: Taking Stock of the Local Carbon Market in India", *The Journal of Environment and Development*, 18/4, 2009, pp. 346–370.
56 Wei Shen, *Understanding the Dominance of Unilateral CDMs in China: Its Origins and Implications for Governing Carbon Market*, Working Paper 149, Tyndall Centre for Climate Change Research, October 2011, http://www.tyndall.ac.uk/sites/default/files/twp149.pdf.
57 Fuhr and Lederer, "Varieties of Carbon Governance in Newly Industrializing Countries", 2009.
58 Leapfrogging proposes that developing nations can 'catch up' to industrialised nations through skipping some of the more dirty stages involved in industrialisation. See Alexandra Mallett, et al., "Section 1: Low Carbon Development Path – Importance,

Perspectives and Trends", *Low Carbon Development Path for Asia and the Pacific: Challenges and Opportunities to the Energy Sector*, The Paper prepared for United Nations Economic and Social Commission for Asia and the Pacific, 2010. Leapfrogging can occur at various levels, including a country's overall development pathway, through the development and production of new technologies in developing countries, and finally, through the use of new technologies. See Raphael Sauter and Jim Watson, *Technology Leapfrogging: A Review of the Evidence*, A Report for DFID, October 2008, https://www.sussex.ac.uk/webteam/gateway/file.php?name=dfid-leapfrogging-reportweb.pdf&site=264.

59 The Pew Charitable Trusts, *Who's Winning the Clean Energy Race?* Philadelphia: The Pew Charitable Trusts, 2014, http://www.pewtrusts.org/~/media/Assets/2014/04/01/clenwhoswinningthecleanenergyrace2013pdf.pdf.

60 Mark Rogers, *Knowledge, Technological Catch-up and Economic Growth*, Cheltenham: Edward Elgar, 2003.

61 This echoes the triple helix model in innovation studies where industry, the academic sector, and governments at various levels (nation, region/state, and local) work together to innovate. The argument is that projects with more sources of leadership and support will be more likely to succeed. See Henry Etzkowitz, Jose Manoel Carvalho de Mello and Mariza Almeida, "Towards 'Meta-Innovation' in Brazil: The Evolution of The Incubator and The Emergence of a Triple Helix", *Research Policy*, 34, 2005, pp. 411–424. Ideally, many advocate for more participatory approaches, engaging the public in the decision-making process, although a number of problems have been identified when attempting to pursue this approach See David Ockwell, *Intellectual property rights and low carbon technology transfer to developing countries – a review of the evidence to date*, Sussex Energy Group/ TERI/ Institute of Development Studies, April 2008, https://www.sussex.ac.uk/webteam/gateway/file.php?name=spru-teri-ids-phase-2-iprs-and-low-c-tt-final.pdf&site=264.

62 National Development and Reform Commission (NDRC), People's Republic of China, "Agreed Minutes of the 1st China–India Strategic Economic Dialogue", 26 September 2011, http://en.ndrc.gov.cn/newsrelease/201109/t20110927_435807.html.

63 CAEP and TERI, *Environment and Development: China and India*.

64 For more details, see Renewable Energy Certificate Registry of India, https://www.recregistryindia.nic.in/.

65 Huang Liming, "A Study of China–India Co-operation in Renewable Energy Field," *Renewable and Sustainable Energy Reviews*, 11, 2007, pp. 1739–1757.

66 Mallett et al., "Section 1: Low Carbon Development Path – Importance, Perspectives and Trends"; Tao Wang and Jim Watson, *China's Energy Transition: Pathways for Low Carbon Development*, Brighton: Sussex Energy Group, 2009, http://www.sussex.ac.uk/Units/spru/environment/CET.pdf.

67 Mallett et al, "Section 1: Low Carbon Development Path – Importance, Perspectives and Trends."

68 The Energy and Resources Institute (TERI), *Towards an Energy Secure Future for India: Summary of Quantitative Analyses*, Project Report 2006RD22, New Delhi: TERI, 2009.

69 Under 'Reference', life continues pretty much as we know it with autonomous efficiency improvements taking place where feasible; increase in use of renewable energy carries on at the same pace; defined policy priorities are implemented with no real sense of urgency. The 'Evolution' scenario sees a determined effort for efficiency improvements both on the supply and demand sides; an accelerated push happens for

renewable energy, nuclear and new technologies such as CTL (Coal to liquids) and GTL (Gas to liquids); energy security concerns are paramount in this scenario. The 'Resolution' scenario honours the Prime Minister of India's commitment that India's per capita carbon emissions would never exceed those of the developed world, and it is optimistically assumed here that the developed world would be able to bring down its emissions to a level of 2 tonnes/capita. The final 'Ambition' scenario considers that India conditionally sets aside its legitimate arguments on "common but differentiated responsibilities" and equitable per capita rights, and takes on even more stringent emission reduction targets. See The Energy and Resources Institute (TERI), Towards an Energy Secure Future for India: Summary of Quantitative Analyses, Project Report 2006RD22, New Delhi: TERI, 2009.

70 Todd Sandler, "Global and Regional Public Goods: A Prognosis for Collective Action", *Fiscal Studies: The Journal of Applied Public Economics*, 19/3, 1998, pp. 221–247.

71 Elinor Ostrom, "A Multi-Scale Approach to Coping with Climate Change and Other Collective Action Problems", *The Solutions Journal*, 1/2, February 2010, pp. 27–36.

72 United Nations World Food Programme, *Report on the State of Food Insecurity in Rural India*, December 2008, http://home.wfp.org/stellent/groups/public/documents/newsroom/wfp197348.pdf.

73 CAEP and TERI, *Environment and Development: China and India*.

74 Speaking in TERI's Climate Change Forum on April 11, 2012, India's Minister for Environment and Forests, Jayanthi Natarajan, stated: "We need to ensure that our people get a fair share of global atmospheric resources, which allows them necessary space to grow and access to food, water and energy. Future arrangements therefore need to be equitable and not just fair and ambitious". She further stated, "Equity does not imply mere parallelism in the actions of countries in future. It is deeper than that and is linked to the potential for growth and sustainable development". See Ministry of Environment and Forests, Government of India, "Speech of Hon'ble Minister for Environment & Forests: From Bali to Durban and Beyond". 11 April 2012, http://envfor.nic.in/downloads/public-information/speech-mef-11-4-12.pdf.

7 Sino-Indian interactions in energy in the 2000s
A Chinese perspective

Zha Daojiong

In international security studies, it is accepted wisdom to treat energy security as a key determinant of a country's foreign policy. According to this approach, because economic growth is invariably dependent upon energy security, ensuring the continuous supply of energy sources, especially oil and natural gas, has become a key foreign policy issue for both China and India. The main factual referent informing such an understanding is that both of these countries are heavily dependent on oil and gas imports. The logical follow up is to ponder how China and India, without ruling out the possibility of joint action, may impact world energy governance.

The view of this chapter is that a single focus on a large economy such as China or India importing oil and gas from the world markets is misleading. A more factually holistic approach is to pay due attention to the notion of energy embedded in an import-dependent country's export of manufactured products. China and India capture more of the attention in the developing world precisely for their respective successes in moving up the industrialisation and urbanisation ladders. As such, their exports of finished products play a more prominent role to further the economic growth of these two economies. With enhanced urbanisation, both the Chinese and Indian economies, in turn, positively contribute to worldwide economic growth by way of increased consumption. Their growth and consumption function as a much-needed driving force to make continued worldwide growth possible, in part because of comparatively low labour costs. As such, it is incomplete to treat either China or India as the final destination for energy movement.

So, in this chapter, the framing of inquiry about China's energy security approaches goes beyond securing the import of oil and gas. After the introduction, the chapter offers an update of some Chinese domestic energy development programmes, while taking note of internal structural challenges the country has to face in the future. The rationale for doing so derives from the recognition that a country's foreign energy policy is an extension of its pursuit of energy development on the domestic front. This part of the chapter also touches upon China's efforts to develop its energy economy through international cooperation and collaboration. In the third part of the chapter, an effort is made to map the contours of interaction between China and India in energy. The author emphasises that what is presented

Sino-Indian interactions in energy in the 2000s 131

here is at best a partial account, due to the fact that comprehensive reviews on the topic are thus far scant. On that basis, the final part of the chapter offers a few thoughts about possible future areas of research on energy as a factor in China–India relations.

Chinese approaches to energy security: an update

As the track record of Chinese economic growth since the 1970s indicates, contemporary China has successfully met its goal of ensuring an adequate supply of energy for its economic development at financial costs commensurate with changes in aggregate national and per capita income, while simultaneously addressing environmental and other concerns associated with energy consumption. The Chinese government's white paper on energy policy, issued in 2012, puts the country's level of aggregate self-sufficiency in energy at 90 per cent.[1] According to statistics compiled by the International Energy Agency, in 2009, imports represented 15.7 per cent of China's total energy consumption.[2] The discrepancy in accounting is not significant enough to overrule the general assessment of domestic supply making up the dominant share of China's total energy consumption. A more pertinent feature is an assessment in the 2013 issue of *BP Statistical Review of World Energy*: China is among the large consuming countries that "saw below-average growth in energy consumption".[3]

One of the key energy policy measures the Chinese central government employs is to issue mandatory goals for energy saving. In the 11th Five-Year Plan (FYP) for economic and social development, issued in 2006, the energy consumption per unit of GDP (energy intensity) was targeted to decline to the tune of 20 per cent by 2010 compared with the 10th FYP period (2005). The grand total is divided by provinces and industry ministries to fulfil their respective shares.[4] Success in implementing the 11th FYP led to the setting of key targets for energy and climate policy for the 12th FYP, which included a 16 per cent reduction in energy intensity, a 17 per cent reduction in carbon intensity (based on the 2005 level) and a 40–45 per cent reduction by 2020, and an increase in non-fossil fuel sources from 8.3 per cent of primary energy consumption in 2011 to 11.4 per cent by 2015.[5]

Granted, actual performance in meeting these targets is subject to a number of contingencies, including those of China's overall economic/financial situation, changes in energy prices, technological breakthroughs, rigour in policy oversight, and international cooperation wherever it applies.[6] By using an energy savings target as a policy instrument, the government has set into motion demand management as a vital part of energy security.

On the production side, China has an energy industry that is as comprehensive as it is possible to be. Driven by the constant necessity to satisfy its consumption needs, virtually every form of domestic energy production – fossil and non-fossil – attracts investment and has government support. About the only exception is food-based bio-fuel production. The low prospect of significant growth in domestic oil production notwithstanding, China has a policy of no competition for land or food when it comes to bio-fuel.[7]

Coal is treated as the foundational source of fuel in China, both in managing on-going necessity and in mapping the country's future energy portfolios. Estimates of the changes in China's energy portfolio by research agencies, both domestic and international, all put the contribution of coal to be over 65 per cent by 2030, against the current level of 72 per cent in aggregate supply. For decades, China pursued coal liquefaction in an attempt to substitute oil.[8] The prospects of switching away from coal to oil in electricity generation are low. Though still a minority voice, some Chinese analysts have begun to warm to the idea that "China's long-term energy reliance on coal will be unsustainable, unless there are dramatic increases in coal reserves".[9] In 2009, China became a net importer of coal, but this has not increased the country's sense of energy insecurity. The economies of scale are going to lead to higher levels of coal imports for the coastal region, in part due to increasing costs in accessing coal further west within the country.

Nuclear power growth continues to be an attractive option for China. Of the 68 nuclear reactors under construction worldwide, 28 are in China. Because fossil fuels still contribute the largest part of China's electricity production – with coal-fired power still making up 80 per cent[10] – and to the incidence of smog in the east (mostly due to coal), further growth in nuclear power has to be a viable option for China. These are the main reasons why, in July 2013, the National Development and Reform Commission announced that the wholesale price of power would be CNY 0.43 per kWh (US$ 0.07/kWh) for all new nuclear power projects, as a way of developing nuclear power and attracting investment in the sector.[11] With advances in technology and with an eye to market factors, the price of power is susceptible to change. This tariff policy ensures a predicable path for the continued growth of the nuclear power industry.

The Fukushima Daiichi nuclear power accident in Japan in March 2011 led to a one-year halt in the 'great leap' of constructing new nuclear power plants, in addition to a comprehensive review of nuclear power plants in operation. A year later, it became clear that China had limited its goal of nuclear power development by the end of 2020 to those projects approved prior to the accident in Japan. By 2020, China is expected to have an installed capacity of 70 million kWh of nuclear power, contingent upon reaching the goal of 40 million kWh in 2015, with enhanced safety standards.[12] It should be borne in mind, however, that China's nuclear economy has always been vigorously debated, and the future development trajectory is likely not to be a straightforward path.[13]

Shale gas extraction, partly due to its revolutionary development in the United States, has received a lot of attention in China. Across the board, Chinese geologists are less sanguine than their American peers in assessing the shale oil reserves in China. Furthermore, there are fierce debates about the accessibility of the deposits and, by extension, whether or not methods and equipment employed in the United States are directly transferrable to China.[14] In late June 2012, authorities concluded that only 40 per cent of the experimental wells produced industrial flows. Nevertheless, the government continues to support the development of the shale industry.[15] As of July 2013, it has become clear that the

2015 target for shale gas production will not be achieved, although some Chinese experts argue that its "long term prospects are still good, even if the short term goal cannot be reached".[16]

The development of renewable energy is vital for China's strategy. The government's target is for 11.4 per cent of primary energy consumption to be from non-fossil sources by 2015 and for this to increase to 15 per cent by 2020.[17] Attractive as the 'renewable' classification is, its path of development is anything but straightforward. The most relevant factor is the continuing competition of interests in the reform of China's electricity market, as wind and solar electricity is more expensive per unit than coal-fired and hydropower power.[18] The good news is that in August 2012, China announced a national feed-in tariff for on-grid solar electricity. In January 2013, China's National Energy Administration targeted an increase in solar power capacity from 7 gigawatts (GW) in 2012 to over 21 GW in 2015. In July 2013, the State Council announced a target of over 35 GW solar power capacity by 2015, to be achieved by yearly additions of 10 GW.[19] China also upgraded its development goal for hydropower. Controversial as hydropower is both domestically and internationally, the World Bank has renewed its efforts to support the growth of the sector in developing countries.[20] In the Chinese context, hydropower is counted as 'renewable'. Furthermore, it is likely that the bulk of growth in Chinese renewable energy will come from hydropower.

Future prospects of China's energy development, nonetheless, depend on how different and competing interests within the country negotiate among themselves to address at least three large structural challenges that are set to remain for the future. The first is that China's energy resource endowment presents a profound material challenge to the pursuit of the twin goals of meeting overall consumption demand and simultaneously seeing rapid reduction of the negative impact of the country's heavy reliance on fossil fuels. China is rich in coal resources but poor in hydrocarbons (oil and natural gas). According to BP, in 2011, as the world's second largest energy consuming economy, China's proven coal reserves stood at 13.3 per cent of the world total. The same numbers for oil and natural gas were 0.9 per cent and 1.5 per cent, respectively.[21] In order to have stable electricity generation, coal has to be the fuel of choice.

The country's geographical distribution of coal reserves – centred in the northern and western parts of the country, thousands of kilometres away from population and industrial centres in the eastern provinces – makes coal extraction and transportation a constant constraint on energy development. China's coal mines are primarily underground ones, making safety maintenance an additional premium. So much so that the central government has consistently retained a separate bureau for handling coal mining safety, even when separating project management from industry regulation has been the norm since the 1990s.[22] Coal still accounts for 70 per cent of China's total primary energy consumption. But reduction of coal use is limited by hydropower already having reached its peak (accounting for 23.1 per cent of the gross installed power capacity in 2010), although Chinese assessments claim that 65 per cent of the country's hydropower resources remain theoretically available.[23] As for renewable sources of electricity such as solar and wind, intermittency in voltage remains a challenge worldwide. In short, a rapid reduction in the country's reliance on coal is certainly desirable but not easily attainable.

Second, since the 1970s, pragmatism has prevailed in China's cooperation with the industrialised economies, yet China risks being a victim of its own success in the future. Taking advantage of the geostrategic window of opportunity presented by the Nixon/Kissinger detente with China in 1971, China intensified its export of coal and other raw materials to Japan in exchange for steel, industrial facilities, and technology.[24] In the early 1970s, China pursued export of crude oil and oil products to its capitalist Asian neighbours.[25] Until the early 1990s, oil assumed an indispensable role in China's total export structure.[26] After the visit by United States Secretary of Energy James R. Schlesinger to Beijing in 1978, China began to systematically pursue involvement by the United States and European countries in its offshore oil development.[27]

Along with trade, China entered into numerous programmes and projects in energy technology cooperation with the industrialised West. International development agencies such as the World Bank and Asian Development Bank funded hundreds of projects that "helped accelerate development of large-scale efficient coal power plants, hydropower, state-of-the-art technologies for controlling power-plant emissions, and international-best-practice environmental assessments of energy projects".[28] The pattern of such interactions is that China sought foreign inputs to increase its energy production, treated energy as an ordinary commodity of export, and along the way worked to improve the technological and managerial knowhow of its own energy companies.

Yet, along with China becoming the second largest economy after the United States, an international consensus has emerged that China's energy companies, its energy science establishment, and its role in financing energy development both inside and outside the country, are to be viewed as peer competitors. As Chinese enterprises become more sophisticated and confident in operating internationally, Western energy enterprises are becoming more cautious in collaborating with their Chinese peers. Successful cases like the tie-up between the Chinese National Petroleum Corporation and BP in developing Iraq's Rumaila oil fields (since 2009) notwithstanding, Western energy and mineral development company executives wonder if the partners of today will become the competitors of tomorrow.[29]

Third, China's involvement in existing world energy governance mechanisms continues to be shallow. China is the world's second largest energy consumer and importer of oil, but not a member of the International Energy Agency (IEA) – the inter-governmental body designed to look after consumer countries' interests. It is more common for Chinese government agencies to dispute the IEA assessments of China's contribution to the fluctuation in world oil and gas prices, rather than the two sides collaborating with each other to address global and domestic concerns. China never joined the Organization of Petroleum Exporting Countries (OPEC), even when it was a net exporter. China only agreed to be an observer in the Energy Charter Treaty mechanism, whose designed purpose is to deal with deliberate interruption by producer states to exploration and production activities and transport routes. The absence of routine contacts between Chinese and major economies' energy policy bureaucrats through such forums, understandably, leaves space for second-guessing about its motives on issues related to world energy governance.

In 2006, China hosted a meeting of the energy ministers of the five major oil-consuming countries (South Korea, India, Japan, and the United States) to discuss energy efficiency and security. However, the initiative has thus far failed to generate much interest from the other major economies. So, how can China and the other major energy-consuming governments generate synergy in world energy governance?

To conclude this part, China continues to pursue both demand management and growth in domestic production of all forms of energy. Development of a particular sector of energy continues to be conditioned by a broad mixture of factors, economic, financial, and technological. What is clear is that there is a greater consensus towards taking quality in energy consumption more seriously. It is no longer possible to justify pursuing growth in total energy supply regardless of the associated environmental and health costs. How to manage the various forces behind the pursuit of goals in quality and quantity is the real challenge for China's policymakers. In addition, China has entered into a totally new external policy environment as it seeks assistance in developing its energy economy at home. Internationally, competition with the industrialised world, at both governmental and corporate levels, is becoming the new normal.

Energy in China–India relations: a sketch

Modern China and India pursued their paths to ensuring their respective energy supply security without a strong footprint of mutual interactions in trading energy commodities. It is commonplace for observers in both countries and beyond to highlight that the two countries have to compete for the same pools of energy resources in the rest of the world. Yet it pays to begin our discussion by trying to track how the two have interacted with each other.

Trade in energy commodities

Chinese statistics record India as a source of refined oil. In 2012, China imported 100,052 tons of refined oil, which accounted for 0.4 per cent of China's total import in this category for the year. The record indicates that India is an occasional source, with 25,300 tons imported in 2000, 31,500 tons in 2005, and 88,000 in 2010.[30] Our research did not locate statistics indicating trade in coal or natural gas between the two economies.

Though statistically insignificant, the fact that there is trade in energy products between China and India is testimony to a measure of normalcy in energy ties between the two economies. After all, the energy geographies of the two countries are such that both are aggregate importers of fossil energy; electricity trade between them is constrained by geography and the availability of spare supply on either side.

Corporate tie-ups and competition in third countries

The international oil and gas exploration and production market has been long dominated by established international oil majors, most of which are of Western origin. When Chinese and Indian oil companies began to join the competition, they had to settle for fields in those countries that are either deemed to be too challenging in either geological/technical or political-diplomatic terms. Still, Chinese and Indian oil corporations have demonstrated that a corporate tie-up is possible.

Sudan was the first major country in which the oil companies of China and India demonstrated their willingness to work together. The opportunity came in 1996, after Chevron (in Sudan since 1978) withdrew due to the Clinton Administration's comprehensive sanctions against the Khartoum regime for its involvement with terrorist networks. When the Greater Nile Petroleum Operating Company (GNPOC) was incorporated in 1997, the China National Petroleum Corporation (CNPC) held the majority (40 per cent) stake, with Petronas Carigali Overseas of Malaysia taking 30 per cent, Arakis of Canada taking 25 per cent, and Sudapet (the national oil company of Sudan) taking 5 per cent. In 2003, ONGC Videsh Ltd. (OVL), a unit of the Indian company Oil & Natural Gas Corporation, became a partner in GNPOC by replacing Talisman (another Canadian company), which had taken over Arakis's share one year earlier. Among other oil projects in Sudan, in 2005, OVL's engineering arm received a build, operate, and transfer contract from Sudanese authorities to construct a 100,000 barrel-per-day (bpd) refinery at Port Sudan. This investment is an integral part of GNPOC's drive toward building up an integrated oil industry in Sudan. After the formal separation of Sudan into two countries in February 2011, both CNPC and OVL chose to stay and work with the new government in South Sudan.[31]

Iran is the second major country to attract China–India cooperation. In November 2004, Iran offered China Petroleum & Chemical Corporation (Sinopec) a stake of up to 60 per cent in the undeveloped onshore Yadavaran field in return for a Chinese commitment to buy some 250 million tons of Iranian liquefied natural gas (LNG) over a 25-year period. Sinopec would also get exclusive rights to buy half of Yadavaran's projected peak output of 300,000 bpd over 25 years. In addition, Iran also offered India's ONGC Videsh a 20 per cent stake in Yadavaran in return for long-term LNG purchases. The Yadavaran project has thus far failed to proceed as was originally envisioned, due to causes both in Iranian domestic politics and in foreign relations over Iran's suspected nuclear weapons programme.[32] In the context of Sino-Indian energy relations, the important fact is that the national oil companies of China and India demonstrated a willingness to enter a geologically attractive project in a (geo)politically complex country like Iran.

Chinese and Indian companies have formed joint ventures in Syria as well. In 2005, CNPC and ONGC jointly bid for and acquired a 37 per cent stake belonging to Petro-Canada in the al-Furat oil and gas fields, the largest oil producing fields in Syria, responsible for half of the country's total production. The significance in this development is that CNPC and ONGC submitted a 50–50 bid, the first time the Chinese and Indian state companies had cooperated in bidding for overseas assets.[33] Other shareholders include Royal Dutch Shell PLC's Syrian subsidiary and the state-owned Syrian Petroleum Co.

In mid-2006, ONGC and Sinopec partnered for a 50 per cent stake in Omimex de Colombia, a subsidiary of Omimex Resources, an independent oil company from the United States. Each pledged to invest US$ 400 million for a 25 per cent stake. The Omimex deal was the third time that Chinese and Indian oil companies acquired land together.[34]

Competition is also a feature in the interactions between Chinese and Indian oil companies in third countries. In August 2005, CNPC beat a joint bid by ONGC and L. N. Mittal for PetroKazakhstan. Also in Kazakhstan, in 2012, ONGC Videsh once again lost to CNPC. ONGC had reached an agreement to purchase ConocoPhillips' 8.4 per cent stake in Kazakhstan's biggest oil field, Kashagan, for US$ 5 billion. However, using the right of first refusal or pre-emption rights, the Kazakh government exercised its option to step in and buy the stake at the price agreed upon by ONGC and ConocoPhillips. Thus, in July 2013, it was announced that Kazakhstan's national oil company, KazMunaiGaz, would buy the 8.4 per cent. This stake would then be sold to CNPC for a reported US$ 5.3–5.4 billion.[35] The Kashagan oil deposits were discovered in 2000 and are thought to be massive. They may constitute the largest field found in the past 30 years, the biggest outside the Middle East, and may match the Ghawar field in Saudi Arabia.[36]

Competition between Chinese and Indian oil companies has also taken place in their respective efforts to enter oil fields in African countries. Sinopec's out-bidding of OVL for Shell's shares in the oil fields in Angola in 2004 is one of the best known instances, perhaps because it was the most noticeable after the Chinese–Indian tie up in Sudan's GNPOC.[37] In 2005, both CNPC and ONGC pursued oil assets in Ecuador. The assets in question were held by EnCana, a firm headquartered in Calgary, Alberta. ONGC was close to acquiring EnCana for US$ 1.4 billion, but the deal fell through when EnCana rejected ONGC's requirement that "EnCana guarantee that the license would not be cancelled, a condition the Canadian firm refused to fulfil, leading to the Indian firm's withdrawal".[38]

A complete recounting of interactions between Chinese and Indian oil and gas companies – in third countries – would require a separate project and is beyond the scope of this chapter. The author's purpose here is to draw attention to details that give a picture of the complex set of actors behind what is generally termed cooperation and/or competition. It is tempting to point to the same developments and question whether or not the Chinese government genuinely wants to see its companies working in collaboration with Indian energy companies.[39] That is a valid question, as the government is an active factor in the country's energy diplomacy. But as the cases above remind us, the outcome of a particular acquisition attempt involves the host country government and international oil companies already established in those societies. In short, it is advisable to guard against simplifying the outcome of a particular case of cooperation or competition and rendering it as

138 *Zha Daojiong*

a manifestation of the nature of the political-diplomatic relationship between the governments of China and India.

Energy cooperation: government frameworks

By most accounts, it was only in the mid-2000s that energy began to feature as a significant topic in government-to-government diplomacy between China and India. For example, in the joint declaration issued during Chinese Prime Minister Wen Jiabao's visit to India in April 2005, Article 9 states, "The two sides agreed to cooperate in the field of energy security and conservation".[40] The declaration also encourages collaboration to explore and exploit oil and natural gas resources in third countries.

Then in January 2006, Mani Shankar Aiyar, the visiting Indian Petroleum and Natural Gas Minister, signed a 'Memorandum for Enhancing Cooperation in the Field of Oil and Natural Gas' with Ma Kai, director of China's National Development and Reform Commission (NDRC). Diplomatic protocol was apparently at work, since the head of China's state energy administration is simultaneously a deputy director of the NDRC. The Memorandum specified five pledges of cooperation: "upstream exploration and production, refining and marketing of petroleum products and petrochemicals, research and development, conservation, and promotion of environment-friendly fuels".[41]

The larger background for these moves in government-to-government diplomacy to highlight energy as an issue area for discussion and collaboration is unprecedented volatility in the world oil trade. For both China and India, together with Japan and Korea, reliance on the Middle East as a source of oil imports means that they have to live with the Asian Premium phenomenon. The historical evolution in contractual designs by Middle Eastern oil exporters is such that crude oil shipped to Asia was priced higher than that to Europe and North America. Although oil traders tend to downplay such differentials, Asian energy economists called for collaborative action among the large importing countries to hedge against its continuation of this practice.[42] Indeed, when New Delhi initiated a meeting of ministers of major East Asian oil and gas importing countries in November 2005, it included on the agenda discussions on the 'Asian Premium' and oil security.

China continued with the momentum set off in Delhi by hosting a meeting of energy ministers from major oil importers India, Japan, Korea, and the United States in December 2006. The purpose was to search for stability in international oil markets. After the outbreak of the financial crisis in the United States and Europe in 2008, however, the momentum seems to have been lost, as stability in the world financial markets consumed the attention of the major economies of the world.

Russia, together with the Central Asian oil producer countries, is important in Chinese and Indian efforts to pursue new sources of external supply. For that purpose, energy has been a standard topic in the trilateral foreign ministers' meetings among China, India, and Russia, since 2002. The Shanghai Cooperation

Organization (SCO) amended its charter to allow observers to apply for full membership in 2011. India has been an SCO observer since 2005 and has worked to gain full membership.[43] Regardless of when this will happen, the point is that Chinese and Indian delegations have ample opportunities to socialise in the SCO and other mini-lateral forums whereby they can hope to have a greater level of influence than in such established energy policy mechanisms as the International Energy Agency and the Organization of Petroleum Exporting Countries.

In terms of government-level energy policy frameworks, a more pertinent issue is how China and India interact with each other in addressing the continuation of energy poverty and the impact of climate change in their respective societies. Similar to the pursuit of fossil fuel energy security, both China and India have launched ambitious renewable energy development goals.[44] In renewable energy and other aspects of energy development, policies adopted in one society cannot be duplicated in another. But a government framework that aims at promoting exchanges between scientists, engineers, and policymakers in energy use can be useful.

Until the 1990s, science and technology (S&T) cooperation between China and India was extremely limited in scope. In part this was due to the rather poor and underdeveloped state of bilateral relations. In addition, neither country offered much by way of advanced technological capabilities, and both instead turned to the industrialised countries for advanced technologies. It was not until the signing of the April 1991 Memorandum of Understanding (MOU) for cooperation in technology transfer, engineering, and consultancy services in the fields of chemicals and petrochemicals that the two governments started to explore the possibility of S&T collaboration. Progress in S&T between the two countries continues to be subject to the fluctuation in overall political-diplomatic relations. However, as is recorded elsewhere, cooperation in energy technologies has, since 2004, featured in government MOUs.[45] A more substantial accounting of Sino-Indian cooperation in energy-related S&T is again beyond the scope of this current effort. The point is that considerations of energy in Sino-Indian relations should include how China and India can take advantage of each other's experiences in addressing energy use in their respective societies, including reducing energy poverty and improving energy efficiency.

To bring this partial recounting to a conclusion, the author sees it possible to reiterate several points. First, trade in energy commodities between China and India is negligible in statistical terms. Still, the very fact that such trade has taken place invites researchers to pay more attention to normalcy in how the two economies relate to each other against the overall backdrop of aggregate energy insufficiency. Second, the national governments of China and India have reached out to each other to promote energy cooperation (with a range of meanings); their national oil/gas companies have in some instances pursued tie-ups in third countries and in other cases competed against each other. The factors behind the outcomes are numerous and often outside the realm of bilateral relations alone. Third, yet by no means least, energy-related science and technology does have its place in cooperation frameworks between the two societies.

Overall, developments highlighted in this part of the chapter ought to drive us to view energy as a mosaic, instead of a straight-jacketed 'cooperation vs. competition' mode of inquiry.

Conclusion: agendas for further research

Based on the preceding discussions, the author offers the following thoughts for consideration in future efforts to appraise energy as a topic for discussion in China–India relations.

First, there needs to be an effort to systematically document how the two countries have interacted with each other. By 'countries', I refer to a multitude of actors: governments, corporations, and science and technology research communities. In this regard, it is necessary to include an accounting of activities and perspectives on the part of both energy and energy-related corporations. The logic behind this call is in reality common sense. Both China and India are in a stage of development that requires far greater levels of attention to the quality in energy use than analysts generally recognise. Related to this agenda, research efforts need to proceed from the recognition that trade and investment in energy-related equipment are as significant as that in energy commodities. For China and India, efforts much be made to facilitate corporate interaction in energy-related activities so that business and engineering entities can maximise their respective competitive niches in each other's society. Doing so will only bring net added value to each side.

Second, based on the first, there is a need to foster a community of energy policy researchers in China and India who find value in resisting over-generalisation about the other country's intentions, particularly when difficulties and disputes arise. Given the nascent history of business and societal interactions between the two countries, Chinese scholars must resist approaches in international commentary that tend to see China and India as unitary actors. In-depth examination of the variety of actors and factors behind a major decision that may have an impact on the other is a priority for a meaningful conversation on narrowing differences in interpretation. This is especially necessary when a third country actor is involved. Hopefully, this chapter makes a positive contribution to such an endeavour.

Third, the evolution of international energy governance affects the welfare of both China and India. The international studies communities of China and India should collaborate in differentiating between the visionary and the pragmatically possible in attempting to affect change. Though not a highlight in this chapter, large consuming countries like China and India face the common challenge of how to become more proactive and effectual in the continuous search for improvement in international energy governance.

In sum, as stated at the outset of this chapter, the author has stayed away from the usual approach in discussing energy in China–India relations by focusing on their aggregate dependence on the rest of the world's markets. Hopefully, the analysis presented in this chapter can serve as a beginning for discussions of energy as a factor in China–India relations from the ground up.

Notes

1. Chinese Government's Official Web Portal, "Full Text: China's Energy Policy 2012", http://www.gov.cn/english/official/2012-10/24/content_2250497.htm.
2. Based on IEA statistics for the People's Republic of China. International Energy Agency (IEA), "2009 Energy Balance for China, People's Republic of", http://www.iea.org/stats/balancetable.asp?COUNTRY_CODE=CN.
3. BP, *Statistical Review of World Energy*, June 2013, p. 1, http://www.bp.com/content/dam/bp/pdf/statistical-review/statistical_review_of_world_energy_2013.pdf.
4. Stephanie Ohshita, Lynn Price and Tian Zhiyu, *Target Allocation Methodology for China's Provinces: Energy Intensity in the 12th Five-Year Plan*, Report, Berkeley: Ernest Orlando Lawrence Berkeley National Laboratory, March 2011. For a case report of the implementation, see Daisheng Zhang et al., "The Energy Intensity Target in China's 11th Five-Year Plan Period – Local Implementation and Achievements in Shanxi Province", *Energy Policy*, 39/7, 2011, pp. 4115–4124.
5. Lan Lan, "Energy, Emissions Goals Appear Cloudy for 2015", *China Daily*, 27 May 2014, http://usa.chinadaily.com.cn/epaper/2014-05/27/content_17544571.htm.
6. Yuan Jiahai, Hou Yong and Xu Ming, "China's 2020 Carbon Intensity Target: Consistency, Implementations, and Policy Implications", *Renewable and Sustainable Energy Reviews*, 16/7, September 2012, pp. 4970–4981.
7. Feng Lianyong, Hu Yan, Charles A.S. Hall and Wang Jianliang, *The Chinese Oil Industry: History and Future*, New York: Springer, 2012.
8. Rong Fang and David G. Victor, "Coal Liquefaction Policy in China: Explaining the Policy Reversal Since 2006", *Energy Policy*, 39, December 2011, pp. 8175–8184.
9. Lin Bo-qiang and Liu Jiang-hua, "Estimating Coal Production Peak and Trends of Coal Imports in China", *Energy Policy*, 38, January 2010, p. 516.
10. Zhao Yinan and Du Juan, "Nuclear Plants to Get the Nod", *China Daily*, 21 April 2014, http://europe.chinadaily.com.cn/business/2014-04/21/content_17449084.htm.
11. "China Sets On-grid Nuclear Power Price", *China Daily*, 3 July 2013, http://europe.chinadaily.com.cn/business/2013-07/03/content_16713340.htm.
12. Zhou Yinan and Du Juan, "Nuclear Plants to Get the Nod".
13. Cheryl S.F. Chi and Ling Chen, "The Sources of Divergent Practices in China's Nuclear Power Sector", *Energy Policy*, 48, September 2012, pp. 348–357.
14. Hu Desheng and Xu Shengqing, "Opportunity, Challenges and Policy Choices for China on the Development of Shale Gas", *Energy Policy*, 60, September 2013, pp. 21–26.
15. "Liu Tienan: Forcefully Push Forward Shale Gas Development", Report in Chinese, *People's Daily*, 26 June 2012.
16. Zhang Dongxiao, quoted in Leslie Hook, "China Set to Miss Target for Shall Gas Field Development", *Financial Times*, 2 July 2013.
17. Wu Wencong, "Premier Vows to 'Declare War Against Pollution'", *China Daily*, 6 March 2014, http://www.chinadaily.com.cn/cndy/2014-03/06/content_17325749.htm.
18. Judith A. Cherni and Joanna Kentish, "Renewable Energy Policy and Electricity Market Reforms in China", *Energy Policy*, 35, July 2007, pp. 3616–3629.
19. Eric Ng, "Power Plan Sparks Rally in Solar Firms", *South China Morning Post*, 17 July 2013, http://www.scmp.com/business/commodities/article/1284266/power-plan-sparks-rally-solar-firms.
20. "World Bank U-turn Brings Hydropower in from Cold", *South China Morning Post*, 11 May 2013, http://www.scmp.com/news/world/article/1234897/world-bank-u-turn-brings-hydropower-cold.

21 BP, *Statistical Review of World Energy*, June 2012, http://www.bp.com/content/dam/bp/pdf/Statistical-Review-2012/statistical_review_of_world_energy_2012.pdf.
22 Xueqiu He and Li Song, "Status and Future Tasks of Coal Mining Safety in China", *Safety Science*, 50, April 2012, pp. 894–898; Xunpeng Shi, "Have Government Regulations Improved Workplace Safety?: A Test of the Asynchronous Regulatory Effects in China's Coal Industry, 1995–2006", *Journal of Safety Research*, 40/3, 2009, pp. 207–213.
23 Xiaolin Chang, Xinghong Liu and Wei Zhou, "Hydropower in China at Present and Its Further Development", *Energy*, 35, November 2010, pp. 4400–4406.
24 Yoshihide Soeya, *Japan's Economic Diplomacy with China, 1945-1978*, Oxford: Clarendon Press, 1998.
25 A. Doak Barnett, *China's Economy in Global Perspective*, Chapter 4, Washington D.C.: Brookings Institute, 1981, pp. 372–494.
26 Larry C.H. Chow, "The Changing Role of Oil in Chinese Exports Since 1974", *The China Quarterly*, 131, 1992, pp. 750–765.
27 Kim Woodard, *The International Energy Relations of China*, Stanford: Stanford University Press, 1980.
28 Eric Martinot, "World Bank Energy Projects in China: Influences on Environmental Protection", *Energy Policy*, 29, June 2001, pp. 581–594.
29 The author is thankful to Tim Lane, China Advisor of Rio Tinto, for sharing this insight.
30 Tian Chunrong, "Survey and Analysis of China's Oil and Natural Gas Import in 2012", Article in Chinese, *International Energy Economics*, March 2013, p. 53.
31 Zha Daojiong, "China's Oil Interests in Africa: International Political Challenges", Article in Chinese, *International Politics Quarterly*, 4, 2005, pp. 53–67.
32 Details of the project are from "Iran Cozies up to China and India", *Energy Compass*, 4 November 2004, p. 1; Kate Dourian and Aresu Eqbali, "Sinopec's Right to Develop Iran Field Tied to LNG Buys", *Platt's Oilgram News*, 82/208, 2 November 2004, p. 1; See also Zha Daojiong, "China and Iran: Energy and/ or Geopolitics", in *Oil and Gas for Asia: Geopolitical Implications of Asia's Rising Demand*, NBR Special Report 41, Washington D.C.: National Bureau of Asian Research, September 2012, pp. 19–28.
33 "ONGC and CNPC Submit Joint Syria Bid", *Energy Compass*, 15 December 2005, p. 1.
34 "Sundeep Tucker, "Sinopec, ONGC buy Colombian stake", *Financial Times*, 15 August 2006.
35 "India Loses US$ 5 billion Bid for Kashagan Oil Field to China", *The Economic Times*, 2 July 2013, http://articles.economictimes.indiatimes.com/2013-07-02/news/40329249_1_kashagan-cnpc-kazakh-law.
36 For an industry description, see "Kashagan Offshore Oil Field Project, Kazakhstan", *Offshore-technology.com*, http://www.offshore-technology.com/projects/kashagan.
37 Vidhan Pathak, "India's Energy Diplomacy in Francophone Africa: Competitive-Cooperation with China", *India Quarterly: A Journal of International Affairs*, 63/2, April 2007, pp. 26–55.
38 "China's Andes Signs EnCana Deal", *Asia Times*, 17 September 2005, http://www.atimes.com/atimes/China_Business/GI17Cb01.html.
39 For example, see P.R. Kumaraswamy, "India's Energy Cooperation with China: The Slippery Side", *China Report*, 43/3, 2007, pp. 349–352.
40 Ministry of External Affairs, Government of India, "Joint Statement of the Republic of India and the People's Republic of China", 11 April 2005, http://www.mea.gov.in/bilateral-documents.htm?dtl/6577/Joint+Statement+of+the+Republic+of+India+and+the+Peoples+Republic+of+China.

41 "China, India Sign Energy Agreement", *China Daily*, 13 January 2006, http://www.chinadaily.com.cn/english/doc/2006-01/13/content_511871.htm.
42 See the debate between Tilak K. Doshi and Adi Imsirovic, "The 'Asian Premium' in Crude Oil Markets: Fact or Fiction?" In Zha Daojiong, ed., *Managing Regional Energy Vulnerabilities in East Asia: Case Studies*, Oxford: Routledge, 2013, pp. 45–47; and Kanekiyo Kensuke and Kobayashi Yoshikazu, "Oil Price Volatility: A Threat to Sustainable Development in East Asia", In Zha Daojiong, ed., *Managing Regional Energy Vulnerabilities in East Asia: Case Studies*, Oxford: Routledge, 2013, pp. 72–86.
43 Meena Singh Roy, "India's Options in the Shanghai Cooperation Organization", *Strategic Analysis*, 36/4, 2012, pp. 645–650. India is expected to join during the July 2015 summit. See "The New, Improved Shanghai Cooperation Organization", 13 September 2014, http://thediplomat.com/2014/09/the-new-improved-shanghai-cooperation-organization/.
44 Aparna Sawhney, "Renewable Energy Policy in India: Addressing Energy Poverty and Climate Mitigation", *Review of Environmental Economics and Policy*, 7/2, June 2013, pp. 296–312.
45 D. Varaprasad Sekhar, "Science and Technology Cooperation between India and China", *International Studies*, 42/3, October 2005, pp. 307–327.

8 What scope for resource cooperation?

An Indian perspective

Arunabha Ghosh

Resource security matters for India and the global economy. This is demonstrated by the rise of new consumers of mineral resources (South–South resource trade is now larger than South–North trade), the continued concentration of large-scale mineral production in a few economies, a step-change in price volatility as compared to three decades ago, the rapid increase in outward foreign investment by BRICS countries in resource-rich economies, and a rising trend of international disputes related to trade in minerals.[1] Against this background, environmental constraints against resource exploration, production, and consumption are also driving the demand for greater resource efficiency.

India, whose per capita consumption of many minerals remains low, has to balance the cumulative demand for greater resource use with the risks of exposing itself to greater price volatility and environmental pressures. In fact, India has to confront three interlocking challenges of sustainable development: securing energy, water, and other minerals to support economic growth; meeting basic needs for food, fuel, and water for a growing population; and managing the environmental constraints and consequences of increased resource use.[2]

India's most pressing priority will be to recognise how vulnerable it is to the linkages between energy, food, water, and climate. The response, in turn, will have to leverage India's strengths in each domain and develop appropriate domestic and international policy positions. India has an especially strong national interest in well-functioning commodity markets. Its growing presence as a 'rule-shaper' and its willingness to engage on a multilateral, rather than solely a bilateral, basis offer it potential to influence the design of robust international regimes for resource security and global public goods.[3]

This chapter reviews India's pressures for securing resources for economic growth, for meeting basic human needs, and the domestic and international environmental constraints it faces. Thereafter, the chapter analyses India's resource nexus – how energy, food, water, and climate change affect each other. It then outlines priorities for the medium-term, both in response to supply constraints as well as demand pressures. These priorities underscore the imperatives for domestic policy as well as reform of global governance. The chapter concludes with reflections on how India and China could cooperate in line with these imperatives.

Energy and critical minerals for growth

India's current development trajectory suggests that, unlike other major economies, all its major sectors will have to grow simultaneously. Agricultural growth, which has been largely stagnant for the past decade, will demand more energy for irrigation and other value-added agro-processing industries. Manufacturing is slated to grow from 15 per cent to 25 per cent of GDP under the new National Manufacturing Policy. And the services sector, already a major contributor to national income, will continue to grow along with rising demand from a rapidly urbanising residential sector. Household energy consumption outstripped that of agriculture for the first time during the last decade and now accounts for a third of all energy use.[4]

Although India is currently a second-tier energy consumer (the United States, China, and the European Union consume much more), between now and 2030, Indian demand is projected to increase more quickly than any other country in the G20. Even under an aggressive, but politically infeasible, global climate stabilisation scenario, India would consume around 60 per cent more energy in twenty years than it does today.[5]

Demand for coal has, on average, been increasing by approximately 7 per cent per year since 2005, up from 5 per cent between 2000 and 2005, with power generation and manufacturing as the main drivers.[6] In addition to problems associated with domestic mining, a lack of port and transportation infrastructure, combined with dysfunctional markets, has hindered imports of coal.[7] Only four major ports handle coal imports, providing a capacity of just 63m tonnes, leaving minor ports to pick up the slack.[8]

There was already an estimated 15 per cent gap between the supply and demand of coal in 2012.[9] Imports (currently accounting for 15 per cent of demand) are growing rapidly and projected to reach 40 per cent by 2030, based on current trends,[10] or sooner (by 2016) if the power sector demand and supply gap is to be closed.[11]

Oil production has remained almost flat over the past decade even as demand is projected almost to double by 2030.[12] India's oil imports will increase four- to six-fold by 2030.[13] As a result, India is exposed to both 'supply' risks (war, strikes, political upheavals in oil exporting countries, deliberate blockades of supplies to India) and 'market' risks (higher and more volatile prices).

Equity oil and gas investments have had limited value. Although overseas production is now around 10 per cent of domestic production,[14] India also has to operate in politically fragile states such as Iran, Iraq, Kazakhstan, Libya, Nigeria, South Sudan, and Venezuela.[15] Joint investments for oil exploration in the South China Sea with Vietnam have created tensions with China.[16] Moreover, little 'equity oil' makes its way back to India, but is instead sold in global markets.[17]

As demand for gas grows (at over 5 per cent each year between now and 2030),[18] India will become more reliant on imports.[19] Substantial investment is needed in liquefied natural gas (LNG) terminals and even transnational pipelines. These pipelines would have to pass through Afghanistan and Pakistan, and would increase competition with China for pipeline gas.[20]

In addition to energy-related fossil fuels, India also needs other critical mineral resources to drive industrial growth. According to the definition of the Committee on Critical Mineral Impacts on the US Economy established by the National Resource Council, "A mineral can be regarded as critical only if it performs an essential function for which few or no satisfactory substitutes exist".[21] No publicly available exercise has been conducted to identify critical minerals for India. The Council on Energy, Environment and Water, an independent research institution, has begun assessing the criticality of 35 minerals based on three criteria: economic importance, supply risks, and environmental constraints. A strategic approach to understanding critical minerals will depend on demand projections, and will factor in supply and environmental risks.

Resources for basic needs

Biofuels, biomass, and waste still take in a large share (33 per cent) of final energy consumption in India, given the lack of access to modern cooking fuels for 772 million people and electricity for 293 million people.[22] As more households demand modern sources of energy, demand for fossil fuels will rise, unless renewable and sustainable sources of fuel along with cleaner cook stoves are deployed on a large scale in the country.

Food security is also of critical importance to India's policymakers. The government passed the Food Security Bill in 2013, which aims to provide subsidised grain to around three quarters of the rural and half of the urban population.[23] The bill is estimated by the government to bring the cost of subsidies to around US$ 16 billion per year; the Food and Agricultural Organisation's projections are much higher.[24]

Even if the government manages to find such large fiscal reserves, its policies would still remain vulnerable to developments in international food markets, as demonstrated by the 2008 food crisis when global food prices rose dramatically. Indian production has grown strongly since the crisis, but total central government subsidies have also doubled in real terms over the past five years.[25]

Food production is intricately linked to water. Over half of India's population lives in areas that are water stressed.[26] Arable land per capita has halved over the past 40 years[27] and farm size is shrinking.[28] In 20 out of India's 29 states, current irrigation infrastructure now exceeds the potential left to be developed, implying the limits of building more canal systems as opposed to focussing on irrigation efficiency.[29] Farmers are, instead, turning to groundwater to maintain productivity, with 61 per cent of land now irrigated by groundwater.[30] In major agricultural states, such as Punjab, Haryana, and Rajasthan, annual groundwater use exceeds annual recharge.

Rising water demand is not unique to agriculture. As with energy, water will also face simultaneously rising pressures from agriculture, industry, and for domestic use. Not only will water demand expand, productive and consumptive sectors will also come into greater competition with each other.[31] By some estimates, India's aggregate water demand could exceed available supply by as much as 50 per cent by 2030.[32]

Resource demand against environmental constraints

Extreme weather events and other environmental disasters further complicate resource pressures. Between 2000 and 2009, an average of around 30 million people was affected by flooding each year, leading to the loss of 17,830 lives.[33] Around three quarters of a million square kilometres of the country are covered by the Drought Prone Area Programme.[34]

Given India's shortage of land, it is vulnerable to deterioration in land quality. Soil erosion affects 0.1 per cent of land in Goa but 21.6 per cent in Rajasthan.[35] Erosion rates range from 5 to 20 tonnes of soil per hectare.[36] By 2050, India will have 18 per cent of the global population with 2.4 per cent of the world's land.[37] In addition to growing water stress, water quality is also poor and will deteriorate as cities grow. Only 31 per cent of municipal wastewater is currently treated.[38]

India is one of the most vulnerable countries in the world to climate change, coming second only to Bangladesh.[39] If global temperatures rise by 2 to 4 degrees, average annual precipitation in India could rise by 7 to 20 per cent per year, while central India and other semi-arid regions could receive 5 to 25 per cent less precipitation.[40]

The nexus and its discontents

Energy, minerals, food, water, and climate form a resource nexus for India, serving as factors that affect each other (Table 8.1). India's resource vulnerability is a function of these interactions.

- *Energy for food.* Agriculture is heavily dependent on oil in India, which accounts for 42 per cent of all agricultural energy.[41] High or volatile crude oil prices drive food inflation and have an impact on the fiscal balance if subsidies are used to cushion some of the shock.
- *Energy for water.* Subsidised energy allows farmers to over-extract water to irrigate their land, leading to both water and energy shortages, and land degradation. With more than 16 million electrified groundwater pump sets in operation, demand for electricity to pump water (in agriculture and in urban areas) will increase. Shortfalls and inefficient water use will build political pressures for continuing subsidies and spur social conflict.
- *Energy impacting climate.* Climate is affected because energy demand in India will post the fastest rate of growth among major economies over the next two decades. Natural gas could partially mitigate the impact, but its use would depend on pricing decisions, infrastructure, and bilateral or multilateral agreements to secure access to gas from other countries.
- *Renewable energy impacting climate.* Renewable energy has a role in climate change mitigation, but it is constrained by policy distortions, access to finance, limited grid connections, and land availability.[42]
- *Food as inputs for energy.* Food markets, in turn, are affected if crops are diverted to produce biofuels. Research on second generation biofuels is

targeting crop residue as feedstock, so that grain markets are not unduly affected.[43] However, inefficient subsidies, such as for corn-based ethanol in the United States, have an impact on global prices for major crops.
- *Food impacting water.* Cropping patterns also affect water use efficiency. For instance, the northern states of Haryana, Punjab, and Uttar Pradesh have almost as much a share of rice production (29 per cent) as the eastern states of Assam, Bihar, Jharkhand, Odisha, and West Bengal (36 per cent), where rice is the staple food.[44] If food security is largely measured by rising stocks of food grains, then continued production of water-intensive crops, like rice, in the northern states, will further deplete water tables. Moreover, wastage of food grains, thanks to inefficient storage and distribution networks, means that the pressure on water increases because more food production is needed to cover up for crop loss.
- *Water for energy.* Nearly 88 per cent of water used in industry is used by thermal power plants.[45] More than 70 per cent of existing and planned thermal and hydropower capacity is already located or will be situated in water-scarce or water-stressed areas,[46] and by some estimates, water demand in the thermal power sector will exceed supply by at least 17 per cent by 2050.[47] Water shortages have shut down power plants (in Chandrapur in 2010, Raichur in 2012 and Parli in 2013 and 2014), raising both energy security risks and the potential for conflict with nearby towns. Also, hydropower links the energy sector with water, causing electricity shortages during times of drought or when water levels in reservoirs are low (as happened in late July 2012 triggering the collapse of the grid).
- *Water for renewable energy.* Many planned concentrated solar power (CSP) plants are likely to be in highly sunny areas, such as in Rajasthan, and demand large quantities of water similar to thermal power plants. Water supply shortages present a key risk to power generation.[48]
- *Water for food.* More than 80 per cent of water is used in agriculture, with groundwater taking a large share. As groundwater levels fall rapidly, food output will be adversely affected unless demand side efficiency measures are adopted. This will, in turn, raise food prices, undermine food security, and threaten farmers' incomes over the long term.
- *Virtual water for food.* Trade in agricultural commodities embeds water that has been used in their production. If water stress increases, food security could be partially achieved by importing higher quantities of food grains. But increasing reliance on virtual water would also involve risks associated with international commodity price fluctuations, foreign exchange pressures, vulnerability to extreme weather events in exporting countries, and threats to the livelihoods of farmers in India.
- *Climate affects everything.* Climate change multiplies risks across all sectors, with energy infrastructure and agriculture vulnerable to extreme weather events as well as rising temperatures and changes in the distribution and extent of rainfall.

Table 8.1 India's resource nexus

Factors	Impacts			
	Energy	Food	Water	Climate
Energy		Oil is 42 per cent of agricultural energy use: price shocks affect food prices	More than 16 million electrified groundwater pumpsets Energy also needed for pumping urban water	Highest growth in energy demand among major economies Natural gas reduces impact of climate change but is also affected by pricing, infrastructure & international agreements Renewables have role in climate change mitigation
Food	Potential feedstock for biofuels; biofuel subsidies in US affect global corn prices		Cropping patterns affect water use efficiency Losses in food storage increase pressure for more water-intensive production	
Water	88 per cent of water in industry is used for thermal power plants Water demand for CSP projects in arid areas Hydropower depends on water levels in reservoirs	More than 80 per cent of water is used in agriculture More than 60 per cent of land is irrigated by groundwater Traded commodities contain virtual water		
Climate	Constrains energy mix options	Extreme weather events & agricultural productivity Longer dry seasons	Affects precipitation Affects glacier melt	

Source: Author.

150 *Arunabha Ghosh*

Priorities for action, consequences of inaction

Despite the complexity of the overlapping and interacting domains of energy, food, water, and climate, the analysis above suggests that India's vulnerabilities are either related to supply constraints or demand pressures. The responses, in turn, will have to be a combination of domestic policies and efforts to strengthen the global governance of resources. India will have to tap into existing strengths while recognising the consequences of inaction (Table 8.2).

Supply constraints: domestic policies

Energy scarcity is *already* hampering India's economy, with the government estimating that the country runs a 7.9 per cent energy deficit (which rises to 13.8 per cent at peak times).[49] India must recognise that a largely supply-focused approach to energy and other resources will be self-defeating. India neither has

Table 8.2 Priorities for action, consequences of inaction

		Supply constraints	Demand pressures
Domestic policies	India's strengths	Business models for distributed generation	Progress in energy efficiency
	Priorities	1 Develop infrastructure to import and transport energy and resources 2 Promote distributed energy infrastructure	4 Promote water use efficiency in agriculture
	Consequences of inaction	Vulnerability in sea lanes; Chinese presence in Indian Ocean Losing out on technological advances; vulnerability to supply shocks	Inter-sectoral & inter-regional conflict over food and water resources Internal security emergencies (Naxalite challenge)
Global governance	India's strengths	High foodgrain production and exports Functioning water treaties	Long period of engagement with climate and trade regimes
	Priorities	3 Participate in development of regional/plurilateral energy regimes	5 Decouple energy access and basic resource needs from mercantilist positions
	Consequences of inaction	Rising risk of resource nationalism and breakdown of global energy markets	'Atmospheric space' for development-related emissions will continue to shrink

Source: Author.

the infrastructure and policies at home to attract significant investment in energy and resources nor the resources to outbid other countries in overseas markets.

Priority 1: develop infrastructure to import and transport energy and resources

There is no avoiding reliance on imports for a range of energy and mineral resource needs. It is imperative for India to build import and transportation infrastructure commensurate with its long-term resource needs. This means greater capacity for coal imports on the western coast, more oil and natural gas terminals on the eastern coast, larger strategic reserves of oil, and greater inland freight and pipeline capacity.

If India does not act strategically, then its vulnerability to external supplies will increase. The intersection between maritime and energy security is a potentially serious source of friction with India's neighbours. About 95 per cent of India's trade by volume (or 70 per cent by value) depends on maritime routes, making it highly sensitive to any risk of interruption.[50] India will need to work with other countries in the region, which also have rising energy demands, for cooperative action in energy supply infrastructure.

Priority 2: promote distributed energy infrastructure

There is also a strong case for promoting distributed energy infrastructure, through a blend of different renewable energy sources and via smart microgrids. This will help to reduce the load on the main grid, offer energy access solutions to those without basic forms of modern energy, and create opportunities for productive uses of renewable energy (such as in small agricultural operations, remote telecom infrastructure, schools and hospitals, etc.). Further, distributed energy, if supported by strong R&D efforts (as is evident in other major economies), could lower the risks for critical infrastructure should the grid collapse or come under attack of any form.

India's strength lies in the range of business models that are already being attempted in distributed generation and in the scale offered by millions of underserved households and enterprises. If this opportunity is ignored, then India will risk missing out on technological breakthroughs and will remain vulnerable to supply shocks to a centralised energy infrastructure.

Supply constraints: global governance

On food, India's size gives it considerable market power. India is a dominant actor in the global rice market and plays an important role in other commodity markets. During the 2008 food crisis, Indian price stabilisation and export controls played an important role in driving food prices higher for other countries, especially for rice.[51] It now plays a critical role in rice markets and is likely soon to be the world's third largest exporter.

Transnational water stress, exacerbated by climate change, might lead to increased tensions with India's neighbours in the future.[52] But the immediate global governance priority for India relates to energy. Global energy markets are constantly changing in character thanks to technological improvements, environmental pressures, rising demand, pricing policies, conflicts, and supply shocks. For the first time since 1995, US domestic crude oil production exceeded imports by two million barrels per day by 2014, and this gap seems set to increase further.[53] Meanwhile, China has become the world's largest oil importer.[54] These developments have profound implications for global security, because they raise questions about the protection of sea lanes, interventions in oil-rich but politically fragile states, the role of markets versus resource nationalism, and so forth.

A world with multiple poles of energy suppliers, energy demanders, and emerging economies has direct implications for coherence between different international organisations.[55] The countries that are members of the multilateral trade regime do not always overlap with those that are part of producers' cartels. Major energy consumers in the Asia-Pacific region have formed the Asia-Pacific Economic Cooperation (APEC) Energy Working Group. There are new calls for bringing together major suppliers *and* users under an Energy Stability Board to coordinate emergency actions and give voice to emerging economies.[56] But it is unclear which forums countries will choose to resolve contradictions and disputes.

Priority 3: actively participate to develop regional/plurilateral energy regimes of which India would be a member

India's participation in energy regimes is limited. It is not a member of most energy-specific regional organisations: it has only observer status at the International Energy Agency since it is not a member of the Organisation for Economic Cooperation and Development; again, as it is not a member of the Asia-Pacific Economic Cooperation, India is also not a member of the APEC Energy Working Group; and there is no multilateral energy regime. India has historically relied on its bilateral relations with oil-producing states to fulfil its energy needs, with the consequence that it is overly reliant on West Asian sources. India, therefore, has an interest in working with other second-tier energy demanders, especially among Asia-Pacific countries, to create a regional or a plurilateral energy regime. Such a forum could emphasise the important role of markets, reduce threats of sudden disruptions of supply, protect overseas investments, increase transparency through shared data, and arbitrate on energy-related disputes. In the absence of a rules-bound system, India's exposure to breakdown in global energy markets will continue to increase, and it will have limited capacity to single-handedly counter resource nationalism.

Demand pressures: domestic policies

As earlier sections have illustrated, India has few strategic advantages vis-à-vis demand for energy, food, and water. Projected demand for resources is high across all sectors, despite recognition of the environmental constraints. That said, efforts to increase energy efficiency are a partial, although imperfect, response to the demand pressures. Energy intensity has gradually eased in manufacturing, falling by about 55 per cent during 1992–2007. Efficiency gains are projected to continue to improve,[57] in part due to the introduction of the Perform, Achieve and Trade (PAT) Scheme, although aggregate demand will still increase rapidly in coming years.

Priority 4: promote water use efficiency in agriculture

There is, however, little action so far on increasing water use efficiency. The National Water Mission has set a target of 20 per cent increase in efficiency of water use in agriculture *and* other sectors, but the benchmarks have not been clearly specified. While there is significant scope to increase industrial recycling and reuse of wastewater, and to plug leakages in urban water supply, the largest returns on investment are likely to come from concerted efforts to increase water use efficiency in agriculture. This is a complex task, involving energy policy reform, use of the latest technologies, improved cropping practices, and participatory irrigation management along with farmers. But the National Water Mission could catalyse action (just as the Solar Mission has done for solar energy) with targets, timelines, transparently selected project interventions, and associated incentives to change behaviour. Water use efficiency in agriculture will have positive spillover impacts on energy demand as well as on food production and security.

Demand pressures: global governance

Ultimately, all resource demand pressures converge through the impact on the global climate. Climate change politics will be increasingly challenging for India. As its emissions grow and 'atmospheric space for emissions' shrink, India will face international pressure to change the way it engages on climate. For twenty years, international climate politics have been strongly influenced by a steadfast alliance between India and China at the heart of the G77 negotiating bloc. Indian per capita emissions are now far below China's. It is likely that the two countries will realign their approach to climate negotiations, but on what terms remains unclear.

Priority 5: decouple energy access and basic resource needs from mercantilist positions

Given India's size, its low per capita resource use, and its projected demand for resources, India is the perhaps the G20 economy that has the greatest incentive to focus international attention on the energy access needs of millions of its citizens. India will have very strong grounds to stand on if it can emphasise the energy, water, food, and other resources required to meet basic needs. This means that resource demand, especially energy demand, in other countries would also have to follow a lower trajectory. This position is different from that of other major economies, including China and the United States, for whom mercantilist interests predominate (such as maintaining high export levels or finding new markets for clean technologies). India, too, will eventually seek technologies that it can acquire and markets in which it can sell its products and services. But its primary aim should be to reform global governance to align with its development needs. Climate negotiations are perhaps the first place to begin drawing such a distinction, but India could also make this the central theme around which to build momentum for its G20 presidency.

Collaboration amidst competition?

Against these imperatives, how could China and India cooperate? Both countries face the imperative of sustaining high economic growth rates. They are expected to account for half of the increase in world energy use until 2040.[58] And both are deeply concerned about energy security (India and China will be importing 92 per cent and 84 per cent of their oil demand, respectively, by 2035).[59]

In response, there are many common features in both countries' energy security strategies. They seek to diversify their energy mix, including using more low-carbon sources (renewables, nuclear, natural gas). They are both building strategic petroleum reserves (China plans a 90-days reserve by 2020; India is trying for a 30-days reserve by 2017). Both countries have energy efficiency goals. And both have tried to diversify sources of energy imports by taking equity stakes in various countries.

There is little doubt that in a number of resource and commodity markets, the two countries will compete. Public enterprises and privately owned firms will seek resources to drive growth, outbidding each other. They also seek explicit government support, financial or diplomatic, to acquire resources. For instance, over the past decade, they have competed over oil and gas assets in Sudan (2002), Iran (2004), Angola (2004), Kazakhstan (2005), Ecuador (2005), Myanmar (2005), Nigeria (2006), and Russia (2006, 2008).[60]

The question is not whether China and India will compete but what form that competition will take. In order to avoid outright conflict as well as manage their respective resource pressures more efficiently, both countries will need to explore avenues for collaboration amidst competition, seeking mutual benefit in certain aspects of resource security.

The case for mutual benefit rests on two main arguments. First, by pooling financial and technological resources, large state-owned oil and gas companies in the two countries could form an unbeatable alliance to address energy security issues. Secondly, this partnership could mitigate concerns in both countries about energy suppliers playing off one against the other, thereby driving up prices. Thanks to the competition, Chinese and Indian companies end up paying much higher premiums for acquiring stakes in overseas resource assets.

In pursuit of these objectives, both countries have sought to cooperate from time to time. In 2004, ONGC bought shares in Sudan's 'Greater Nile Project',

What scope for resource cooperation? 155

in which CNPC had a stake since the late 1990s. By April 2005 they issued a declaration that included cooperating on energy security, exploration, and exploitation of resources in other countries. In December 2005, India's Oil & Natural Gas Corporation (ONGC) and the China National Petroleum Corporation (CNPC) joined hands for the first time to purchase oil assets in Syria. In January 2006, the countries signed a 'Memorandum for Enhancing Cooperation in the Field of Oil and Natural Gas', which included upstream exploration and production, refining, and marketing of petroleum products and petrochemicals, research and development, conservation, and promotion of environment-friendly fuels. The agreement also called for trading in oil and joint bidding in third countries.[61] And in June 2012, ONGC and CNPC signed an MOU to strengthen partnerships in Myanmar, Syria, and Sudan and jointly explore assets in other countries. India's hope has been that it is "better to cooperate than compete".[62]

In other words, the record of the past decade demonstrates that competition and collaboration co-exists between India and China. Despite joint efforts, the two countries do not share much information and are unlikely to hold back their individual efforts. For instance, in August 2013, China and India held their first bilateral dialogue on Central Asia. The expectation of the dialogue is to share more information and find joint opportunities for energy cooperation.[63] But the dialogue also took place just weeks after Kazakhstan barred ONGC Videsh from purchasing a stake in the Kashagan oil field and awarded it to China instead.[64]

A more fruitful basis of cooperation could draw upon each country's core strategic priorities. Based on the priorities outlined in the previous section for India, there are a number of promising areas in which India could work with China to improve the infrastructure for transporting fuels, promote distributed energy sources, and reform global governance of climate and energy regimes.

Create opportunities for joint private sector investment in ports and pipelines

Both China and India have not limited themselves by geography in seeking new energy supplies. Their agreements with other countries stretch from South America to West Asia, from the Bay of Bengal to the South China Sea, and from Russia and the Pacific to Central Asia. The 2012 MOU was geared not only for jointly bidding for fields but also for investing in infrastructure development. Investments in third countries could help companies from both countries develop experience in working together and gradually build trust. CNPC and ONGC have expressed interest in building an oil pipeline from South Sudan to the Kenyan coast.[65] ONGC's overseas arm, ONGC Videsh, has a stake in the gas pipeline from Myanmar into southwestern China. Within its immediate region, India is considering building gas pipelines from West Asia, Central Asia and Myanmar, forming what one scholar calls a 'T-vision' for its energy strategy.[66]

At the dialogue on Central Asia in August 2013, China and India discussed the challenges of implementing the Turkmenistan–Afghanistan–Pakistan–India (TAPI) pipeline. Some have suggested that in addition to forming joint consortia for building pipelines in third countries, China and India could also envision a network of pipelines, which they could share to tap resources in Russia, Central Asia, and West Asia.[67] Further downstream, in 2008, the Gas Authority of India Limited (GAIL) took a stake in China Gas Holdings Limited in order to collaborate on operating city gas pipeline networks, coal gasification, and liquefaction projects.[68] As these efforts grow, they could partially mitigate strategic concerns in both countries about the development of energy-related infrastructure in their respective neighbourhoods (the Indian Ocean or the South China Sea).

Another idea is to use each other's equity oil and gas stakes through swap arrangements. Some commentators have suggested that India's gas production in the Sakhalin fields in Russia could be used by China in exchange for India accessing the latter's supplies from the Middle East, thereby reducing energy transportation costs for both countries. Similar propositions have been made regarding energy cooperation with Japan. The challenge is that there is very little public information, including for experts who have served on regulatory bodies in India, about whether such swaps have been attempted or been successful.[69]

Strengthen business models for distributed energy infrastructure

Both countries have also signed MOUs in 2000 and 2003 to increase cooperation in renewable energy. They share vast potential in solar, wind, hydropower, and biomass-based energy. Both are already among the top five countries in terms of installed renewable energy capacity. Most of India's wind capacity is along coastal areas with severe challenges of corrosion. Meanwhile, China's potential is largely inland in the northern and north-western parts, with the challenge of cold temperatures. These technological challenges could serve as a basis for joint R&D.[70] For wind projects, private agreements have already been signed, including a proposed investment of US$ 3 billion by India's Reliance Power and China's Ming Yang Wind Power Group. India's National Solar Mission, one of the world's largest solar schemes, has seen prices being driven down, in part thanks to the low cost of panels manufactured in China.[71] Indian companies have also looked to China for financing renewable energy ventures. Lanco Infratech secured US$ 2 billion worth of loans from the China Development Bank.[72]

However, grid-connected renewable energy projects are also attracting trade disputes, because of accusations of unfair government support (financial transfers, tax incentives, tariff barriers, access to low-cost land, water and credit, etc.).[73] India has launched investigations to impose anti-dumping duties against Chinese solar panels. Major Indian manufacturers claim to have been forced to shut operations entirely or have more than 50 per cent of capacity lie idle.[74] There are also cases against China launched by the United States and the European Union. China, in turn, has filed retaliatory cases. Promoting renewable energy will require concerted effort to avoid or prevent trade disputes, but the effort has to go beyond bilateral deals.[75]

Greater potential for cooperation in renewable energy, perhaps, lies in distributed energy solutions. China also has some of the largest programmes for clean cook stoves, an area of particular interest to India given that traditional biomass still accounts for 33 per cent of India's primary energy. India, meanwhile, has perhaps the world's largest decentralised solar energy programmes.[76] The advantage of distributed generation solutions is that the focus is less on technology and manufacturing and more on business models that could serve a variety of energy needs for the poor. India already has 250 firms providing off-grid energy services. These businesses range from selling products like lanterns to installing home systems (solar panels, biogas plants) to developing micro-grids.[77] Indian firms and social entrepreneurs could develop business models for distributed generation in remote regions in China that have struggled to get connected to the grid. Meanwhile, Chinese firms could be encouraged to establish manufacturing facilities in India, to counter opposition within some quarters about the dumping of renewable energy products.

Initiate dialogues on regional and global energy governance

If China and India were to collaborate on a regional energy regime, it would greatly soothe concerns about resource nationalism. It would also send signals to energy markets that the two countries are keen on working through market mechanisms rather than primarily relying on equity investments in overseas energy sources.

In order to deepen cooperation, however, there is need to improve communication. A regional energy order (if not a formal regime) could offer regular information on oil and gas purchases, long-term contracts, and spot market prices. It could facilitate discussions on how each country's strategic reserves could be used to instil confidence in energy markets to mitigate short-term supply shocks. Further, other major energy demanders among emerging economies, especially in Asia, might also wish to join a China–India partnership. The objective would be to present an Asian market and collectively press for a reduction in premiums charged on energy supplies to the Asia-Pacific region.[78]

Both countries have an interest in ensuring stability in global energy markets. They are observers at the International Energy Agency (IEA) and more recently have secured observer status in the Arctic Council, an important forum given that an Arctic free of summer ice (as a result of climate change) could become a major alternative for prospecting and shipping energy and other mineral resources within the next decade. China and India's cooperation in Asian energy markets could give the two countries greater voice in influencing reforms in the IEA and elsewhere.

Focus on climate adaptation, not only mitigation

Much of Chinese and Indian cooperation in climate negotiations has been on resisting pressure to cap emissions. In the lead-up to the Copenhagen climate change summit, China and India agreed to undertake cooperative activities on mitigation, technology development and demonstration, energy efficiency, renewable energies, clean coal, methane recovery, afforestation, and transportation and sustainable habitats, among others.[79] India's then environment minister proclaimed, "There is virtually no difference in Indian and Chinese negotiating positions".[80] Yet climate negotiations are entering a crucial phase for the design of the post-2015 climate architecture. With growing divergence in the countries' economic models and resource demands, this unity might come under strain. With China already the world's largest emitter of greenhouse gases and India's per capita emissions a fraction of China's, both countries will need to consider alternatives to climate mitigation.

A less explored avenue for collaboration is adaptation (including food and agriculture) and joint technological development. There are, no doubt, grave concerns about intellectual property and financing of technology development, especially in line with each country's industrial policies. But such concerns are not insurmountable. There is a need to set targets for solving problems that are common to both countries' energy and climate challenges: increasing efficiency of solar panels and the sustainable use of biomass to reduce black carbon emissions; developing drought-resistant crop varieties and flood-resistant urban and rural infrastructure; and increasing water use efficiency in agriculture. Such targets could galvanise research institutions and enterprises to collaborate on joint R&D activities. Such activities were envisioned under an MOU signed between the governments of Maharashtra and Guangdong in October 2010; the US$ 125 million India–US Joint Clean Energy R&D Centre, operationalised in April 2012, demonstrated how consortia of organisations from two countries could focus on common problems.[81]

Finally, there will be areas where collaboration will be unlikely in the near future, particularly in the nuclear arena. China and India have a long history of suspicion over each other's nuclear programmes. In 2008 China tried to block an waiver from the Nuclear Suppliers' Group for India. It has also increased its nuclear cooperation with Pakistan. As with oil and gas, the two countries are also seeking stakes in uranium-rich countries, such as Australia, Canada, Kazakhstan, and Namibia. Despite joint declarations and statements in 2006, 2008, and 2013 to increase cooperation on civilian nuclear energy,[82] the existing situation is one of empirical competition and rhetoric cooperation.

Conclusion

There have been several attempts in the past decade to increase cooperation between China and India, via government declarations, joint ventures among state-owned energy companies, and even private sector collaborations. Most of these efforts have been driven by a supply-side logic, namely to secure more resources abroad. But the success of these efforts will depend on commercial considerations. Equity oil and gas resources do not guarantee that the fuels reach the investing country's shores. Investments in coal or uranium reserves affect taxes and other export restrictions in mineral-rich countries. These obstacles imply that along with cooperative efforts, competition will also persist between China and India.

India's best bet would be to find areas of convergence between its national priorities and China's advantages. This chapter has suggested that investing in third countries' energy transportation infrastructure could gradually open the space for investing in each other's pipelines and port facilities. Similarly, rather than limit each other's renewable energy deployment with trade disputes, both countries have complementary assets (in technology and business models) for distributed energy. Further, as the main sources of future energy demand, China and India would do well to consider how to strengthen regional and global energy regimes through information exchanges, use of strategic reserves, and collaboration with other countries to reduce price pressures in Asia. Finally, on climate change and related pressures for food security and water management, the two countries need to give more attention to adaptation. This would include, among other things, joint R&D on new crop varieties, water use efficiency in agriculture, disaster prevention and management, and urban and rural infrastructure.

The nexus between energy, food, water, and climate is not easy to understand. Nor is it easy to develop strategic responses to the interconnected challenges. The priorities for India outlined in this chapter – infrastructure to transport energy and resources; distributed energy generation; plurilateral energy regimes in which India could actively participate; water use efficiency in agriculture; and an emphasis on the developmental as opposed to the mercantilist needs for energy and resources – cannot be implemented overnight. Instead, by drawing attention to the most pressing resource security challenges, relevant actors in government, industry, and civil society could be brought together to collectively channel their energies and efforts to lay the ground for long-term resource security, inclusive development, a growing but responsible international stature for India, and a more realistic approach to cooperation with China.

Notes

1 Bernice Lee, Felix Preston, Jaakko Kooroshy, Rob Bailey, and Glada Lahn, *Resources Futures: A Chatham House Report*, London: Royal Institute of International Affairs (Chatham House), December 2012, pp. xiii, 16–17, 31, 36, 59, 100–102, http://www.chathamhouse.org/sites/files/chathamhouse/public/Research/Energy,%20Environment%20and%20Development/1212r_resourcesfutures.pdf.

2 Arunabha Ghosh and David Steven, "India's Energy, Food, and Water Security: International Cooperation for Domestic Capacity", in Waheguru Pal Singh Sidhu, P. B. Mehta and B. Jones, eds., *Shaping the Emerging World: India and the Multilateral Order*, Washington, D.C.: Brookings Institution Press, August 2013.

3 Arunabha Ghosh et al., *Understanding Complexity, Anticipating Change: From Interests to Strategy on Global Governance*, Report of the Working Group on India and Global Governance, New Delhi: Council on Energy, Environment and Water, 2011, http://ceew.in/pdf/CEEW_WGIGG_Report.pdf.

4 Arunabha Ghosh, "Industrial Demand and Energy Supply Management: A Delicate Balance", *Empowering Growth: Perspectives on India's Energy Future*, The Economist Intelligence Unit, October 2012, pp. 26, 30, http://www.economistinsights.com/sites/default/files/downloads/Empowering_Growth.pdf.

5 Calculations based on IEA & EIA energy demand projections to 2030. International Energy Agency (IEA), *World Energy Outlook 2011*, Paris: IEA, 2011, http://www.iea.org/publications/freepublications/publication/WEO2011_WEB.pdf.; Energy Information Administration (EIA), *International Energy Outlook 2011*, Washington, D.C.: EIA, 2011.
6 IEA, World Energy Outlook 2011.
7 Krittivas Mukherjee, "New Pricing May See Cut in Higher Grade Coal Imports", *Reuters*, 2 February 2012, http://www.reuters.com/article/2012/02/02/india-coal-idUSL4E8D156X20120202.
8 Ghosh, "Industrial Demand and Energy Supply Management: A Delicate Balance", p. 29.
9 Ajoy K. Das, "Coal Shortage Causes India's Electricity Generation to Slump", *Mining Weekly*, 17 May 2011, http://www.miningweekly.com/article/coal-shortage-causes-indias-electricity-generation-to-slump-2011-05-17.
10 McKinsey & Company, *Environmental and Energy Sustainability: An Approach for India*, Mumbai: McKinsey & Company, August 2009.
11 Planning Commission, Government of India, *Report of the Working Group on Power for Twelfth Five Year Plan (2012–17)*, New Delhi: Ministry of Power, January 2012, Ch. 7, p. 5, http://planningcommission.gov.in/aboutus/committee/wrkgrp12/wg_power 1904.pdf.
12 IEA, World Energy Outlook 2011.
13 Planning Commission, Government of India, *Integrated Energy Policy: Report of the Expert Committee*, New Delhi: Ministry of Power, August 2006, http://planningcommission.nic.in/reports/genrep/rep_intengy.pdf.
14 Ministry of Finance, Government of India, "Economic Survey 2011–12", http://www.indiabudget.nic.in/survey.asp.
15 Lydia Powell, "Do India's Equity Oil Investments Make Sense?" *Energy News Monitor*, VIII/43, New Delhi: Observer Research Foundation, 10 April 2012, http://www.observerindia.com/cms/sites/orfonline/modules/enm-analysis/ENM-ANALYSISDetail.html?cmaid=35815&mmacmaid=35813.
16 S. Anilesh Mahajan, "World Wide Woe – ONGC Videsh's Overseas Woes: Could the Problems have been Avoided?" *Business Today*, 19 August 2012, http://businesstoday.intoday.in/story/overseas-problems-of-ongc-videsh-other-oil-companies/1/186797.html; Rakesh Sharma, "ONGC to Continue Exploration in South China Sea", *Wall Street Journal*, 19 July 2012, http://online.wsj.com/article/SB10000872396390444464304577536182763155666.html.
17 Powell, "Do India's Equity Oil Investments Make Sense?"
18 Powell, "Do India's Equity Oil Investments Make Sense?"; Anne-Sophie Corbeau, *Natural Gas in India*, Working Paper, Paris: International Energy Agency, 2010.
19 EIA, International Energy Outlook 2011.
20 Anil Jain and Anupama Sen, *Natural Gas in India: An Analysis of Policy*, Working Paper, Oxford: Oxford Institute for Energy Studies, April 2011.
21 Committee on Critical Mineral Impacts on the U.S. Economy et al., *Minerals, Critical Minerals, and the U.S. Economy*, Washington, D.C.: The National Academies Press, 2008, http://www.nap.edu/openbook.php?record_id=12034.
22 International Energy Agency (IEA), *World Energy Outlook 2012*, Paris: IEA, 2012.
23 "Parliamentary Panel Clears Food Security Bill", *NDTV*, 11 January 2013, http://www.ndtv.com/article/india/parliamentary-panel-clears-food-security-bill-316322.
24 Ministry of Finance, Government of India, *Economic Survey 2011–12: Agriculture and Food*, New Delhi: Ministry of Finance, 2012, http://www.indiabudget.nic.in/es2011-12/

What scope for resource cooperation? 161

echap-08.pdf; Food and Agriculture Organization (FAO), *Food Outlook: Global Market Analysis*, May 2012, http://www.fao.org/fileadmin/user_upload/newsroom/docs/Final%20web%20version%202%20May%20(2).pdf.
25 Ministry of Petroleum and Natural Gas, Government of India, *Basic Statistics on Indian Petroleum and Natural Gas 2010–11*, New Delhi: Ministry of Petroleum and Natural Gas, 2012, p.36; International Monetary Fund (IMF), "Nurturing Credibility While Managing Risks to Growth", *Fiscal Monitor*, 16 July 2012, http://www.imf.org/external/pubs/ft/fm/2012/update/02/pdf/0712.pdf; IMF, *India: Staff Report for the 2012 Article IV Consultation,* 22 February 2012, http://www.imf.org/external/pubs/ft/scr/2012/cr1296.pdf.
26 Günther Fischer, Harrij van Velthuizen, Mahendra Shah, and Freddy Nachtergaele, *Global Agro-ecological Assessment for Agriculture in the 21st Century: Methodology and Results*, Laxenburg: International Institute for Applied Systems Analysis, January 2002, http://www.iiasa.ac.at/publication/more_RR-02-002.php; Ministry of Finance, Government of India, *Economic Survey 2011–12: Human Development*, New Delhi: Ministry of Finance, 2012, http://www.indiabudget.nic.in/es2011–12/echap-13.pdf.
27 The World Bank, "Data: Arable land (hectares per person)", http://data.worldbank.org/indicator/AG.LND.ARBL.HA.PC.
28 Pulapre Balakrishnan, Ramesh Golait, and Pankaj Kumar, "Study No. 27: Development Research Group – Agricultural Growth in India Since 1991", Department of Economic Analysis and Policy, Reserve Bank of India, Mumbai, http://rbidocs.rbi.org.in/rdocs/content/pdfs/85240.pdf.
29 Martin A. Burton, Rahul Sen, Simon Gordon-Walker, Anand Jalakam, and Arunabha Ghosh, *National Water Resources Framework Study*, Research Report Submitted to the Planning Commission for the 12th Five-Year Plan, New Delhi: Council on Energy, Environment and Water and 2030 Water Resources Group, October 2011, p. 152, http://ceew.in/pdf/CEEW-WRG10Oct11.pdf.
30 Ibid., p. 219
31 Ibid., p. 314; Upali A. Amarasinghe, Tushaar Shah, Hugh Turral, and B.K. Anand, *India's Water Future to 2025–2050: Business-as-Usual Scenario and Deviations*, Research Report 123, Colombo: International Water Management Institute, 2007, http://lib.icimod.org/record/13329/files/3740.pdf.
32 2030 Water Resources Group, *Charting Our Water Future: Economic Frameworks to Inform Decision-making*, 2009, p. 9, http://www.mckinsey.com/client_service/sustainability/latest_thinking/charting_our_water_future.
33 Ministry of Statistics & Programme Implementation, Government of India, *Compendium on Environment Statistics India*, 2011, http://mospi.nic.in/mospi_new/upload/compendium_2011_30dec11.htm.
34 Ibid.
35 Planning Commission, Government of India, *Eleventh Five-Year Plan 2007–12*, 2008, http://planningcommission.nic.in/plans/planrel/fiveyr/11th/11_v3/11th_vol3.pdf.
36 Ministry of Environment and Forests, Government of India, *State of Environment Report – India 2009*, New Delhi: Ministry of Environment and Forests, 2009, p.13, http://moef.nic.in/downloads/home/home-SoE-Report-2009.pdf.
37 Ibid.
38 Food and Agriculture Organization of the United Nations, "Aquastat Database", 2013, http://www.fao.org/nr/water/aquastat/data/query/index.html?lang=en.
39 Maplecroft, "Big Economies of the Future Most at Risk from Climate Change", 21 October 2010, http://www.energy-enviro.fi/index.php?PAGE=13&PRINT=yes&ID=3337.

40 Divya Sharma and Sanjay Tomar, "Mainstreaming climate change adaptation in Indian cities", *Environment and Urbanization*, 22/451, 2010, http://eau.sagepub.com/content/22/2/451.full.pdf.
41 Derek Headey and Shenggen Fan, *Reflections on the Global Food Crisis: How Did It Happen? How Has It Hurt? And How Can We Prevent The Next One?* Research Monograph 165, Washington D.C.: International Food Policy Research Institute, 2010, http://www.ifpri.org/sites/default/files/publications/rr165.pdf.
42 Council on Energy, Environment and Water and Natural Resources Defense Council, *Laying the Foundation for a Bright Future: Assessing Progress Under Phase 1 of India's National Solar Mission*, Interim Report, April 2012, http://ceew.in/pdf/CEEW-NRDC-Concentrated%20Solar%20Power_Sep12.pdf; Council on Energy, Environment and Water and Natural Resources Defense Council, *Concentrated Solar Power: Heating Up India's Solar Thermal Market under the National Solar Mission*, September 2012, http://ceew.in/pdf/CEEW-NRDC-Concentrated%20Solar%20Power_Sep12.pdf.
43 See the example of collaborative R&D on second generation biofuels under the US$ 125 million India-US Joint Clean Energy R&D Centre: Council on Energy, Environment and Water, "India-U.S. Joint Clean Energy Research and Development Centre (JCERDC)", http://ceew.in/JCERDC.
44 Directorate of Economics and Statistics, Department of Agriculture and Cooperation, Ministry of Agriculture, Government of India, "Data on Area, Production and Yield of Major Crops for 2012–13", http://eands.dacnet.nic.in/StateData_12–13Year.htm.
45 WWF-India and Accenture, *Water Stewardship for Industries: The Need for a Paradigm Shift in India*, New Delhi: WWF-India, March 2013, p. 15, http://awsassets.wwfindia.org/downloads/water_stewardship_report_final_edited_1.pdf.
46 World Resources Institute, *Over Heating: Financial Risks from Water Constraints on Power Generation in Asia*, 2010, p. 5, http://pdf.wri.org/over_heating_asia.pdf.
47 WWF-India and Accenture, *Water Stewardship for Industries*, p. 16.
48 Council on Energy, Environment and Water and Natural Resources Defense Council, *Concentrated Solar Power*, p. 19.
49 Planning Commission, Government of India, *Eleventh Five Year Plan 2007–12*.
50 Business Portal of India, "National Level Infrastructure: Maritime Transport", http://www.archive.india.gov.in/business/infrastructure/maritime_transport.php.
51 David Dawe and Tom Slayton, "The World Rice Market in 2007–08", in Adam Prakash, ed., *Safeguarding Food Security in Volatile Global Markets*, Rome: Food and Agriculture Organization of the United Nations, 2011, http://www.fao.org/docrep/013/i2107e/i2107e13.pdf.
52 Walter W. Immerzeel, Ludovicus P. H. van Beek, and Marc F. P. Bierkens, "Climate Change Will Affect the Asian Water Towers", *Science*, 328/5984, June 2010, pp. 1382–1385.
53 US Department of Energy, "US Oil Production and Imports", http://energy.gov/maps/us-crude-oil-production-surpasses-net-imports.
54 Javier Blas, "China Becomes World's Top Oil Importer", *Financial Times*, 4 March 2013.
55 Arunabha Ghosh, "Seeking Coherence in Complexity? The Governance of Energy by Trade and Investment Institutions", *Global Policy*, 2 (Special Issue), September 2011, pp. 106–119.
56 David G. Victor and Linda Yueh, "The New Energy Order: Managing Insecurities in the Twenty-first Century", *Foreign Affairs*, 89/1, January/February 2010, pp. 71–72.
57 IEA, World Energy Outlook 2011.

What scope for resource cooperation? 163

58 "India, China to Lead Rise in World Energy", *Business Standard*, 26 July 2013, http://www.business-standard.com/article/news-ians/india-china-to-lead-rise-in-world-energy-113072600196_1.html.
59 IEA, World Energy Outlook 2011, p. 92.
60 Wu Fuzuo, Yazhou Nengyuan Xiaofeiguo jian de Nengyuan Jingzheng yu Hezuo: Yizhong Boyi de Fenxi (Energy Cooperation and Competition among Asian Energy Consuming Countries: A Game Theory Analysis), Shanghai: Shanghai People's Publishing House, 2010, Chapter 4, "Sino-Indian Autonomous Cooperation in Energy Game".
61 "China, India Sign Energy Agreement", *China Daily*, 13 January 2006, http://www.chinadaily.com.cn/english/doc/2006-01/13/content_511871.htm.
62 Rakesh Sharma, "India, China to Explore Energy Assets", *The Wall Street Journal*, 19 June 2012, http://blogs.wsj.com/dealjournalindia/2012/06/19/ongc-cnpc-to-renew-pact-on-cooperation/.
63 Shubhajit Roy, "India, China to Hold Dialogue on Central Asia on Aug 12–13", *The Indian Express*, 10 August 2013, http://www.indianexpress.com/news/india-china-to-hold-dialogue-on-central-asia-on-aug-1213/1153537/.
64 Ananth Krishnan, "Amid Energy Competition, India, China Hold First Central Asia Dialogue", *The Hindu*, 15 August 2013, http://www.thehindu.com/news/national/amid-energy-competition-india-china-hold-first-central-asia-dialogue/article5024973.ece.
65 Rakesh Sharma, 2012.
66 Ma Jiali, "The Energy Cooperation between China and India in the Post-Crisis Era", *Contemporary International Relations*, 20/2, March-April 2010, http://www.cicir.ac.cn/chinese/Article_1923.html.
67 Bhupendra Kumar Singh, "Energy Security and India-China Cooperation", *International Association for Energy Economics*, 2010, p. 19.
68 Sanjay Jog, "GAIL Explores Investment Scope in China", *Financial Express,* 4 October 2008, http://www.financialexpress.com/news/gail-explores-investment-scope-in-china/369085/1.
69 Sudha Mahalingam, "Crude and Not Sweet at All", *The Hindu*, 6 August 2013, http://www.thehindu.com/opinion/lead/crude-and-not-sweet-at-all/article4992779.ece.
70 Toufiq Siddiqi, "China and India: More Cooperation than Competition in Energy and Climate Change", *Journal of International Affairs*, 64/2, Spring/Summer 2011, pp. 73–90.
71 Council on Energy, Environment and Water and Natural Resources Defense Council, *Laying the Foundation for a Bright Future: Assessing Progress under Phase 1 of India's National Solar Mission*, Interim Research Report, April 2012, http://www.nrdc.org/international/india/files/layingthefoundation.pdf.
72 "Renewable Energy, Rail Deals Inked at Sino-Indian Talks", *The Standard*, 26 November 2012, http://www.thestandard.com.hk/breaking_news_detail.asp?id=28285.
73 Arunabha Ghosh and Himani Gangania, *Governing Clean Energy Subsidies: What, Why, and How Legal?* Geneva: International Centre for Trade and Sustainable Development, August 2012, http://ictsd.org/downloads/2012/09/governing-clean-energy-subsidies-what-why-and-how-legal.pdf.
74 Shreya Jai and Dilasha Seth, "India Might Impose Anti-dumping Duty on US, China, Malaysia, Taiwan, Major Importers of Solar Cells", *Economic Times*, 3 July 2013, http://articles.economictimes.indiatimes.com/2013-07-03/news/40352160_1_chinese-solar-imports-anti-dumping-duty-domestic-industry.

75 Arunabha Ghosh and Ricardo Meléndez-Ortiz, "Want Clean Energy? Avoid Trade Disputes", *Business Standard*, 15 April 2013, http://www.business-standard.com/article/opinion/want-clean-energy-avoid-trade-disputes-113041500023_1.html.
76 Huang Liming, "A Study of China–India Cooperation in Renewable Energy Field", *Renewable and Sustainable Energy Reviews*, 11, 2007, p. 1753.
77 Council on Energy, Environment and Water, *Developing Effective Networks for Energy Access: Implementation Roadmap*, Report for the United States Agency for International Development, August 2013.
78 J. Nandakumar, *India-China Energy Cooperation: Attaining New Heights*, IDSA Comment, New Delhi: Institute for Defence Studies and Analyses, 28 November 2005, http://www.idsa.in/idsastrategiccomments/IndiaChinaEnergyCooperation_JNandakumar_281205.
79 Press Information Bureau, Government of India, "India and China signs Agreement on Cooperation on Addressing Climate Change", 21 October 2009, http://pib.nic.in/newsite/erelease.aspx?relid=53317.
80 Gaurav Singh and John Duce, "China, India Sign Climate Change Cooperation Accord (Update)", *Bloomberg News*, 21 October 2009, www.bloomberg.com/apps/news?pid=newsarchive&sid=aFyFHkF6C3Fs.
81 Both initiatives were facilitated by the Council on Energy, Environment and Water (CEEW).
82 "India, China Focus on Civil Nuke Cooperation", *The New Indian Express*, 21 May 2013, http://newindianexpress.com/nation/India-China-focus-on-civil-nuke-cooperation/2013/05/21/article1599048.ece.

Part III
Water

9 Towards riparian rationality
An Indian perspective

Uttam Kumar Sinha

Water has emerged as a contentious issue between India and China with complex inter-relationships among the social, environmental, economic, and political dimensions of hydrology. As riparian neighbours and the world's two most populous countries, the waterscape is characterised by familiar challenges in the planning, design, and management of water resources in terms of quantitative, qualitative, and uneven distributions. Global warming, rainfall pattern shifts, and expanding demand have further combined to put pressure on water. There are also worrying signs that the growing water scarcities in India and China, which have amongst the lowest per capita availability of water, present the largest threat to food security.[1] With population increase and corresponding consumption patterns, it is projected that by 2030 the demand for water will be 50 per cent higher in both India and China.[2]

The leadership in both the countries have from time to time acknowledged the water problem as an existential threat. In 1998, then Deputy Prime Minister Wen Jiabao expressed concern that the "very survival of the Chinese nation" is threatened by the looming water shortage.[3] Indian Prime Minister Manmohan Singh, in his first Independence Day address in 2004, highlighted the issue of water and raised it as one of the *saat sutras* (seven sectors) needing attention.[4]

At the same time, the political significance of water between India and China becomes crucial not only because of the supply-demand imbalance but also because the two countries share some significant glacial-fed rivers that originate from the Tibetan plateau and include the Indus and Sutlej on the western side. The Brahmaputra, on the eastern side of the plateau, is a precipitation-based river. Nine key tributaries of the Ganges flow from Nepal into India; of these the biggest – Karnali, Gandaki, and Kosi – originate from Tibet.

Among these rivers the Brahmaputra, known as the Yarlung Tsangpo in Tibet, has become a source of anxiety for India. As a lower riparian, India's concerns revolve around future plans of water diversion and a series of dam projects undertaken by China on the Yarlung. Both will lead to flow fluctuations and impact the local economy and ecology. The uses of the Yarlung/Brahmaputra are also related to competing claims over Arunachal Pradesh.[5] As scientific evidence on the impact of global warming on the Himalayan/Tibetan glaciers mounts, worries also arise over the lack of shared information on the hydrological alterations occurring as a result of these changes.

While lower riparian angst and apprehensions beleaguer India, China's promotion of large-scale, capital-intensive water projects with classic slogans like "big diversions, big irrigation" continues. Going by the 2011–2015 energy sector blueprint released in January 2013, far from restraining itself, Beijing plans to construct more hydroelectricity dams on the Nu (Salween), Lancang (Mekong) and Yarlung river basins.[6] These are not only internationally shared rivers but are also in ecologically and seismically sensitive areas. The blueprint is a reassertion of an aggressive 'supply-side hydraulic' approach of increasing storage capacity by building dams and reservoirs, making water transfers, and prospecting and extracting groundwater. This approach is the result of a combination of factors that includes food and energy needs, plans to meet the low carbon-intensity goals of the 12th Five-Year Plan (2011–2015), and the intensive lobbying of the dam builders and electricity companies. By 2015 it is expected that some 120 gigawatts of hydroelectricity projects will be installed nationwide.[7]

This chapter outlines India's concerns over China's upstream actions from three interconnected features: dams and diversions, the resultant hydropolitics and power asymmetry, and the impact of climate change on the glaciers in the Tibetan plateau. The chapter argues that it is essential for India to bring water issues into the core of the bilateral discussions with China and to use all diplomatic tools to push towards a structured water dialogue that allows for lower riparian apprehensions and fears to be recognised and discussed. Equally important will be the need for both countries to study carefully the projections of future trends in water availability, flow patterns, and changes in climatic variables. Though certainly not easy, water as an area for mutual cooperation potentially opens up new possibilities based on sharing the benefits of the flow rather than merely determining and dividing the volume. The 'water rationality' view or 'water as a unifier' view would require a greater emphasis on hydro-diplomacy, exploring alternative institutional arrangements and effective dispute settlement mechanisms.

Dams and diversions

No region with shared international water is exempt from water-related controversies and disputes. China's water need and India's concern will be a recurring theme in the two countries' relations. Rivers are deeply subjective in terms of where, what, and how they are being used. With no legally binding treaty, apart from norms and principles as expressed in the 1966 Helsinki Rules and the 1997 UN Convention on the Law of the Non-Navigational Uses of International Watercourses (UN Watercourses Convention), rivers are an unruly resource. Further, projections of a looming water crisis both in India and China raise questions about the availability and distribution of water as well as legal difficulties in water management. It is now a common national security refrain that a stable supply of water is paramount to a country's political, social, and economic stability. From a *realpolitik* prism, the preciousness of water often translates into possessiveness and, at times, resource aggressiveness.

China's demand for water is growing even as supplies are limited. In addition, water in China is unequally distributed, leading the country to push ahead with invasive water diversion plans going back to 1988 to the idea of *Shou-tian* or 'reverse flow' of the Tibetan rivers.[8] Water projects have been part of the popular political consciousness since the founding of the People's Republic of China (PRC) in 1949. Chinese engineers, who are a leading voice in decision-making, firmly believe that the diversion of rivers into the water-scarce northern and western regions is crucial for growth and stability. The diversion on the Yarlung Tsangpo is part of the planned South-North Water Transfer Project (SNWTP).[9] There are questions related to the technical, economic, and seismic feasibility of the project, but it has not been shelved. China prefers to maintain a diplomatic silence on its water diversion plans even though water could be an important threat multiplier and creates down-riparian fears.

China's growing requirement for energy is increasingly bringing water into the development process. The 12th Five-Year Plan's priorities in the area of energy include accelerated construction of coal bases across western China, stabilising oil output and increasing gas output, developing oil and gas pipe networks and storage facilities, and improving the power grid.[10] These water-intensive industrial activities will require an enormous amount of water. The SNWTP diversion of the Yarlung and other rivers, including the Lancang and the Nu, will probably get a reboot as the west-to-east coal-based industries develop. Given China's uneven water distribution, its energy needs and its food requirements, it is difficult for Chinese planners not to consider water diversion as an option.

Upstream diversion of water is hugely scary for down riparian states and not surprisingly is regarded as a malign act. India has been deeply concerned over the planned diversions on the Yarlung, but since the project has not yet come to fruition, and increasingly seems difficult to achieve, these concerns have somewhat diminished. The more immediate concern is over the major dams and storage projects that have started and are being planned on the Yarlung, in order to "push forward vigorously the hydropower base construction".[11] China has proposed the construction of three dams on the middle reaches of the Yarlung: a 640 MW dam in Dagu; a 320 MW dam at Jiacha; and a third dam at Jiexu, the capacity of which is not known. These three dams, along with the 510 MW dam in Zangmu, which began in 2010, are part of a series of damming projects on the Yarlung.

For the Chinese, who are used to water projects on a gigantic scale, the capacity of the planned dams is 'small'; from an Indian perspective, however, these projects are sufficiently large to be storage dams, especially if the purpose is for flood control and irrigation, as is the Zangmu.[12] Run-of-the-river (ROR) projects, as the Chinese planners officially describe them, can be misleading. The basic principle of the ROR dams is to return the waters to the river after it passes through the turbines. But what if they are not returned? A mechanism therefore is necessary to 'trust and verify'.

Given the political equation between the two countries, China could well exploit its upper riparian position against India. It suits Beijing to be ambiguous and not show enthusiasm towards formal arrangements on sharing design-related and hydrological information. Moreover, Chinese hydrologists explain that "the Brahmaputra has plenty of water; it won't make any difference to India".[13] Even the Indian Water Resource Ministry has now openly stated, to allay unnecessary fears, that the Yarlung enters India (as the Siang in Arunachal) with 78 billion cubic metres (bcm) of water and then is then 629 bcm when it enters Bangladesh.[14] On the question of Yarlung diversion (if it ever comes about), the Central Water Commission has suggested "a 50 per cent reduction of the 31.25 bcm currently available in the non-monsoon season and a reduction of 50 per cent in power generation in the Upper Siang project".[15] The figures suggest that India's concerns are not so much about water scarcity as they are about flood water release in the monsoon. The solutions for Indian planners are essentially two-fold: build storage dams at various locations and effectively put in place flood mitigation programmes.

India and China: the hydropolitics

Water relations can never be permanently settled since flows in rivers are not constant. The flows in turn are determined by seasonal variations and usage, particularly those that are non-consumptive in nature. Interventions and diversions on rivers also impact flow. Political relations can easily be impacted by the changing quantitative and qualitative nature of the river. Varied interpretations on the use of river water have resulted in claims and counter-claims. Upper riparian nations essentially base their claims on 'absolute territorial sovereignty', i.e., the right to use rivers unilaterally regardless of lower riparian concerns. The lower riparians, on the other hand, claim 'absolute territorial integrity' of rivers, arguing that upstream actions should not affect the water flow downstream. Taken together, the two sets of claims are incompatible. There are, however, accepted legal norms of 'equitable utilisation' and the 'no-harm rule' that riparian states work with and that they use to frame negotiations and treaties in order to overcome differing positions.[16] More often than not, however, these norms are difficult to achieve given state politics and power equations. This also holds true for a nation's entitlement to a "reasonable share of water".[17]

India and China share a number of interests, yet the bilateral relationship is marked by inconsistency. At one level, trade between the two is promising and pushing forward in spite of odds;[18] at another, the boundary issue remains vexing and irksome. Similarly, India's position on the Dalai Lama is a longstanding annoyance for China; for India, Chinese strategic reach in the subcontinent is worrisome. At the international level, while the two converge as BASIC (Brazil, South Africa, India, and China) countries in the climate change negotiations, at various other forums they have divergent views. India and China simultaneously cooperate, contest, and compete. Water relations have to be viewed and understood from this triangular perspective.

As economic powers, both countries are also 'planetary powers', consuming resources at a high rate with a heavy ecological footprint. Water is central to their development and growth. The need for water in the food-energy nexus as well as for safe drinking will continuously challenge development goals. As two critically important riparian countries in Asia, it is troubling that there is an absence of institutionalised water cooperation. This is even more so with a climate future projected to be hotter and drier and directly impacting water resources.

Thinking about water critically does not mean lapsing into a discourse about the inevitability of 'water wars'. History is on the side of water cooperation. The record is that even rival states resolve their water conflicts. A good case in point is the 1960 Indus Waters Treaty between India and Pakistan and the historic water treaty between Israel and Jordan in 1994 in which water was seen as a positive-sum game. India and China hydro-relations are evolving and thus offer considerable scope for framing water as a resource for cooperation and an opportunity for joint work at the scientific and societal levels. Peace building and cooperative returns, however, can best be achieved by assessing the vulnerability and strength of the hydrology in which China and India coexist.

For India, hydro-diplomacy will be a vital component of its neighbourhood policy, which from an expanded hydrological point of view cannot exclude China. It is not easy to ignore the competitive nature of water between the two and the significance of the Himalayan watershed, from where the shared rivers originate, as the hydrological fault line.

Climate change and Himalayan glaciology

In the coming years, the effects of climate change will begin to be felt, if they have not already been consequential. First, the food–energy–water nexus will be impacted by changes in temperature.[19] Second, rapid ecological change will instigate states to act, even if unilaterally, to secure resources and territorial sovereignty.

Rivers carve the length and breadth of the Himalaya mountain system, physically linking upstream and downstream users. The glaciers, the dazzling source of these rivers, are vulnerable to various exogenous impacts including global warming. Planning any water resource utilisation policy will have to take into account the assessment of the impact of climate change in terms of seasonal flow and extreme events.

The middle-latitude, high-altitude Himalayan glaciers have the largest reservoir of snow and ice outside the Polar Regions. This area is now commonly referred to as the 'Third Pole'. The Karakoram glaciers are fairly stable, while the glaciers in the western, central, and eastern Himalayas are shrinking. Of these, the western glaciers have shown the highest rate of retreat.[20] China's mountain-glacier systems include the Himalaya, Karakoram Tien Shan, and Altay mountain ranges covering an area of about 59,425 sq. km. The glaciers in India are located in the Himalaya and cover about 8,500 sq. km.[21]

Scientific observations point to the possibility that 90 per cent of the Himalayan glacier melt is directly caused by black carbon soot and other industrial processes.[22] Other studies point to the presence of debris such as pebbles and rocks as an additional factor. Projections into the 2030s suggest warming throughout the Himalayan region by 1.7 to 2.2 degrees centigrade and a likely increase in precipitation by 5 to 13 per cent.[23] The impact will gradually shrink glaciers and reduce water runoff. In the short term, ironically, the melting water from the glaciers and seasonal rains could cause flooding. Hydrologists widely agree that the Asian rivers are fed by three sources: precipitation (rainfall), snow melt, and melting glaciers. The IPCC 4th Assessment Report in 2007 generalised and overestimated the Himalayan glacial melt contribution to the rivers. Studies thereon on the glaciers suggest that there are 662 glaciers contributing to the Yarlung Tsangpo/Brahmaputra, considerably less than the Indus Basin (3,538) and the Ganges Basin (1,020).[24] The glacial melt contribution to the rivers varies considerably. The eastern rivers like the Brahmaputra receive 30 per cent of melt water to the total flow, while the Ganges and Indus basins receive 50 per cent and 80 per cent of melt water respectively.[25] In the dry season, this is enormously valuable. Many recent studies on the overall glacier retreat and additional melt focus on water-dammed glacier lakes (GLOF) that have the potential of generating dangerous outbursts of flooding.[26]

India and China: contrasting riparians

The deeply political question of "who gets how much water, how and why"[27] influences the behaviour of the riparian. China and India, given their hydrological position and dependence on the Himalayan rivers, are critical players in the hydropolitics of the region. India is simultaneously an upper, middle, and lower riparian. China's hydrological position, on the other hand, is one of upper riparian advantage. India's middle riparian position increases its dependency (and thus its water insecurity) on the headwaters of the rivers' sources such as the Brahmaputra, Indus, and Sutlej, which originate in the Tibetan plateau. China is also water insecure, but its insecurity relates to the uneven distribution of waters domestically, with most of the water in the south (Tibet Autonomous Region). In terms of per capita water availability, China ranks among the world's lowest.

The territorial source of the Himalayan and other Chinese rivers makes China the world's most independent riparian country.[28] This hydrological position gives it enormous latitude in shaping larger political equations with its riparian neighbours. India, on the other hand, given its middle riparian position and its longstanding commitment to bilateral river treaties, has to assiduously balance the anxiety and concerns of its lower riparians (Pakistan and Bangladesh) without compromising its own water requirements. China, in contrast, has no formal commitment and therefore is not bound by any water distribution and sharing agreements with its neighbouring countries.[29] In fact, China was one of the three countries that did not approve of the 1997 UN Watercourses Convention.[30] On the Mekong River basin, China is only a dialogue partner in the Mekong River Commission (MRC), which was formed by lower riparian countries – Cambodia, Laos, Vietnam, and Thailand in 1995. Though China's non-binding participation in the Mekong basin has increased, it is unlikely that it will join MRC as an active member because it does not want to formally commit to any water-sharing arrangement.

For India, as a Himalayan basin state, being water-dependent on China is a hydrological reality and shapes the country's fears and perceptions. Apprehensions, in fact, are widespread. For example, the Mekong lower riparian countries remain suspicious of China's upstream hydroelectricity projects. Likewise, Kazakhstan and Russia are concerned over China's diversion of the Irtysh and Ili rivers. In the case of Pakistan and Bangladesh, India is seen as an upper-riparian aggressor.

While China has no formal water-sharing arrangements with the lower riparian countries, India has several treaties to address water issues with its neighbours, including the 1960 Indus Water Treaty with Pakistan and the 1996 Ganges Treaty with Bangladesh. With Nepal and Bhutan, treaties have been signed to share the benefits of water. Treaties commit India to a dialogue-based water-sharing approach and diplomatically become an important part of its neighbourhood policy. China, in contrast, tends to take a strategic view of water and given its hydrological position uses water as leverage and a bargaining instrument in framing its regional policies.

A snapshot of the riparian dynamics in the Himalayan watershed suggests that while there is considerable lack of trust on water issues between states, there exists a greater possibility of states overcoming impasses and reaching river water-sharing agreements with India than with China. The future water challenge in the Himalayan watershed is to draw China into a water dialogue.

Towards water dialogue

China perplexes the world. Its continued economic growth stirs the academic and research community into asking whether China will be the next superpower and how the political landscape will change with its ascendancy. On transboundary water issues, the question of whether China can be a constructive upper riparian is crucial for the lower-basin states, including India. Views on this range from alarmist and fearful to circumspect. There is also a quiet acceptance of China as the hydrological *supremo* and the reality of building political relations first and foremost to quell any hydro-aggression. All in all, these arguments make for a fascinating debate on China's hydrobehaviour.

Before any formal water cooperation can be achieved, an understanding on water issues has to be developed, and this requires diplomacy that is holistic, bold, and imaginative. Mechanisms for water cooperation have already been established between India and China, and for the time being it is unrealistic to expect a treaty from China.

In 2002, India and China signed a Memorandum of Understanding (MOU) on the sharing of hydrological information on the Yarlung/Brahmaputra in flood season. Under this MOU, the two sides regularly exchanged data, from 1 June to 15 October, on water levels, discharge, and rainfall, at the Nugesha, Yangcun, and Nunxia stations, which were utilised in the formulation of flood forecasts by India's Central Water Commission. This particular understanding ended in 2007. A second agreement, with the same provisions and with a validity of five years, was signed in 2008 and was again renewed for five years in 2013. China has provided the requisite information since the monsoon season of 2010.[31] With regards to the Sutlej (Langquin Zangbu), in April 2005 an MOU was signed on sharing hydrological information in flood season for a period of five years; this was renewed in 2010.[32] In November 2006, during the visit of President Hu Jintao to India, the two countries agreed on the constitution of an Expert-Level Mechanism (ELM) to discuss wider cooperation, including emergency management.[33] The ELM meets once a year alternately in Beijing and New Delhi and essentially focuses on the exchange of hydrological information and the smooth transmission of flood season hydrological data. It is very selective and limited but forms the base on which future water cooperation can be further developed.

During the visit of Chinese Premier Li Keqiang to India in May 2013, serious time and discussion was given to water issues. India's proposal of a joint mechanism for better transparency on the dams being constructed on the Yarlung was diplomatically appreciated but failed to elicit a clear commitment from China. As noted above, the Chinese followed the tested 2002 MOU format and renewed the pact on twice-daily sharing of hydrological data of the Brahmaputra River during the monsoon. The MOU says, "China will provide to India twice a day the hydrological data of the Brahmaputra River in the flood season between 1 June to 15 October".[34] A forward step was taken by signing a new MOU for cooperation in "ensuring water-efficient irrigation".[35] In October 2013, when Indian Prime Minister Manmohan Singh visited Beijing, the two countries reached further understanding to strengthen water cooperation on provisions of flood-season hydrological data and emergency management. It was also agreed that starting in 2014, flow information provided by China would now commence from May 15 instead of June 1.[36]

The mechanism apart, any hydro-relations with China cannot ignore the power asymmetry in the basin. Clearly China does not want a permanent mechanism on water issues. By reviewing and renewing the MOU and various agreements, China dictates the proceedings as an upper riparian. Thus, China is effectively mixing 'cohesion and compliance' with 'attraction and intimidation', what the Marxist political philosopher Antonio Gramsci famously termed "a mix of force and consent".[37] As China aspires to be a global leader, it will also have to adjust and earn the respect of its neighbouring riparians. One way forward is to play a leadership role and develop a rules-based system that will help build an image of a non-threatening partner and careful listener.[38]

India as a lower riparian to China and as an upper riparian to Pakistan and Bangladesh needs to express concern over China's upstream utilisation of water and make it a core issue of bilateral talks. Raising concerns is perfectly acceptable in inter-state relations. A typical way is to argue for the application of international water laws, even if they are non-binding. Advocating such norms alerts and sensitises the international community, in spite of the fact that issues of 'equitable utilisation' and 'limited sovereignty' are always difficult and uncomfortable to agree upon. The principle of 'information exchange, notification, and consultation' is crucially important in dealing with China given the nature of the dams and water diversions. For example, withholding data on the flows of the rivers or on plans for building storage structures or dams or projects that divert water come under the 'no-harm rule' of the UN Watercourses Convention.

India's own water-sharing treaties with its lower riparians – Pakistan and Bangladesh – takes due account of the need for transparency. Under the Indus Waters Treaty, the Permanent Indus Commission meets regularly on river projects and also undertakes site and field inspections. The Ganges Treaty with Bangladesh has provision for a Joint Committee, which examines difficulties arising over the implementation of the sharing arrangement. India of course cannot ask China to reconsider signing the 1997 UN Watercourses Convention as India itself had abstained from voting in favour of it during the General Assembly debate and has not yet ratified it. The only plausible course for India now is to push for a water dialogue, hoping gradually that this will mature into a water-sharing treaty with China.

India's riparian relations with China are exceptional and critical. The country is dependent on the Brahmaputra in the east and the Indus and the Sutlej on the western side. The Ganges too depends on Tibetan waters. Some figures indicate that about 354 billion cubic meters (bcm) of water flows into India from the Tibet plateau.[39] If the goal of diplomacy is to turn potential water conflict into constructive engagement, then a water dialogue with China is necessary.

It is critical for India to articulate its middle riparian position, first to change the perception in the neighbourhood that India is a 'water hegemon', as is often expressed by Pakistan and Bangladesh, in spite of the robustness of the water treaties with these two countries, and second to draw China into the South Asian water equation through a multilateral basin approach, thereby sensitising China to downstream concerns and upstream responsibilities. Hydro-diplomacy has to be well nuanced and not always framed in legalistic terms but rather with a view to managing and engaging China.[40] This has significant political value when dealing with China over Tibetan water resources. By raising the question, however contested it might be, that China alone cannot be the stakeholder to the waters in Tibet, India creates the opportunity to articulate an ecological perspective and principles of resource conservation.

By terming water resources in Tibet as a 'commons', India draws international attention and could possibly prompt China into a water dialogue with the downstream countries on ways to preserve and share the benefits of the Tibetan waters.[41] It needs to be remembered that China has a strong environmental constituency, with activists, scientists, and journalists, who despite the odds are sensitising local people and authorities to ecological issues and principles. In 2007, President Hu Jintao called for more "scientific development" on water issues, including "securing more clean drinking water, improving water conservation, water pollution prevention, restricting excessive water resources exploitation and cutting water waste".[42]

Tibet's ecology has been a key issue for civil society and powerful environmental groups like the International Union for Conservation of Nature (IUCN) that are campaigning for Tibet as a vulnerable area to be protected from rampant resource exploitation. China has ratified the 1972 UNESCO World Heritage

Convention, and, in 2003, 1.7 million hectares in Yunnan province, where the upper reaches of the Yangtze, Lancang (Mekong), and Nu (Salween) run parallel, was declared a World Heritage site.[43] In 2004, several NGOs in China protested against developmental projects on the Nujiang River, prompting Wen Jiabao to take a difficult decision to halt the project pending a comprehensive environmental assessment. Likewise, environmentalists campaigned in 2008 to preserve the Tiger Leaping Gorge from the impact of a proposed dam. The government had to respond by moving the site of the dam away from the gorge.[44]

Warming and glacial melting have prompted unprecedented global pressure and action in areas where vulnerability is high. Tibet draws particular attention. It is becoming increasingly clear that rivers have more ecological functions than just providing water. The interaction of rivers and flood plains is one such vital function. Tibet, with its weather patterns and hydrology systems, glacial conditions, and forest and soil functions, has an essential influence over Asia, providing sustenance to some of the world's most productive agricultural zones. No one expects Tibet to become a protected area, but it is in China's interest as well as the interest of other riparian states to factor the ecosystem into Chinese water schemes (an example is the Three Parallel Rivers of Yunnan Protected Areas). It is also vital to involve local communities who integrate ecological values into everyday life and have long worried over Beijing's blatant mismanagement of the environment.

China's environmental activists, scientists, and journalists responding to the science of climate change and global warming have become a significant constituency in sensitising Chinese citizens and authorities as well as the world at large on Tibet's diverse cultural and ecological wealth. This constituency could turn out to be an effective lobby, helping China's leaders steer the country towards sustainable development and better management of water resources. An environmentally conscious regime in Beijing, concerned with the impact of global warming, would be more open to conciliatory approaches to hydrological conflicts and would perhaps be more acceptant of broad-based basin management of the Tibetan rivers.

Another important element of hydro-diplomacy would be for India to initiate a lower riparian coalition stretching from the Ganges-Meghna-Brahmaputra basin to the Mekong in order to draw China into a water dialogue. India's hydro-diplomacy has to ensure that the coalition is not seen as a counter-force or a challenger or even a pressure group, but rather a concerned group seeking to open channels of communication and transparency with China on upstream usage based on the principles of 'equity' and 'no-harm'.[45]

To redefine a vital resource like water as a 'commons' should be an important part of the water dialogue between India and China in spite of the political sensitivity to such an approach in Beijing. As noted earlier, it is in everyone's long-term interest, including China's, that Tibet's water resources are monitored as a sensitive ecosystem. India and China can together evolve a scientific community of glaciologists, hydrologists, seismologists, and climatologists studying and observing, collecting, and comparing data, and building a knowledge base that helps harmonise development with nature. India and China have become observers in the Arctic Council, and their endeavours to observe and share notes on the geo-physical changes in the Arctic could be a positive experience for the study of the glaciers of Tibet.

Way forward

Benefit sharing that shifts away from a volume-driven approach is widely regarded as a rational solution to contentions over water. While this is attractive, it is certainly not easy to implement. Identifying the benefits can itself be a contentious exercise involving trade-offs and rigorous economic accounting. The immediate derivable benefits between India and China on the Yarlung/Brahmaputra are the mitigation of floods and the potential for joint hydropower generation. These would add positively to the two countries' development activities. A case in point is the Itaipu dam between Brazil and Paraguay. Despite tough negotiations at times, the two countries signed what is the world's largest and most successful hydro-energy cooperation in 2009.

The accuracy and regular availability of credible hydrological data are vital to the effectiveness of any transboundary water arrangement. India and China would need to collaborate on data generation and constantly upgrade data-sharing mechanisms based on the MOU signed in 2002. For India, accurate hydrological data is imperative to ensure early detection and effective flood management. This will also help in removing irritants over differences in data, which both sides use to justify their preferences.

Conclusion

China's upper riparian position and its enormous domestic requirements make water a critical resource and fundamental to its development. Its upstream actions evoke different levels of concern. China's quest to dominate the flow will continue with hydraulic manipulations and civil engineering interventions. The enthusiasts of such a paradigm, which Karl Wittfogel described as leading to a "hydraulic society",[46] have "emptied water of its historical, cultural and ecological properties."[47]

This chapter has emphasised that water relations between India and China have very limited conflict potential. It argues that mechanisms (MOUs) are in place since 2002 that allow for India to get hydrological data on the Brahmaputra and the Sutlej. In the backdrop of no universally recognised international water law, the chapter's other emphasis is on the effect of power relations and the exertion of power by the hegemon. China is undeniably more powerful than its competitors both in terms of structural power and hydrological position and thus can establish its preferred form of interaction over transboundary water. Hence, there appears to be limited scope for action beyond working within the established MOUs.

There is, however, space for a hydro-diplomacy that engages China in a broad-based water dialogue and that aims at not only a bilateral but also a multilateral, basin-wide approach. The principles of 'information exchange, notification and consultation' and 'no harm' are sound points on which to consistently engage China. While Beijing will continue to enjoy its riparian position and determine relationships based on power, India's counter approach should be to take a bold stride towards creating awareness about water resources and the ecological significance of Tibet. The water dialogue between India and China should use science and research capacities to provide the knowledge backbone needed for water management.

Water cannot be viewed in isolation. It is interconnected and interlinked with fundamental facets of human existence. Water in India-China relations is no longer an underdeveloped issue. As global powers, India and China have to balance water output with social equity, environmental protection, and sustainable economic development.

Notes

1 The per capita water availability, measured in cubic meter/person/year, on average from 2003–2007, was 2,138 for China and 1,719 for India. See Aquastat, "Computation of Long-term Annual Renewable Water Resources by Country (in km3/yr, average): China", *Food and Agriculture Organization of the United Nations*, 1 August 2013, http://www.fao.org/nr/water/aquastat/data/wrs/readPdf.html?f=WRS_CHN_en.pdf; Aquastat, "Computation of Long-term Annual Renewable Water Resources by Country (in km3/yr, average): India", *Food and Agriculture Organization of the United Nations*, 1 August 2013, http://www.fao.org/nr/water/aquastat/data/wrs/readPdf.html?f=WRS_IND_en.pdf.
2 McKinsey and Company, *Charting our Water Future: Economic Frameworks to Inform Decision Making*, Munich: 2030 Water Resources Group, 2009, http://www.mckinsey.com/client_service/sustainability/latest_thinking/charting_our_water_future.
3 "Drying Up", *The Economist*, 19 May 2005, http://www.economist.com/node/4000643.
4 See "Prime Minister's Independence Day Address", *Prime Minister's Office*, 15 August 2004, http://pib.nic.in/newsite/erelease.aspx?relid=29937.
5 China refers to Arunachal Pradesh as 'South Tibet' (*Zangnan*) and bases its claim on historical ties between the Lhasa and Tawang monasteries. These claims are frequently reiterated, giving the impression that Arunachal for China is now also about acquiring the vast water resources there. See IDSA Task Force Report, *Water Security for India: The External Dynamics*, New Delhi: Institute for Defence Studies and Analyses (IDSA), 2010, p. 48, http://www.idsa.in/sites/default/files/book_WaterSecurity.pdf.
6 Li Jing, "Ban Lifted on Controversial Nu River Dam Projects", *South China Morning Post*, 25 January 2013, http://www.scmp.com/news/china/article/1135463/ban-lifted-controversial-nu-river-dam-projects.
7 Ibid.
8 The area south of the Yangtze River "accounts for roughly 36 per cent of Chinese territory and has 81 per cent of its water resources. The territories north of the Yangtze make up 64 per cent but have only 19 per cent of water resources". See IDSA Task Force Report, *Water Security for India: The External Dynamics*, 2010, p. 48. The idea of 'reverse-flow' was the brainchild of hydrologist Guo Kai.
9 SNTWP has three routes of diversion: the central, the eastern, and the western. The first two routes are on the internal rivers. The western route is planned on the Yangtze River and would divert about 200 billion cubic meters (bcm) of water annually.

10 12th Five-Year Plan, http://www.cbichina.org.cn/cbichina/upload/fckeditor/Full%20 Translation%20of%20the%2012th%20Five-Year%20Plan.pdf. See also APCO Worldwide, *China's 12th Five-Year Plan: How it Actually Works and What's in Store for the Next Five Years*, 10 December 2010, http://www.export.gov.il/UploadFiles/03_2012/ Chinas12thFive-YearPlan.pdf;
11 Quoted in Ananth Krishnan, "China Gives Go-ahead for Three New Brahmaputra Dams," *The Hindu*, 30 January 2013, http://www.thehindu.com/news/international/ china-gives-goahead-for-three-new-brahmaputra-dams/article4358195.ece.
12 Himanshu Thakkar, "Chinese Checkers", *Hindustan Times*, 12 February 2013, http://www.hindustantimes.com/editorial-views-on/ColumnsOthers/Chinese-checkers/ Article1-1010765.aspx.
13 Zhou Wei, "Divided Waters in India", *Chinadialogue*, 20 September 2011, http://www.chinadialogue.net/article/show/single/en/4539-Divided-waters-in-China.
14 Standing Committee on Water Resources (2009-2010), *Fourth Report*, August 2010, p. 43, http://wwfenvis.nic.in/files/Water%20Resources/Working%20of%20 Brahmaputra%20Board.pdf.
15 "Parched Tiger to Thirsty Dragon: 'No Concerns about Dams on Brahmaputra'", *Water Politics*, 8 February 2011, http://www.waterpolitics.com/2011/02/08/parched-tiger-to-thirsty-dragon-no-concerns-about-dams-on-brahmaputra/.
16 "The rule of 'equitable utilisation', based on the concept that an international drainage basin is a coherent legal and managerial unit, embodies a theory of restricted sovereignty under which each nation recognises the right of all riparian nations to use water from a common source and the obligation to manage their uses so as not to interfere unreasonably with like uses in other riparian nations". The subordinate 'no-harm rule' requires that states "take all 'appropriate measures' to prevent the causing of significant harm to other watercourse nations". See Water Encyclopedia, "Law, International Water", http://www.waterencyclopedia.com/La-Mi/Law-International-Water.html.
17 This is enshrined in the UN Convention on the Law of the Non-Navigational Uses of International Watercourses (1997), which has been ratified and came into force on August 17, 2014. The Convention also includes the "no-harm rule", which states that riparian nations should take all "appropriate measures" to prevent causing harm to other watercourse nations. See United Nations, *Convention on the Law of the Non-navigational Uses of International Watercourses*, Adopted by the General Assembly of the United Nations, 21 May 1997, https://treaties.un.org/doc/Treaties/1998/09/19980925%20 06-30%20PM/Ch_XXVII_12p.pdf.
18 India and China bilateral trade peaked in 2011 with USD 73.9 billion but fell by 12 per cent in 2012 to USD 66.47 billion. The expected target is to reach USD100 billion by 2015. See Ananth Krishnan, "India's Trade with China Falls 12%", *The Hindu*, 10 January 2013, http://www.thehindu.com/business/Economy/indias-trade-with-china-falls-12/article4295117.ece.
19 As noted by John Beddington, UK Chief Scientist on March 18, 2009. See Ian Sample, "World Faces 'Perfect Storm' of Problems by 2030, Chief Scientist to Warn", *The Guardian*, 18 March 2009, http://www.guardian.co.uk/science/2009/mar/18/perfect-storm-john-beddington-energy-food-climate.
20 Study carried out by the Department of Geography, University of California Santa Barbara.
21 H.C. Nainwal, "Retreat of Himalayan Glaciers: Examples from Garhwal Himalaya", http://nidm.gov.in/idmc/Proceedings/LandSlide/A2-8,%20Nainwal%20H%20C.pdf.
22 Recent studies indicate that the accumulation of black carbon is accelerating the shrinking of the Himalayan glaciers, and the carbon is not only coming in from the

East (China) but largely from South Asian countries. See Wu Wencong, "Third Pole Glaciers Shrinking, Affected by Black Carbon", *China Daily*, 25 March, 2013, http://www.chinadaily.com.cn/china/2013-03/25/content_16341312.htm.
23. Ministry of Environment and Forests, Government of India, "Climate Change and India: A 4X4 Assessment", November 2010, p. 12, http://www.moef.nic.in/downloads/public-information/fin-rpt-incca.pdf.
24. WWF, "An Overview of Glaciers, Glacier Retreat, and Subsequent Impacts in Nepal, India and China", *WWF Nepal Program*, 1 March 2005, p. 30.
25. UNEP Global Environment Alert Services (GEAS), September 2012, http://na.unep.net/geas/getUNEPPageWithArticleIDScript.php?article_id=91
26. For example, see International Centre for Integrated Mountain Development (ICIMOD), *Glacial Lakes and Glacial Lake Outburst Floods in Nepal*, Kathmandu: ICIMOD, 2011.
27. Mark Zeitoun and Jeroen Warner, "Hydro-hegemony – a Framework for Analysis of Trans-boundary Water Conflicts", *Water Policy*, 8, 2006, pp. 435–460.
28. Independence here refers to the sources of rivers originating in China's territory, so that China is not dependent on the sources of the headwaters from other countries.
29. None of China's riparian treaties address water distribution and sharing arrangements on the transboundary rivers. With Kazakhstan on the Irtysh and Ili rivers, China has agreements on flooding (2001) and on water quality (2011). China has a number of procedures, protocols, and agreements with Russia on navigation (1905), delimitation of border (1915), hydropower (1956), protection and regulation (1994), and flooding and water quality (2008). On the Brahmaputra it has MOUs on hydrological information and on the Lancang-Mekong it has basin cooperation. For details, see Sophie le Clue, "Water Treaties – A Question of Rights", *China Water Risk*, 12 April 2012, http://chinawaterrisk.org/resources/analysis-reviews/water-treaties-a-question-of-rights/.
30. The other two were Turkey and Burundi.
31. See Ministry of Water Resources, Government of India, "India-China Co-operation", http://www.wrmin.nic.in/forms/list.aspx?lid=349.
32. Ibid.
33. Ibid.
34. Gargi Parsai, "India, China Renew Flood Data Pact on Brahmaputra", *The Hindu*, 20 May 2013, http://www.thehindu.com/news/national/india-china-renew-flood-data-pact-on-brahmaputra/article4732965.ece.
35. Ibid.
36. Uttam Sinha, "India-China Hydrorelations", *China–India Brief 15*, Lee Kuan Yew School of Public Policy, 23 October – 12 November 2013, http://lkyspp.nus.edu.sg/cag/publication/china-india-brief/china-india-brief-15.
37. Antonio Gramsci, *Selections from the Prison Notebooks of Antonio Gramsci*, Quintin Hoare and Geoffrey Nowell Smith, eds., and trans., New York: International Publishers, 1971; See also Mark Zeitoun, Naho Mirumachi, and Jeroen Warner, "Transboundary Water Interaction II: The Influence of 'Soft Power'," *International Environment Agreements: Politics, Law and Economics*, 11/2, 2011, p. 164.
38. The phrase is similar to the one expressed by David Shambaugh: ". . . most nations in the region now see China as a good neighbour, a constructive partner, a careful listener and a non-threatening partner." See David Shambaugh, "China Engages Asia: Reshaping the Regional Order," *International Security*, 29/3, winter 2004–2005, p. 64.
39. IDSA Task Force Report, Water Security for India: The External Dynamics, p. 44.
40. Sujit Dutta, "Managing and Engaging Rising China: India's Evolving Posture", *Washington Quarterly*, 34/2, 2011, pp. 127–144.

Towards riparian rationality 181

41 Uttam Kumar Sinha, "Tibet's Watershed Challenge", *The Washington Post*, 14 July 2010, http://www.washingtonpost.com/wp-dyn/content/article/2010/06/13/AR2010061303331.html.
42 Hu Jintao, "Hold High the Great Banner of Socialism with Chinese Characteristics and Strive for New Victories in Building a Moderately Prosperous Society in All", *China.org.cn*, 25 October 2007, http://www.china.org.cn/english/congress/229611.htm.
43 See United Nations Educational, Scientific and Cultural Organizations (UNESCO), "Three Parallel Rivers of Yunnan Protected Areas", http://whc.unesco.org/en/list/1083.
44 "Paradise Lost at Tiger Leaping Gorge", *China Digital Times*, 7 November 2008, http://chinadigitaltimes.net/2008/11/paradise-lost-at-tiger-leaping-gorge/.
45 The community of co-riparian states is an important principle in the waters of an international river. According to Salman M.A. Salman, "The basis...is that the entire river basin is an economic unit, and the rights over the waters of the entire river are vested in the collective body of the riparian states, or divided among them either by agreement or on the basis of proportionality. Clearly, this is an ideal principle that overlooks sovereignty and nationalism (p. 627) . . . ". See Salman M.A. Salman, "Helsinki Rules, the UN Watercourses Convention and the Berlin Rules: Perspective on International Water Law," *Water Resources Development*, 23/4, December 2007, pp. 625–640. Also, "'Equality' and 'No harm' principles are based on 'limited territorial sovereignty' and 'limited territorial integrity' as opposed to 'absolute territorial sovereignty' and 'absolute territorial integrity' (p.50)". See IDSA Task Force Report, *Water Security for India: The External Dynamics*.
46 For Wittfogel, state control of water for purposes of irrigation was central to the Asiatic mode of production. One of the consequences of this is the institution of a powerful bureaucracy. See Karl A. Wittfogel, *Oriental Despotism: A Comparative Study of Total Power*, New Haven: Yale University Press, 1957.
47 Rohan D'Souza, "From Damming Rivers to Linking Waters: Is this the Beginning of the End of Supply-Side Hydrology in India?" in Terje Tvedt, Graham Chapman and Roar Hagen, eds., *A History of Water, Volume 3: Water, Geopolitics and the New World Order*, London: IB Tauris, 2011, p. 357.

10 A river flows through it
A Chinese perspective

Selina Ho

The lack of a comprehensive framework between China and India for managing their shared water resources is a source of instability in Sino-Indian relations and for the region as a whole. The nature of water, the water problems in both China and India, and climate change, set against the backdrop of historically tense relations between the two countries, increase the potential for conflict. However, the path to greater hydrological cooperation between China and India is fraught with difficulties. The benefits of cooperation to India are clear – as lower riparian, it is in India's interest to lay down water sharing and water usage principles with China. For China, the incentives are less obvious; from its perspective, there are substantial sovereignty and autonomy risks, and limited political and economic gains, to be derived from cooperating with India.

China's historically acrimonious and currently uneasy relations with India shape its policies towards the rivers it shares with India, particularly the Brahmaputra. It does not see it in its interest to establish any formal joint development and water sharing arrangements with India. While it does not want relations with India to deteriorate, it also does not expect a warm and substantive relationship to develop in the near future, given the countries' historical baggage and India's emergence as a competitor. China is thus unwilling to give up the strategic advantages that its position as upstream riparian offers over India.[1] It wants to maintain the status quo in the Brahmaputra, that is, to continue developing the water resources within its territory without interference and serious disruption to its ties with India. It seems that China will only consider any significant forward movement in cooperation with India on water management when there is substantial progress towards resolving the other outstanding issues between them, namely, Tibet and territorial disputes.[2] Moreover, China takes an absolutist stance on its sovereign rights to develop the water resources that flow through its territory. It believes it is not accountable to other riparians for its actions and plans.

However, despite the obstacles to deepening cooperation in the form of joint development and water sharing arrangements, there are areas where China and India can work together to increase confidence and trust. At the present moment, China's aims are to peacefully co-exist with India and keep ties with India on an even keel, so as to maintain stability along its borders with India. India's rising influence and alignment with the United States also explain Chinese motivations for maintaining equanimity with India. There are indications that China is beginning to reassess India's strategic value, and Chinese leaders have recently taken steps to place greater emphasis on the country's ties with India. For instance, Li Keqiang made India one of the first countries he visited as Premier in May 2013. For these larger political reasons, China takes into consideration Indian concerns in the Brahmaputra and has made attempts, albeit limited ones, to minimise conflict over water. This bodes well for stepping up cooperation in less sensitive areas, such as enhancing the Memorandums of Understanding (MOUs) on sharing hydrological data, strengthening dialogue on water pollution, flood control, and disaster management, and cooperating in research on the impact of global warming on the Himalayan glaciers.

This chapter focuses on Chinese perspectives on riparian politics with India. It first explains why water is a potential source of conflict between China and India. The chapter then examines Chinese policies towards transboundary rivers in general and the Brahmaputra in particular. It concludes by assessing the prospects for riparian cooperation between China and India. Comparisons with China's cooperation with the Indochina states in the Mekong and Kazakhstan in the Ili and Irtysh rivers are made to understand Chinese calculations of the risks and benefits of cooperation.

Water as a political and security issue in Sino-Indian relations

Rivers are subject to competing interests because they can be used in a variety of ways by multiple users. They are a source of drinking water and are important for navigation, transportation, flood control, irrigation, and hydropower generation. Rivers can also be diverted to supply areas suffering from water shortages. Entire communities living along rivers are dependent on the 'river economy' for their livelihood. As a result, there are often conflicts over how rivers should be used. For instance, building dams to generate hydropower affects flood levels and navigation. Diverting water from one area to another pits one group of users against another. Water is neither a pure public good nor a private good. It is often described as a "common pool resource", which is defined as "sufficiently large natural or manmade resources that it is costly (but not necessarily impossible) to exclude potential beneficiaries from obtaining benefits from their use".[3] Consumption by one party not only reduces the benefits to other parties but can also result in negative externalities for others. Downstream users are especially vulnerable to the actions of upstream users in terms of pollution, extraction, or impoundment, which may affect the amount and quality of water available to downstream users. The tug of war between upstream and downstream users is often over the principles of usage – upstream users emphasise "equitable use" while downstream users stress "no appreciable harm".

As a World Bank report, *Reaching Across the Waters*, puts it:

> Water management, by definition, is conflict management. Water, unlike other consumable resources that are scarce, fuels all parts of society, from

biologies to economies to aesthetics and spiritual practices... Water management has multiple objectives and is based on reconciling co-existing and competing interests. Within a nation, these interests include domestic and industrial users, agriculturalists, hydropower generators, tourism and recreation beneficiaries, and environmentalists – any two of whom may be at odds. The complexity of finding mutually acceptable solutions increases with the number of stakeholders involved. When international boundary issues are factored in, the difficulty grows substantially yet again.[4]

In international politics, rivers have significant impact on relations between states. Water disputes are a non-traditional security issue and a form of low-intensity conflict.[5] While wars arising out of water disputes alone are rare, conflict short of armed violence is a regular occurrence between parties, whether within or between states, sharing water resources. Water is also often embroiled in conflicts between states even if it is not the root cause of conflicts. For instance, in the history of Malaysia and Singapore, Malaysia's occasional threat to "turn off the tap" was a constant source of insecurity for Singapore, which was dependent on Malaysia for most of its water supply. Israel and its neighbours have also been involved in water-related skirmishes even though water is not the root cause of conflicts between them. Rivers link upstream and downstream riparians, creating an unequal balance of power, usually in favour of the upstream riparian. In China's case, its position as the dominant power in Asia further increases the power asymmetry with other riparians.

For China and India, disputes over water resources add another layer of complication to historically tense relations, marked by border wars, unresolved territorial disputes, and mutual distrust. Water has emerged as the greatest resource constraint for both China and India's economic and global ambitions. According to the World Bank, China's water crisis costs China about 2.3 per cent of its GDP, of which 1.3 percentage points is due to water scarcity and 1 percentage point is the result of water pollution.[6] As for India, the annual cost of environmental degradation, including the lack of an adequate water supply, is estimated to be 5.7 per cent of GDP.[7] Both countries suffer from severe water shortages. By national available water resource per capita, China is just slightly above the water stress level, with about 1,800 to 2,000 cubic meters per capita on average.[8] Of even greater concern to Chinese policymakers is the uneven distribution between the north and the south: areas south of the Yangtze River have 81 per cent of China's water resources while areas north of the Yangtze have only 19 per cent.[9] Rapid economic growth, industrialisation, and urbanisation further shrink water resources by creating problems of water pollution.

A report commissioned by the 2030 Water Resources Group, *Charting Our Water Future*, shows that China's water supply will reach 619 billion cubic meters compared to an expected demand of 818 billion cubic meters in 2030.[10] In other words, with no change in consumption and usage patterns, demand will outstrip supply in the next two decades; by 2030, China will experience a water shortage of about 25 per cent.[11] India is already suffering from water stress, with an average per capita water availability of 1,545 cubic meters.[12] Rapid population growth, economic development, and urbanisation are increasing water demand, which is expected to increase to 833 cubic kilometres and 899 cubic kilometres by 2025 and 2050, respectively.[13] India is expected to be water scarce by 2050.[14]

The waters of the Himalaya are therefore an invaluable resource for both China and India. The countries share significant water resources originating from the Tibetan plateau, namely the Indus, Sutlej, and Brahmaputra rivers, with the Brahmaputra and its tributaries being the most significant with a mean annual run-off volume of 165.4 cubic kilometres.[15] It is estimated that about 354 billion cubic meters of water flow from Tibet into India, of which 131 billion cubic meters are accounted for in the Brahmaputra.[16] China's position as the upstream riparian in these river systems flowing from Tibet is a source of insecurity for India. India fears that China's water diversion plans and dam-building activities would reduce the flow of water to India, visiting enormous ecological and economic costs upon India as a result. More importantly, there are fears that China's upper riparian position would give it significant political leverage over India: India worries that China would use threats to withhold water to pressurise India and extract political and territorial concessions.

Water politics between China and India are often conflated with larger territorial and political issues between the two countries. India views with suspicion Chinese funding of major Pakistani infrastructure projects such as the Diamer-Bhasha dam on the Indus and the Bunji hydro-project at the intersection of the Indus and the Gilgit in Kashmir. It sees China using these projects to extend its reach into India's neighbourhood. Water as a resource dispute is also mixed with territorial disputes between China and India. India believes that "water occupies centre stage in China's interest in Tibet".[17] It also suspects that China claims Arunachal Pradesh in order to lay its hands on the state's rich water resources, which are estimated to be almost 200 million cusecs.[18] India's beliefs are fuelled by Chinese actions – in 2009, China blocked an Indian request for a loan from the Asian Development Bank because it was earmarked for a watershed development project in Arunachal Pradesh.

China's plans to construct more dams along the Brahmaputra as part of its 12th Five-Year Energy Plan (2011–2015) and the widespread speculation that China plans to divert the waters of the Brahmaputra for the western route of its South-North Water Transfer Project increases Indian suspicions of Chinese intentions. China's opaque decision-making structure and belief that it does not need to explain its actions to other riparians create further anxiety for India. China is seen as unilateral in its actions, particularly in building dams, and unforthcoming in terms of information sharing.

Environmental degradation and the impact of climate change on the Himalayan glaciers lend urgency to, and intensify the political and security dimensions of, water issues between China and India. According to a report by India's Institute of Defence Studies and Analyses:

186 *Selina Ho*

> In spite of the abundance, inadequate water supplies in rural Tibet have led to widespread water-borne diseases and high incidence of hepatitis. The impact of global warming on the glaciers and the melting of permafrost is also alarming. According to the IPCC [Intergovernmental Panel on Climate Change], glaciers in the [Tibetan] plateau are receding at a faster rate than anywhere else in the world.[19]

Global warming is believed to influence the water and energy cycle of the Tibetan plateau, reducing runoff on the plateau source areas of large Asian rivers.[20] In the short term, melting glaciers mean "greater river flows, floods, landslides, and glacial lake outbursts. In the longer term . . . it will mean the loss of glaciers and with them the loss of year-round regulated water flow through the lowlands of Asia".[21] China and India need to work together in order to tackle these urgent issues.

The character and nature of water, the water shortages in China and India, the geopolitics of water between China and India, and the urgency of climate change, all add friction to Sino-Indian relations. The next section examines Chinese policies with respect to transboundary rivers, focusing specifically on the Brahmaputra.

Chinese policies on transboundary waters

China accords low priority to the management of international rivers. It does not have an overarching policy or institutional framework dedicated to managing transboundary rivers. Only one article in its revised 2002 Water Law deals with the international rivers running through its territories:

> Where any international treaty or agreement relating to the international or border rivers or lakes, concluded or acceded to by the People's Republic of China, contains provisions differing from those in the laws of the People's Republic of China, the provisions of the international treaty or agreement shall apply, unless the provisions are the ones on which the People's Republic of China has declared reservation.[22]

The government structure for managing international rivers is also weak. There appears to be no dedicated government agency that is empowered to resolve international river disputes. The Department of International Cooperation, Science and Technology, under the Ministry of Water Resources (MOWR), is tasked to carry out cooperation and exchanges with its foreign counterparts on international river issues, formulate policies to manage transboundary rivers, and coordinate negotiations.[23] The Department's focus, however, appears to be conducting science and technological exchanges with water organisations in other countries. Moreover, the MOWR is an inward-looking government agency not equipped to deal with the complexities of managing relations with other riparian states. Its priority is internal water issues, with flood control as its most important responsibility. It therefore does not appear to have the mandate to resolve water disputes with other riparians.

The other government agency that could be well placed to manage international river disputes is the Ministry of Foreign Affairs (MOFA). However, the issue of international river disputes does not rank high on its list of priorities: MOFA established the Department of Boundary and Ocean Affairs in 2009 to manage Chinese territorial and maritime disputes but did not include international river disputes among its responsibilities. Without a strong central government body dedicated to international rivers, the management of transboundary rivers is usually left to the discretion of provinces. For instance, Yunnan province drives China's policy on the Mekong and represents the central government in Mekong forums.[24]

The lack of attention towards international rivers on the part of Chinese policymakers is not surprising, given China's position as the "upstream superpower"[25] of Asia. Less than one per cent of China's water has its source in other countries, and the country's outflows "are over 40 times as great as its inflows".[26] China enjoys the benefits of being an upstream riparian without having to worry about the negative externalities of its actions. It thus has little incentive to consider the effect of its actions on others. Moreover, China is more concerned about its internal water disputes, between and within provinces, which have direct repercussions for China's domestic stability and continued economic growth.[27]

As a result of the lack of an overarching framework for dealing with international rivers, China manages its international rivers in the larger context of its overall relations with other riparian states. Any form of cooperation is usually bilateral and seldom multilateral. For instance, it is one of three countries (the other two are Turkey and Burundi) that rejected the 1997 UN Convention on the Law of the Non-Navigational Use of International Watercourses. It is also not a participant of the 1992 UN Economic Commission for Europe Convention on the Protection and Use of Transboundary Watercourses and International Lakes, which was made open to all UN member countries. China's policies towards its water disputes with India are therefore dependent on its attitude towards India and the overall state of their relations.

Chinese policies towards the Brahmaputra

Following an acrimonious relationship during most of the 20th century, Sino-Indian relations were normalised and diplomatic relations re-established in 1978. Chinese policies towards India since then have been motivated by three main goals: stabilising its border with India; expanding opportunities for bilateral trade and investment; and diluting India's alignment with the United States.[28] Attempts have been made by both sides to improve relations but relations remain tense and marked by mutual suspicion. China traditionally perceives India as a regional power without global reach, while it sees itself as a global power. This traditional lack of regard for India belies the image of a rising India, a potential competitor to China's own global ambitions. Both countries have among the world's fastest-growing economies and militaries. They also compete in Africa,

Latin America, and other parts of Asia for influence and for resources to fuel their growth.

While these new areas of competition arise, traditional rivalries and perceptions remain, resulting in ambivalence in China's policies towards India. Relations between the countries are also characterised by a classic security dilemma, which makes it difficult for one party not to view the actions of another as being directed against it. For instance, India sees China as conducting "a string of pearls" strategy in the Indian Ocean to encircle India, while China sees India's development of its northeast as challenging its claims in the area.

Despite the uneasiness and mutual distrust between the countries, Sino-Indian relations nevertheless flourished in other areas, especially in economic terms. China is India's largest trading partner while India is among China's top ten trading partners, although a large trade deficit in favour of China is a sore point for the Indians. Economic complementarity between them, that is, China's strengths in manufacturing and infrastructure, and India's in services and information technology, has led to the coining of the term "Chindia".[29]

It is in this larger context of Sino-Indian relations that riparian politics between the two, particularly in the Brahmaputra, is played out. China's main interest in the Brahmaputra is in harnessing the river for hydropower. Its key project thus far is the construction of a large 3,260 meter dam in Zangmu, less than 200 kilometres from the Indian border. In addition, there is also reportedly a plan to construct a dam more than twice as large as the Three Gorges Dam, the 38-gigawatt Motuo Dam, at the Great Bend, which is located just before the Brahmaputra enters Indian territory.[30] In its 12th Five-Year Energy Plan (2011–2015), China declared its intentions to build another three dams along the Brahmaputra – Jiexu, Dagu, and Jiacha.

China's decision-making on the Brahmaputra is complicated and inextricably linked with larger national issues, namely Tibet, territorial disputes with India, and the possibility of diverting the waters of the Brahmaputra for the western route of the South-North Water Transfer Project. Tibet is a national security concern that naturally garners the attention of top Chinese leaders and multiple bureaucratic agencies. Decision-making is therefore likely to be complex. In addition, as noted in the previous section, border disputes between China and India are mixed with the water resource dispute between them, particularly in the disputed area of Arunachal Pradesh.

The possibility of diverting the waters of the Brahmaputra for the western route of the South-North Water Transfer Project further adds to the complexity of Chinese policies towards the Brahmaputra. The idea of diverting the water of the Brahmaputra has been mooted in some quarters of the People's Liberation Army (PLA) and certain academic think tanks, although top Chinese leaders and both the MOFA and MOWR have repeatedly denied that China has such intentions.[31]

MOWR officials are aware of the difficulties of the project and have spoken out against it. MOFA, whose interest is in keeping Sino-Indian relations on a stable footing, is also likely to be against the project. Given the technical difficulties, and the associated financial and ecological costs, it is unlikely that the Chinese would carve out tunnels in the Himalaya in order to build the western route. As a result of the existence of multiple parties with diverging interests in decision-making on the Brahmaputra, Chinese policies towards the Brahmaputra lack clarity and appear evasive and uncooperative.

However, it would be erroneous to view the Chinese attitude towards India on the issue of the Brahmaputra as completely uncooperative and disregarding of Indian sentiments. In the larger interest of ensuring peaceful relations with India, China has sought to address Indian concerns. It has time and again reassured the Indians, including in statements by high-level officials, that it has no intention of diverting the water of the Brahmaputra. China has also claimed that the dams it is building are "run-of-the-river" and will not affect the flow of the Brahmaputra. It has propounded a positive view of the impact of its dams, saying that dams can help increase the amount of water during the dry season and provide flood control during the rainy season.

All these are attempts to 'desecuritise' water conflicts so as to maintain stable ties with India. According to Sebastian Biba, the clearest attempts at "assuaging rhetoric" took place in spring 2010, following an official Chinese announcement that the Zangmu Dam was indeed being built, this after months of denial.[32] Biba gives an account of these actions and statements by Chinese officials and hydropower companies:

> The China Huaneng Group, a state-owned hydropower company in charge of the Zangmu Hydropower Station project, was quick to announce that, first, '[t]he river will not be stopped during construction' and that, second, '[a]fter it [i.e. the dam] comes into operation, the river water will flow downstream through water turbines and sluices. So the water volume downstream will not be reduced'. Even more importantly, during a Sino-Indian strategic bilateral dialogue around the same time, Chinese Vice Foreign Minister Zhang Zhijun assured the Indian delegation that the project 'was not a project designed to divert water' and would not affect 'the welfare and availability of water of the population in the lower reaches of the Brahmaputra'. During the same meeting, China reportedly also expressed its willingness to continue exchanging hydrological data with India to minimise the risks of any future dispute. All this was topped by Chinese Premier Wen stating during a visit to India in late 2010 that China takes seriously India's concern about the transborder rivers, and we are ready to further improve the joint working mechanism. [. . .] I would like to assure our Indian friends that all upstream development activities by China will be based on scientific planning and study and will never harm downstream interests.[33]

These public statements are Chinese attempts to control the damage to its relations with India as a result of the Zangmu Dam. Furthermore, while MOUs are a dime a dozen between China and India and not always faithfully adhered to, the fact that China signed two MOUs in 2013 alone is a sign of increasing Chinese attention to Indian concerns.[34]

190 *Selina Ho*

Prospects for cooperation

Currently, there are limited mechanisms for riparian cooperation between China and India (see Table 10.1). These consist of a series of MOUs on hydrological data sharing. Specifically, China agreed to provide India with information about water level, discharge, and rainfall from its three monitoring stations on the Brahmaputra as well as the Sutlej. An expert-level mechanism was also established in 2006. The expert group meets annually to discuss cooperation and coordination on information sharing and emergency management. However, the terms of the MOUs are very limited; China only agrees to provide hydrological data for

Table 10.1 Existing Sino-Indian cooperation on transboundary rivers

Date	Frameworks	Details
2002, renewed in 2008 and 2013	MOU on Hydrological Data Sharing on the Brahmaputra River/Yalu Zangbu	China agreed in a MOU signed in 2002 to provide hydrological information, namely water level, discharge, and rainfall, from 1 June to 15 October every year. The 2002 MOU expired in 2007 and was renewed in 2008 for another five years. In May 2013 during Premier Li Keqiang's visit to India, the MOU was further extended till 2018. In October 2013, during Prime Minister Manmohan Singh's visit to China, a new MOU on Strengthening Cooperation on Transboundary Rivers was signed. China agreed to share data from 1 May instead of 1 June. Under the MOU, China and India also agreed to "exchange views on other areas of mutual interest".
2005, renewed in 2010	MOU on Hydrological Data Sharing on River Sutlej/Langquin Zangbu	China agreed to provide hydrological information during flood season. An Implementation Plan was additionally signed in 2011 for China to provide hydrological information, data transmission method, and cost settlement.
2006	Expert-Level Mechanism	The expert group, made up of representatives from both sides, discussed interaction and cooperation on provision of flood season hydrological data, emergency management, and other issues on an annual basis. The first meeting was held in 2007, and meetings were held every year subsequently.

Source: Government of India, Ministry of Water Resources, "India-China Co-operation", http://www.wrmin.nic.in/forms/list.aspx?lid=349.

the Brahmaputra and Sutlej from May/June to October each year. China has also refused to allow Indian experts to visit dam sites on the Brahmpuatra on the premise that these were "run-of-the-river" projects. The MOUs are not legally binding, and there is no oversight body that can ensure implementation.

The question then is, how can both riparians be encouraged to increase their current levels of cooperation? For India, as lower riparian, the benefits of greater cooperation are clear. Locking in China on water-sharing and allocation principles serves its interest. The Brahmaputra is important to India in two respects: as a source of available fresh water and for hydropower generation. It accounts for 29 per cent of the total runoff of India's rivers and about 44 per cent of India's hydropower potential.[35] Like China, India has plans for a series of dams along the Brahmaputra. For instance, it plans to build more than 100 large dams in Arunachal Pradesh "to exploit a potential generating capacity of over 50,000 megawatts".[36] India is also planning to divert water to link up all its major river systems – in December 2012, it announced progress on plans to connect 37 rivers through 31 links with 9,000 kilometres of canals.[37] Given the Brahmaputra's centrality to India's plans, India needs to ensure that the Brahmaputra's flow is uninterrupted.

For China, as upstream riparian, there are few incentives for cooperation. The World Bank's *Reaching Across the Waters* listed five categories of risks that riparians have to deal with when considering joint cooperation in international rivers. These include capacity and knowledge, accountability and voice, sovereignty and autonomy, equity and access, and stability and support risks.[38] For China, the risks to sovereignty and autonomy, in terms of both territory and resources, are most important. China rejects a multilateral framework for managing transboundary rivers because it does not want its sovereignty and freedom of action to be circumscribed by external parties.

China believes that it has exclusive use of all resources that originate on its soil. It has stayed as a dialogue partner of the Mekong River Commission (MRC), refusing to be a full member, because it does not want to be constrained by the MRC's aquatic environmental standards and dam-building restrictions. For China, the Brahmaputra is an even more sensitive issue to its sovereignty concerns since the river is intertwined with the Tibetan issue and the border disputes with India. Not only must China see lowered risks to its sovereignty and autonomy if it were to cooperate on shared waters, it also needs to perceive positive political and economic gains from cooperation. With this risk-benefit framework in mind, the rest of this section assesses two potential areas of cooperation: joint development and water sharing.

The idea of joint development has been raised by various quarters in India. In this regard, China's participation in the Greater Mekong Subregion (GMS) has been held up as an example of the fact that China is not unaccustomed to such arrangements.[39] The GMS is the only organisation in the Mekong River that includes all six riparians of the Mekong – China, Thailand, Cambodia, Laos, Vietnam, and Myanmar. Initiated by the Asian Development Bank in 1992, the GMS focuses on constructing power, transport, and communication networks in the region.

China was willing to join the GMS because the GMS programmes focus on economic and infrastructure development, and not on sensitive aquatic environmental issues and restrictions on dam-building like the MRC. China sees the GMS as a useful platform for improving the lives of the people of Yunnan. It seems therefore that a similar programme on the Brahmaputra could benefit the Tibetan population and help China develop its poor western provinces as part of its "Go West" policy. For China, joint cooperation in the Brahmaputra in a form similar to the GMS that focuses on hydroelectric projects could be an attractive option.

The possibility of a Sino-Indian bilateral water treaty and the setting up of a river commission similar to the Indus River Commission between India and Pakistan has also been discussed among scholars and experts. A bilateral water-sharing arrangement will go a long way towards setting up a mechanism that will ensure predictability in managing water resources between China and India, reducing the possibility of misperceptions and miscalculations. That there has been gradual movement between China and Kazakhstan on managing their shared rivers, the Ili and Irtysh rivers, suggests that China is not entirely closed to the idea of bilateral water management/sharing arrangements. In 2001, China took the unprecedented step of setting up a joint river commission with Kazakhstan. In early 2011, China also signed an agreement with Kazakhstan on water quality protection. Both sides have also agreed to move forward plans to regulate the distribution of shared water resources. In 2011 as well, China finalised an agreement with Kazakhstan for a joint water diversion project on the Khorgos River.

China's cooperation with the Indochina states in the Mekong River, and Kazakhstan in the Ili and Irtysh rivers, is largely the result of the depth of its relations with these countries. China sees low risks to its sovereignty in cooperating in the Mekong and in the case of the Ili and Irtysh rivers, while putting in place safeguards for its ability to act autonomously, particularly in the Mekong, by limiting cooperation in forums that could restrict its freedom of action. At the same time, there are significant political and economic advantages that China derives from cooperation.

The Indochina states are traditionally in China's sphere of influence, politically, economically, and culturally. There has been a long history of cooperation and engagement between them. Through various multilateral forums, the Southeast Asian countries engage China in a set of relationships that builds confidence and trust. China's multilateral cooperation in the Mekong River Basin is a natural extension of these networks of interdependency. Similarly, in Central Asia, China is a dominant actor. The Shanghai Cooperation Organization enables China to exert its influence over the region. In this context, China is willing to adopt a step-by-step approach to strengthening water cooperation with Kazakhstan.

Furthermore, Kazakhstan is the major player in Central Asia and its security partnership with China is vital for China's role in the region. Kazakhstan is crucial for China's fight against separatism, extremism, and terrorism. China also has significant economic and energy stakes in Kazakhstan: the country is an important source of oil imports to China as well as a transit state for the Turkmenistan-China natural gas pipeline. China thus has ample strategic reasons to be more cooperative with Kazakhstan in managing their shared water resources. In sum, China's cooperation with Kazakhstan is unusual and unlikely to be replicated with other riparians.

Joint development and a bilateral water management/sharing arrangement between China and India are a non-starter at the present moment. In contrast to its relations with Indochina states and Kazakhstan, China's relations with India suffer from a trust deficit and are often thorny. India has never historically been in China's sphere of influence. Culturally, there is little understanding between them. China sees India as a regional power while it sees itself as a global power. It does not place relations with India in the same category as its relations with the United States, Europe, Russia, and even Japan. Although a potential competitor, China has a low regard for India: to China, India's democracy and form of government are messy, and Indian society backward and disorderly. Hence, it considers comparisons with India to be demeaning. While it does not want relations with India to deteriorate, it also does not see significant improvements in its relations with India, as the outstanding issues between them – Tibet, the Dalai Lama, and border disputes – are intractable. A 2012 Pew Survey is particularly revealing of Chinese attitudes towards India.[40] In the survey, only 23 per cent of Chinese have a positive opinion of India, as against a 62 per cent negative opinion. Additionally, only 39 per cent of Chinese view relations with India as one of cooperation, significantly down from 53 per cent in 2010.

The lack of trust between China and India is not helped by the fact that there are no robust multilateral mechanisms in South Asia that engage China. South Asian geopolitics and the lack of regional mechanisms for dealing with conflict in South Asia make it difficult for water conflicts to be resolved. The South Asian Association for Regional Cooperation (SAARC) is the only existing multilateral mechanism in South Asia. However, it is a forum that discusses the least controversial issues. Furthermore, China is not a part of SAARC.[41] The avenues for confidence-building are therefore missing, presenting a big obstacle for enhancing riparian cooperation. Water issues between India and its co-riparians are often dealt with bilaterally. But even in these agreements, South Asian politics occasionally intrudes. For instance, India and Pakistan interpret the Indus Treaty differently and view the water allocation arrangements as unfair. Moreover, while the Ganges Water Treaty greatly reduces friction between India and Bangladesh, problems related to the Teesta River water sharing and India's plans to construct the Tipaimukh Dam on the Barak River have created further bilateral issues.

In the Brahmaputra, therefore, not only are the risks of cooperation to China's sovereignty and autonomy substantial, China also does not gain significant political and economic benefits from cooperating with India. In China's view, any significant movement towards joint development and water sharing is contingent on improvements in other aspects of its relations with India. Tibet is a security and sovereignty issue, and any proposal for jointly developing resources in that area would be a hard sell to the Chinese. Moreover, China is reluctant to give up the strategic advantages it enjoys as upstream riparian; should relations with

India significantly deteriorate in an extreme worst-case scenario, water is a tool that China can wield against India. There are also limited economic gains from cooperating with India on joint hydroelectric projects. China's infrastructure building skills, particularly in constructing dams, are superior to India's, and its financial muscles are also stronger.

Conclusion

Transboundary rivers as an issue in Sino-Indian relations present opportunities for both conflict and cooperation. Left on its own, without a comprehensive and effective framework for managing shared water resources, transboundary rivers can create huge rifts in relations. Yet, water can be a great unifier in many ways. Civilizations and cultures have been built around rivers; for neighbours that share water resources, rivers can be a means to enhance understanding as well as the exchange and flow of goods, people, and ideas. There are potential areas in which riparian cooperation between China and India can be enhanced. However, there are also tremendous difficulties that are part of the larger complexities of the relationship between the two countries. Developing an overarching independent transboundary river policy on both sides that is not subject to the vagaries of broader political relations would provide a firm basis for cooperation. Delinking the management of shared water resources from other contentious issues between China and India is therefore a first step towards greater water cooperation. It would, however, take substantial political will and effort from top policymakers on both sides to move in this direction.

The government apparatuses on both sides also need to be organised to deal with transboundary rivers. China, in particular, does not pay sufficient attention to managing its international rivers. This could prove costly for China in the long run, as its water resources and those of its neighbours become more stressed in the future. However, the problem is not only on China's side. Although India's apparatus for managing international rivers is better developed than China's, given that it has bilateral water treaties with Pakistan, Bangladesh, and Nepal, like China's MOWR, the Indian Ministry of Water Resources' main priority is intra-state water disputes and the development of integrated river basin management within its borders. For instance, its 2002 National Water Policy dealt only with water issues as they pertain to India internally.

Despite the current dim prospects for in-depth cooperation between China and India on water issues, there is a silver lining to the difficulties. The Chinese leadership's increasing focus on environmental issues and sustainable growth, specifically "sustainable use of water resources" as encapsulated in its 2011 No. 1 Policy Document on water resources reform,[42] could provide greater incentive for Chinese policymakers to look for ways to manage the country's international rivers more efficiently, including cooperation with its neighbours. Moreover, as India rises and becomes a serious competitor to China, China will be forced to re-examine its ties with India. There are indications that Chinese leaders have begun to reassess India's strategic value, as signified by the fact that Li Keqiang made India his first official trip overseas as Premier. India's alignment with the United States is also a source of concern for China, incentivising China to minimise conflicts and strengthen relations with India. China's "peripheral diplomacy", launched by President Xi Jinping in a work conference in October 2013, suggests that it intends to place greater weight on improving relations with its neighbours, including India. Xi has also declared that his "historic mission" is to further the strategic partnership between China and India.[43]

As China gradually adjusts its attitudes and policies towards India, there are opportunities for both sides to move closer on water issues. Both countries should work towards strengthening dialogue and cooperation in less sensitive areas, which will help build trust and confidence between them. Implementation of the hydrological data-sharing MOUs should be more rigorous and the terms of the MOUs enhanced. The signing of an MOU during Indian Prime Minister Manmohan Singh's trip to China in October 2013 that extends the period in which China would share hydrological data with India shows that China may be amenable to increased cooperation in this area. The expert-level mechanism that has been established should expand the range of issues discussed to include flood control and disaster management.

China and India could cooperate on protecting the waters of the Himalaya against environmental degradation. In addition, they could also collaborate on research into the impact of climate change on the Himalayan glaciers. China and India signed an MOU in October 2009, ahead of the 2010 UN Climate Conference in Copenhagen, agreeing to cooperate on climate change issues internationally, as well as in the area of research on the effects of climate change in the Himalaya. The MOU should be given greater substance, and a task force established to help spread costs and bring together expertise from both sides. This step-by-step approach to increasing cooperation on water issues will help enhance prospects for establishing joint development and water-sharing arrangements between China and India in the longer run.

Notes

1 Interview with experts in a Chinese think tank, 11 February 2014.
2 Ibid.
3 Roy Gardner, Elinor Ostrom, and James Walker, "The Nature of Common-Pool Resource Problems," *Rationality and Society*, 2/3, 1990, p. 335.
4 Ashok Subramanian, Bridget Brown, and Aaron Wolf, *Reaching Across the Waters: Facing the Risks of Cooperation in International Waters*, Washington, D.C.: The World Bank, 2012, p. 10.
5 Low-intensity conflict is defined by the US Army as "a political-military confrontation between contending states or groups below conventional war and above the routine, peaceful competition among states". US Army and US Air Force, *FM 100–20/AFP 3–20: Military Operations in Low Intensity Conflict*, Washington, DC: Department of the Army, 1991, http://www2.gwu.edu/~nsarchiv/NSAEBB/NSAEBB63/doc4.pdf.
6 Jian Xie et al., *Addressing China's Water Scarcity: Recommendations for Selected Water Resource Management Issues,* Washington, D.C.: The World Bank, 2009, p. xxi.

7 The World Bank, *India: Diagnostic Assessment of Select Environmental Challenges: An Analysis of Physical and Monetary Losses of Environmental Health and Natural Resources, Volume 1*, Washington, D.C.: The World Bank, 2013, p. iv.
8 Ministry of Water Resources, The People's Republic of China, *2007–2008 Annual Report*, www.mwr.gov.cn/english/2007–2008.doc. Water availability of 1,000–1,700 cubic meters per person is regarded as a situation of water stress; less than 1,000 cubic meters indicates extreme water stress.
9 Jintian Yang, Chazhong Ge, and Shuting Gao, *Corporatisation of Urban Water Supply and Wastewater Treatment Facilities in China*, 2000, http://www.caep.org.cn/english/paper/CORPORATISATIN-OF-URBAN-WATER-SUPPLY-2000-by-GE-Chazhong.pdf.
10 Andrea Hart, "Water Demand-Supply Gap Rising At Alarming Rate, Report Shows", *Circle of Blue*, 2 December 2009, http://www.circleofblue.org/waternews/2009/world/news-water-demand-supply-gap-rising-at-alarming-rate-report-shows/.
11 Ibid.
12 Press Information Bureau, Government of India, "Per Capita Water Availability", 26 April 2012, http://pib.nic.in/newsite/erelease.aspx?relid=82676.
13 WWF India, "Indian industry underestimating water related risks in a new research from WWF-India and Accenture", 5 March 2013, http://www.wwfindia.org/news_facts/?8640.
14 IDSA Task Force Report, *Water Security for India: The External Dynamics*, New Delhi: Institute for Defence Studies and Analyses (IDSA), 2010, p. 5.
15 Brahma Chellaney, *Water: Asia's New Battleground*, Washington, DC: Georgetown University Press, 2011, p. 152.
16 IDSA Task Force Report, *Water Security*, p. 40.
17 Ibid., p. 45.
18 Ibid., p. 44.
19 Ibid., p. 47.
20 See, for example, Kun Yang, Hui Wu, Jun Qin, Changgui Lin, Wenjun Tang, and Yingying Chen, "Recent Climate Changes over the Tibetan Plateau and their Impacts on Energy and Water Cycle: A Review", *Global and Planetary Change*, 112, 2014, p. 89.
21 Environment and Development Desk, Department of Information and International Relations, Central Tibetan Administration, *The Impacts of Climate Change on the Tibetan Plateau: A Synthesis of Recent Science and Tibetan* Research, 2010, p. ii, http://www.tew.org/archived/2010/climatechangereport.pdf.
22 "Water Law of the People's Republic of China", *China.org.cn*, http://www.china.org.cn/english/government/207454.htm.
23 Ministry of Water Resources, The People's Republic of China, "Department of International Cooperation, Science and Technology", http://www.mwr.gov.cn/english/d07.html.
24 Selina Ho, "River Politics: China's Policies Towards the Mekong and the Brahmaputra in Comparative Perspective," *Journal of Contemporary China*, 23/85, January 2014, pp. 16–17.
25 James E. Nickum, "The Upstream Superpower: China's International Rivers," in Olli Varies, Cecilia Tortajada and Asit K. Biswas, eds., *Management of Transboundary Rivers and Lakes*, Berlin: Springer, 2008.
26 Ibid., p. 230.
27 Ho, "River Politics", p. 5.

28 Evan S. Medeiros, *China's International Behavior: Activism, Opportunism, and Diversification*, Santa Monica: Rand Corporation, 2009, p. 142.
29 Coined by Jairam Ramesh, Indian Member of Parliament. See "'Chindia' still vibrant idea", *The Economic Times*, 27 March 2014, http://articles.economictimes.indiatimes.com/2014-03-27/news/48630342_1_india-and-china-chinese-state-run-global-times-chinese-public-opinion.
30 Jonathan Holslag, "Assessing the Sino-Indian Water Dispute", *Journal of International Affairs*, 64/2 Spring/Summer 2011, p. 3.
31 Ho, "River Politics", p. 10.
32 Sebastian Biba, "Desecuritization in China's Behavior towards its Transboundary Rivers: the Mekong River, the Brahmaputra River, and the Irtysh and Ili Rivers," *Journal of Contemporary China*, 23/85, January 2014, p. 38.
33 Ibid.
34 One MOU, signed in May 2013, is to renew an expiring MOU; the other, signed in October 2013, extends the period for sharing hydrological data. See Table 10.1.
35 Biba, "Desecuritization", p. 38.
36 Brian Orland, "Brahmaputra Dams Promise Prosperity but at a Big Cost", *The New York Times*, 5 March 2013, http://india.blogs.nytimes.com/2013/03/05/brahmaputra-dams-promise-prosperity-but-at-a-big-cost/?_php=true&_type=blogs&_r=0.
37 Press Information Bureau, Government of India, "River Linking Projects", 4 December 2012, http://pib.nic.in/newsite/erelease.aspx?relid=89898.
38 Subramanian et al., *Reaching Across the Waters*, p. 3.
39 Institute for Defence Studies and Analyses, *Water Security*, p. 50.
40 Pew Research Global Attitudes Project, "Growing Concerns in China about Inequality, Corruption", 16 October 2012, http://www.pewglobal.org/2012/10/16/chapter-2-china-and-the-world/.
41 China is an observer at SAARC meetings. See South Asian Association for Regional Cooperation (SAARC), "Cooperation with Observers," http://saarc-sec.org/Cooperation-with-Observers/13/.
42 Martin Griffiths, Jin Hai and Liu Dengwei, "Water Security in China and Europe: Lessons and Links", *Water21*, International Water Association, June 2013, http://www.iwapublishing.com/water21/june-2013/water-security-china-and-europe-lessons-and-links.
43 Ananth Krishnan, "My Mission is to Better India Ties: Xi", *The Hindu*, 21 March 2014, http://www.thehindu.com/todays-paper/tp-international/my-mission-is-to-better-india-ties-xi/article5812635.ece.

Conclusion
Ways forward for China–India cooperation

Kanti Bajpai, Huang Jing and Kishore Mahbubani

Over ten chapters, our authors make an assessment of the conflicting and common interests of China and India in relation to economics, environment, energy, and water. They describe the state of interaction between the two countries but also outline policy options which address the differences between them as well as the opportunities for cooperation in these four areas. The chapters link their assessments of the past and present to prescriptions for the future. An underlying theme of the volume is that China and India can indeed cooperate, that the need and opportunities for collaboration have to be articulated more systematically and creatively, that geopolitical and functional concerns are inter-related, and that it will take leadership to bring the two countries more decisively together. Here we attempt to pull together the key recommendations on cooperation in each of the chapters and conclude with some general observations about the possibility of cooperation that we abstract from the chapters as well as the conference discussions in Singapore where the papers were originally presented.

Cooperating in economics

We begin with economics, which has been at the heart of China–India cooperation thus far. The chapters by Prem Shankar Jha, Zhao Gancheng, Sanjaya Baru, and Hu Shisheng make a number of proposals for China–India cooperation with regard to investment, bilateral and regional trade, and the reform of global financial institutions. Jha argues that although the Chinese and Indian models of development have produced rather brittle economies that could be at risk in the years to come, there is at least one substantial possibility of cooperation. Essentially, China's vast supply of liquid capital could help build Indian infrastructure. Jha's suggestion is strongly supported by both Baru and Hu in their analyses of China–India trade.

China's financial reserves have been estimated at US $3.82 trillion at the end of 2013.[1] The Jha, Hu and Baru proposal is for China to deploy some of these massive reserves in Indian infrastructure projects. Over the next five years alone, India's infrastructure needs funding to the tune of US $1 trillion.[2] With China looking to diversity its portfolio of investments, the Indian infrastructure sector is increasingly attractive. Thus, in response to an Indian request going back to 2012, in February 2014 a Chinese planning group submitted an ambitious proposal whereby China would have invested up to US $300 billion – fully one-third of India's funding requirements – in Indian infrastructure projects including in railways, roads, telecom, and nuclear and solar power.[3] As Xi Jinping's visit to India approached, the Chinese offer had seemingly been reduced to US $100 billion. In the event, China offered only US $20 billion – far lower than early estimates suggested but nonetheless an enticing promissory note.[4]

Having said this, it is useful to think about the reasons why Chinese investment was apparently whittled down from $300 billion to $20 billion. Decision-making on the Chinese side is opaque, so it is hard to know what may have transpired in Beijing, but a number of hurdles likely got in the way on the Indian side, even though New Delhi had solicited the investment in the first place. For one thing, key ministries in India, including the Ministry of Home Affairs and the Ministry of Defence, were concerned about the implications of such massive Chinese investments in infrastructure, particularly if the infrastructure was located near the disputed borders in India's northeast and Kashmir.[5] A second hurdle was economic. One view is that Chinese investment will help correct the trade deficit, but an opposite view is that infrastructure investment might actually widen the gap. As Biswajit Dhar, Director General of Research and Information System for Developing Countries (RIS), New Delhi, notes: "Allowing Chinese investment into [the] infrastructure sector looks a bit dodgy from the look of it as it will lead to higher import content, [which is] likely to worsen the trade deficit between the two countries".[6] A third hurdle may have simply been the capacity of the Indian bureaucracy to respond to such a large offer. As at least nine different ministries were involved in negotiations with the Chinese side, considerable coordination was required, and this probably failed to occur in time.[7] China, sensing the difficulties, may have therefore backed off, concluding that notwithstanding India's dire need for infrastructure funding, it is not geared to absorbing large investments.

This suggests that the two governments will have to plot a careful course. Beginning slowly and with smaller amounts is a sensible strategy. Steering clear of infrastructure investments in the border areas such as the northeast and Kashmir would also seem to be a sensible decision. There are many other parts of India where Chinese investments would be better utilised. Getting the Chinese to build infrastructure such as industrial parks, in which they themselves then set up manufacturing units, would help bridge the trade deficit rather than increase it. Finally, India has to improve its ability to coordinate between various arms of its bureaucracy and between New Delhi and the state capitals if it is to absorb large amounts of Chinese investment funding.

Trade has been the greatest success story of China–India relations since the early 1990s, burgeoning from a mere US $200 million to nearly US $70 billion in the past few years. However, the trade deficit – chronically in favour of China – has introduced a fresh set of tensions in the relationship. Strictly speaking, on economic grounds, it should not matter that India runs a deficit with China. As Amitendu Palit points out, India runs a deficit with 16 of its top 25 trading partners.[8]

The deficit with China has become politically charged, however. This is partly because of geopolitical tensions and competition with China, but it is also partly because, as Baru notes in his chapter, there are business interests in India that fear imports from China and are frustrated by their inability to penetrate the Chinese market. These interests are working with Indian business associations and the Indian media to draw attention to the deficit and in particular to what they consider to be unfair business practices on the part of Chinese enterprises. Not surprisingly, the largest number of Indian complaints to the World Trade Organization regarding "dumping" is directed towards China.[9] Chinese analysts, including Hu, generally regard Indian complaints as being exaggerated and political in nature and retort that the deficit arises largely from India's weakness in manufacturing rather than from Chinese trade malpractices.

Baru and Hu consider the deficit and propose a number of remedies. These include FDI from China to offset the trade deficit, collaborating in the global supply chain, the easing of Chinese regulations for India's pharmaceutical exports, cooperating in third markets, and upholding WTO trading norms against the new trans-regional norms being negotiated by the US in Europe and the Asia-Pacific which act as protectionist barriers against Chinese and Indian exports.

The Indian government has already suggested that one way of dealing with the deficit is through greater Chinese investments in India. While this would certainly lower the deficit, Chinese FDI in India cannot by itself solve the problem given the magnitude of the gap. Palit has shown the average flow of FDI into India is US $30 billion, while the deficit with China in 2013–14 was US $36 billion. He concludes that it is unrealistic to suppose that China can commit to inflows of US $30 billion every year.[10]

The notion of Indian and Chinese companies working together in global value chains is an attractive one, though it largely depends on public and private sector enterprises taking the initiative. However, the two governments might be able to help in identifying promising areas of collaboration and making it easier for businesses on both sides to work together. This might involve everything from issuing business and work visas more readily, to organising trade fairs, to lowering restrictions on investment flows, to providing industrial parks and free trade zones. It is also important for both sides to re-examine their trade regulations and trade infrastructure to ensure that obstacles to the flow of goods and services are reduced if not eliminated, including in areas where the other side has a comparative advantage, such as pharmaceuticals in the case of India.

Cooperating in third markets is a much greater challenge. Once again, the initiative for this probably resides with businesses rather than governments, but governments can help identify opportunities and niches. China and India have tried to cooperate in the area of energy markets but so far with no great success (as we note below). As for forging a common position against the new trans-regional trade agreements, this appears increasingly unlikely, as Beijing begins to soften its stance towards membership in the TPP.[11] It is unclear why China seems to be reconsidering its position towards the TPP, but part of the reason is geopolitics. There is a view in China that the TPP is part of the US's strategy to contain burgeoning Chinese power.[12] Others see economic motives behind the TPP, with the US trying either to respond to China's manufacturing dominance by keeping it out of a major trade pact or getting China to open its markets to the US by eventually bringing it into the pact on American terms.[13] In either case, the strong labour standards and other social clauses in the pact would strengthen Washington's hand. From Beijing's viewpoint, joining the TPP would bring China "inside the tent" and position it to influence the nature of the agreement.

In these circumstances, the choices for India are threefold: push harder for the Regional Comprehensive Economic Partnership (RCEP), move towards Free Trade Area of the Asia-Pacific (FTAAP) membership, and open talks on the TPP. How likely is each of these? First, New Delhi will almost certainly persist with the RCEP since that is the most congenial regional trade agreement given India's political economy. Second, India could at the same time begin to explore the possibility of joining the FTAAP. As India has moved closer to joining APEC, with Chinese and US support, the FTAAP would be a fairly natural move. Third, India could consider joining the TPP at some point as well. TPP membership at this stage looks the most remote since it promises to have much more stringent requirements, particularly social clause requirements. In each of these cases, New Delhi will need to deal with China. On the TPP, it may be worthwhile for India to use the Strategic Economic Dialogue with China to get a clearer sense of Beijing's thinking. If Beijing indicates that it is interested in moving forward on membership, then New Delhi's attitude to the TPP may have to change. Like China, it may have to consider membership, or the two countries may decide to approach the TPP together.

China and India have both complained that global financial institutions are dysfunctional because they respond to the priorities and political preferences of the rich industrialised countries and do not accommodate the views of the rising powers as well as the developing countries. Cooperation between Beijing and New Delhi would seem to be a rational project. Thus, Zhao argues that China and India could cooperate within multilateral institutions such as the IMF and World Bank on issues such as Special Drawing Rights (SDRs) and voting shares, the selection of IMF and World Bank heads, and in institutions such as the G20 and particularly BRICS.

China and India would both like their quotas (denominated in SDRs) and voting shares in the IMF to be increased. Changes in the quotas and voting shares were agreed upon in the reforms of 2010. However, they have still not entered into force. The two countries have asked publicly for reform, as recently as September 2013 during the 6th China–India Financial Dialogue in Beijing.[14] Amongst the key countries which have not accepted the reforms is the United States. Without US acceptance, the IMF cannot reach the acceptance threshold required for entry-into-force. As things stand, China and India's joint stand may be in danger of breaking. The IMF appears to be on the verge of including the yuan as part of the SDR basket of currencies (along with the dollar, yen, pound, and euro).[15] If the yuan is accepted as part of the SDR basket, it will in effect become a reserve currency, and the internationalisation of the renminbi will have taken a big step forward. Beijing may well be less vociferous about the need for fundamental reform in this situation.

China and India have also made clear that they would like to see the US and Europe loosen their stranglehold of the directorship of the World Bank and IMF, respectively. After Dominique Strauss-Kahn stepped down as Managing Director of the Fund in 2011, Christine Lagarde of France was elected head, in keeping with the norm that a European should lead the Fund. At the time, China and India, along with Russia, Brazil, and South Africa, criticised the norm.[16] Beijing called for "fairness, transparency and merit" in the selection of the new head, but it did not rock the boat.[17] New Delhi certainly made it clear that it would like to see a non-Western candidate in the fray.[18] In the end, both powers conceded that it was not possible to appoint a non-European Managing Director, presumably in recognition of the fact that the voting structure in the body militates against this.[19] While China and India drew back from an outright and protracted challenge in 2011, they may well respond differently in the future. If so, the question is whether or not the two powers will coordinate on a preferred candidate, perhaps including someone from China or India.[20]

China and India have cooperated in international institutions, including in the G20 and BRICS, particularly after the global economic crisis of 2008. As the economic crisis receded, the G20 lost its verve and relevance. BRICS, by contrast, has gradually grown in importance, from a "talk shop" to a more active organisation. Its biggest initiative is the New Development Bank, which was launched at the Brazil summit in 2014. China and India have been central to the setting up of the bank, essentially striking a deal between them to assuage the concerns of Brazil, India, Russia, and South Africa on China dominating the institution.

The deal showed that pragmatism and good sense can prevail between China and India. In deference to the anxieties of the smaller economies in BRICS, including itself, India pressed for an equal vote for each power based on equal contributions to the subscribed capital fund of US $100 billion. At the same time, it was agreed that China would contribute the largest amount – US $41 billion – to the contingent reserve arrangement (CRA) of US $100 billion, with Brazil, India, and Russia contributing US $18 billion each and South Africa US $5 billion. Also in a gesture to China, Shanghai was chosen as the headquarters of the bank. To placate New Delhi, which had wanted to host the bank, the first head of the institution will be Indian.[21] Leadership of the bank will thereafter rotate every five years, though the Indian head will get a six-year term.[22]

The latest instance of China–India cooperation is the Asian Infrastructure Investment Bank (AIIB). Membership has quickly expanded beyond Asia to include all major economies except the US, Japan, and Canada as founding members. As we noted in the Introduction, the AIIB is a Beijing-led initiative, with India a founding member. Again, as in the New Development Bank, there are fears of Chinese dominance and worries about the Bank's mission, rules, and decision-making procedures, but New Delhi appears comfortable with the institution and its ability to help shape it by being in at the inception.

China's new-found economic activism has also led it to propose two new silk routes, one land and one maritime, which would connect Asia with Europe. Beijing is pressing hard to establish the Belt and Road Initiative and has committed up to US $900 billion to the project, including funding from the AIIB and the Silk Road Fund. The Chinese government is keen to get Indian participation, but New Delhi has so far held off, fearing that the initiative will draw large parts of Asia, including South and Southeast Asia, firmly into China's economic and political orbit, improve its access to natural resources, and provide it with ports and other infrastructure that will help encircle India.[23] To bring India in, Beijing has suggested India can choose the extent and nature of its involvement. It has also said that the silk routes are compatible with India's idea of a new Spice Route and its Mausam initiative. The Spice Route seeks to link India with countries in Europe, and Mausam is aimed at Sri Lanka, the Seychelles, and Mauritius.[24] In spite of two summits between Xi Jinping and Narendra Modi in 2014 and 2015, and China's attempts to entice India, New Delhi has not been persuaded to join. The problem for India is that by staying out of the scheme, it risks being isolated and giving China freedom to shape the idea to its advantage. The pressure to join will therefore intensify.

To conclude, China and India have moved steadily forward to increase their mutual economic interactions, from the Rajiv Gandhi 1988 visit to Beijing onwards. The biggest current challenge is the trade deficit. China is more than ever aware of the political symbolism of the chronic deficit as well as the domestic interests in India lobbying against open trade. It has promised to help reduce the trade gap. India has shown considerable patience so far in dealing with the issue, but looking ahead it has to improve its own manufacturing and export performance. Much bigger than trade is investment, primarily from China to India. Here not just bilateral flows but also multilateral flows (from the New Development Bank, AIIB, and silk routes scheme) could involve the two countries in exciting cooperative ventures in the future.

Cooperating on environment and energy

The economic discussions in the first four chapters are followed by four chapters on environment (climate change) and energy, two areas that have grown in salience over the past decade as global warming has forced itself on to the international agenda and as China and India have rapidly industrialised. While China–India interactions here have not been as extensive and deep as in economics, they could be of considerable significance in the decades ahead, with signs of conflict and opportunities for cooperation already apparent.

As the chapters show, China–India cooperation in international climate change negotiations has been fairly substantial thus far, but its future is uncertain. Thus Arunabha Ghosh notes, with the "growing divergence in their economic models and resource demands", China and India's climate change cooperation "might come under strain". That time may have arrived. The China–US climate change deal of November 2014 is a signal that the two superpowers are ready to work together and that China–India cooperation may be a sideshow. China and the US will collaborate on CO2 capture and storage (CCS) and will increase funding to the US-China Clean Energy Research Centre. They have also pledged to work together at the Conference of the Parties to UNFCCC in Paris in December 2015.[25]

China and India have of course reaffirmed their commitment to climate change cooperation, but this increasingly appears to be fairly nominal. The joint statement on climate change issued during Prime Minister Narendra Modi's visit to China in May 2015 merely affirms their existing positions on bilateral and multilateral efforts to combat climate change and all said and done is a rather anodyne document.[26] That the US and China will lead, and India will go its own way substantially, is reinforced by recent US–India interactions on climate change. There was hope that the US and India too would strike a climate deal when President Barack Obama visited India in January 2015. In the event, the two countries were unable to agree on a deal that was in any way comparable to the US–China agreement, in large part because New Delhi was unwilling to commit itself to a date by which its emissions would peak. As a result, the two sides merely agreed on a range of bilateral deals on technology and research and committed themselves to signing a five-year Memorandum of Understanding (MOU) on "Energy Security, Clean Energy and Climate Change".[27]

Does this mean the end of China–India cooperation on climate change negotiations? Not necessarily. It continues to be in the interest of both governments to use each other in dealing with other parties. Beijing and New Delhi will find it useful to confront the US and other Western powers on issues such as commitments on emission limits, transfer of technology, and funding of the Clean Development Mechanism (CDM). They may also want to close ranks against those developing countries which regard China and India as part of the climate change problem rather than its solution.

Much more promising than climate change cooperation is the prospect of energy collaboration, to which we now turn. Abstracting from the four chapters, we suggest that there is agreement on the following broad areas of possible cooperation: renewable energy; research cooperation; and collaboration in third countries.

What are the prospects of cooperation in renewable energy? The four chapters agree that there is considerable scope. Thus, Pan Jiahua advocates a new, ecologically sustainable approach for development and recommends China–India cooperation within the renewable energy sector, including Chinese hydropower from its Tibetan rivers. Arabinda Mishra and Neha Pahuja show that China and India's carbon mitigation programmes are based mainly on renewable energy and suggest that the two countries can work together on decentralised energy projects. China has great competence in decentralised biogas, stove, and solar systems while India has great experience in decentralised solar systems. Ghosh too urges cooperation in decentralised energy. India is increasingly experimenting with combinations of different renewables and the use of smart microgrids. Ghosh argues that supporting business models are vital for decentralised energy, and India could share its experiences with China. Ghosh also recommends cooperation in wind energy, where India could learn from China's mostly inland wind power systems and China from India's mostly coastal system.

The two countries seem quite well placed to cooperate on renewables, with China potentially being a huge supplier and India a huge buyer. Pan's idea of hydropower cooperation is an intriguing one given the fears of China–India conflict over shared river waters. If it is technologically and economically viable, however, such cooperation could help transform the countries' hydrological relationship for the better and contribute to energy security, particularly in their respective borderlands. China is far and away the global leader in renewable energy and so could play a major part in India's energy future. According to the International Renewable Energy Agency (IRENA), China has 70 per cent of the world's solar manufacturing capacity and employs 3.4 million workers in the renewable energy sector, with 1.6 million in the photovoltaic solar sector alone. It also leads in the number of jobs in wind, solar heating and cooling, small and large hydropower, and biomass and biogas.[28]

At the same time, India's demand for renewable energy is massive. It has set a target of 100 gigawatts of solar power and 60 gigawatts of wind power by 2022, which is roughly five times its present renewable energy capacity.[29] While Indian capacity in these two areas is growing, it is clear that the country cannot meet those targets through domestic production. India's solar power potential has been estimated at 750 gigawatts while its current capacity is only 3 gigawatts.[30] Domestic manufacturing capacity at present is only 700–800 megawatts. Thus, India has recently indicated that it will launch a tender for a 15 gigawatts solar project, roughly equivalent to half its current total renewable energy capacity.[31] It is estimated that India will also need US $220 billion in funding for its 2022 targets of solar and wind power.[32] Clearly, China, given its massive manufacturing capacity and sovereign funds, could be a vital partner in respect of both solar and wind energy infrastructure (and other renewables) and energy financing.

China and India could work together not just on existing renewable energy technologies but also on future technologies. In his chapter, Pan suggests that China and India can cooperate in research on ecologically sound development practices in agriculture and industry. He gives the example of emerging Chinese agricultural practices that are more ecologically responsible, including the use of biodigester wastes as fertilizers. These experiments might be adapted to India. Mishra and Pahuja recommend that the two countries collaborate on energy research, especially in biomass and solar energy. They also urge the two countries to work together in supporting research into biotechnology applications in agriculture. As climate change leads to global warming and extreme weather events, food security will be threatened. Biotechnologies might help develop crops that are more resistant to heat and other extreme weather phenomena and might produce seed variants that boost food output. China and India could lead the way in addressing Asia's food security challenge. Ghosh's chapter draws attention to the linkages between food, water, energy, and climate. He argues that perhaps even more than climate change mitigation, the two countries should be thinking seriously about cooperation on adaptation. On mitigation, he notes that in the run-up to the 2009 Copenhagen negotiations on climate change, Beijing and New Delhi had agreed to a rich programme of cooperation including technology demonstrations, energy efficiency, renewables, clean coal, methane recovery, afforestation, and transportation and sustainable habitats. On adaptation, he suggests that the menu of cooperation could include water efficiency, drought resistant crops, and flood infrastructure for rural and urban settings, amongst others.

While these are potentially fruitful areas of research cooperation – and surely there are more – the record is rather poor. Why so? Part of the answer is geopolitics – that is, mistrust between the two governments arising from a sense of insecurity vis-à-vis the other that has led them to restrict scientific and technical contacts. For example, both governments look upon official links between national research institutions with suspicion, fearing that the other will get more out of the interaction. Part of the answer, though, is cultural and historical – namely, the tendency of Chinese and Indian officials, scientists, and engineers to look for research collaboration and inspiration primarily from the advanced industrialised countries. Another related factor is ignorance of each other's scientific and technical capacities. Zha therefore argues that at this stage the two governments can do at least three things to overcome the lack of mutual knowledge – foster a community of energy policy researchers who would carefully disentangle why cooperation has succeeded or failed in the past; invite an international studies community to examine the possibility of cooperation going forward; and promote exchange between Chinese and Indian scientists, engineers, and policymakers.

A final dimension of energy cooperation is working together in third countries. Interestingly, none of the chapters in this section are particularly sanguine about the prospects for collaboration here. While there is a record of cooperation in third countries, as both Ghosh and Zha Daojiong point out, it is rather modest, and there have been many occasions of competition. Ghosh notes that China and India cooperated in Sudan (2005) and Syria (2005) and came to agreements on the whole range of petrochemical cooperation in 2006. In 2012, Ghosh notes, the ONGC and CNPC agreed to joint exploration in Myanmar, Syria, and Sudan. On the other hand, they competed in Sudan, Iran, Angola, Kazakhstan, Ecuador, Myanmar, Nigeria, and Russia between 2002 and 2008.

As Zha shows, in competitive situations, India has usually been bested by China. The important point he makes, though, is that the cases of cooperation and the cases of outright competition need careful analysis. It may well be that geopolitical competition between China and India accounts for the negative record. However, Zha notes, a number of other factors are at work, including the role of host governments and international oil companies present in those third countries.[33] He remains cautiously optimistic about the possibility of future collaboration. Ghosh, by contrast, feels that China and India are better off trying to collaborate on the construction of energy infrastructure such as ports and pipelines as envisaged in the 2012 Memorandum of Understanding signed by the two governments. They might also agree to swap arrangements – India's gas production from the Sakhalin fields for Chinese gas from the Middle East – with attendant savings on transportation costs.

Crucial to the prospects, however, is the role of the giant Chinese and Indian oil companies. As Zha suggests, and as Luke Patey has shown in his book on the China National Petroleum Corporation (CNPC) and ONGC Videsh Limited (OVL) in Sudan, much depends on the interests, influence, and interactions of these semi-autonomous companies, whatever the directives of the two governments. The CNPC in particular is no ordinary oil company, as it possesses enormous prestige and power in Chinese politics and within the Communist Party.[34] Zha suggests that while Chinese and Indian oil companies have so far mostly been unsuccessful in the joint acquisition and operation of oil fields in third countries, this may not be altogether a dead end. More important for Zha, though, is promoting trade and investment in energy-related equipment so that Chinese and Indian companies can carve out market niches. Ghosh, in contrast, argues for a bigger programme of cooperation, including joint consortia for pipeline construction in Russia, Central Asia, and West Asia, swapping each other's oil and gas acquisitions, as well as joint development of energy infrastructure worldwide.

In sum, cooperation in energy could benefit both countries. There are attractive possibilities, particularly in renewable energy and more generally in joint research in various energy-related fields. Three areas not dealt with at any length in this volume suggest that the scope of cooperation could significantly expand: shale gas and shale oil deposits, nuclear energy, and smart cities. China is reputed to have shale gas deposits larger than the US and Canada combined (even if these deposits are difficult to exploit with current technology).[35] It also has the third largest recoverable shale oil deposits in the world, at 32,000 billion barrels.[36] India has about 5 per cent of China's technically recoverable shale gas deposits.[37] Its shale oil deposits are relatively small, at 3,800 billion barrels.[38] If China chooses to export shale gas and oil, India could be one of its biggest markets. Zha and Ghosh both briefly refer to the possibility of nuclear energy cooperation. China and India do have a minor history of cooperation. In 1995, China provided low-enriched uranium for India's Tarapur reactor when the US and France on non-proliferation grounds refused to provide fuel for the reactor (which the Americans had built in the 1950s).[39] Most recently, the China–India joint statements of 2014 and 2015 both refer to civilian nuclear energy cooperation in the interest of increasing clean energy consumption. One area of possible collaboration is in new civilian reactor technologies. China is working closely with Westinghouse to develop the new generation AP1000 reactors.[40] India could eventually access the new reactor technology from China. China and India could also cooperate on smart cities, which incorporate energy saving technologies, designs, procedures, and programmes. Both countries are looking to build smart cities on an unprecedented scale as they increasingly urbanise. China has more than 300 smart city proposals on the table, and India under Narendra Modi has projected up to 100 smart cities.[41]

Cooperating on river waters

The third area of potential cooperation is river waters, a shared resource that has become the object of some contention between China and India. Both India and China face a growing absolute scarcity of water as well as a relative scarcity alongside steadily increasing demand. So far, Chinese rhetoric and action on water issues have been more cooperative than competitive, but India remains concerned over Chinese dam building on the Yarlung Tsangpo/Brahmaputra and the possibility of Chinese water diversion on the Yarlung.

Uttam Kumar Sinha points out that while China and India cooperate on the sharing of hydrological data pertaining to the Brahmaputra as well as the Sutlej rivers, the question ahead is whether they can and should do more. Sinha argues that, in the absence of any formal agreements on water sharing and water harnessing, India must continue to engage China through "hydro-diplomacy", both bilaterally and regionally. Sinha notes that while India has a history of formal riverine agreements with its South Asian neighbours, China has avoided this mode of conflict management and cooperation. In his view, it is time for Beijing to consider formal understandings with India (and others) and integrated basin development.

Selina Ho by contrast looks at the prospects of future hydrological cooperation in the absence of a comprehensive framework to manage shared water resources. While Ho is not terribly optimistic, she suggests that delinking hydrological issues from other contentious issues would be helpful, even if difficult. In addition, she suggests that both countries, but especially China, need to build domestic capacity in dealing with international river water negotiations. The current understanding on data sharing could be enhanced and, for the future, the two sides need to explore the possibility of cooperating on the Himalayan glaciers that are threatened by climate change.

Ho contends that China only cooperates on international water issues – as it has with Kazakhstan in the case of the Ili and Irtysh rivers and with Southeast Asia in the case of the Mekong River – when it sees little risk to its sovereignty and autonomy, when it regards its interlocutors as much weaker, when there are larger strategic issues at stake, and when it has deep cultural ties with the other party. China's position on the Yarlung is also intrinsically linked with the Tibet issue and the still-unresolved border dispute with India. Further, the substantial trust deficit that exists between the two countries, along with a lack of discernible economic and political advantages for China, renders further bilateral cooperation in river water issues unlikely. This is a position that Sinha would not disagree with.

As Sinha and Ho note, there are broadly three concerns in India and amongst other lower riparians in South Asia. The first is that glacier melt in Tibet and the Himalayas will lead to flooding and rising sea levels and later could be the cause of diminished water flows. The second is that Chinese dam-building will have downstream ecological and water flow effects. The third is that China will seek to divert the Yarlung northwards to its drier provinces as part of its massive South-North Water Transfer Project.

Glacier melt is the most obvious common interest between China, India, and other lower riparians. The causes of glacier melt are complex but clearly climate change, local micro-climatic conditions, and human practices are key factors that need to be monitored. As both Sinha and Ho note, glacier melt is a key bilateral concern. Yet the prospects of cooperation here may not be great in part because the causes are global (climate change) but also in part because the latest scientific evidence suggests that glacier melt is not as alarming in this region as the International Panel on Climate Change (IPCC) had originally suggested, and that in any case the amount of melting varies between the Karakoram mountains in the west and the central and southeast Himalayan areas.[42]

China's dam-building activities on the Yarlung have caused a fair amount of worry in India. It has built a series of large dams at various points along the Yarlung, and there are plans for more. While Beijing has insisted that these pose no danger to countries downstream because they are run-of-the-river projects, India in particular is worried at least in part because of the lack of transparency in planning. Yet, officially, New Delhi has accepted that the dams have not in fact reduced the flow of water. In 2011, Foreign Minister S.M. Krishna stated publicly that:

> India trusts statements when the Government of China at the highest level assures the Prime Minister on the dam. . . . We trust but we also verify. We have verified Chinese claims on the dam being a run-of-the-river power project which does not store water. We are convinced that it is a run-of-the-river project. We constantly keep our surveillance across the border.[43]

The great fear is that China will build a dam at the so-called Great Bend on the Yarlung, a project that some suggest will be bigger than the Three Gorges, which may affect India.

Even more worrying for India is the possibility that China will divert the waters of the Yarlung northwards to its drier provinces. Beijing has insisted that it is not pursuing the Yarlung version of the diversion plan. *The Times of India* of October 25, 2006 reported perhaps the first official denial of any plans to divert the Yarlung, quoting Chinese foreign ministry spokesman Liu Jianchao to the effect that "China has no such plans to build a dam and divert water from Yarlung Zangbo (Brahmaputra) to the Yellow River".[44] In 2009, as Indian worries continued to grow and be expressed in public, Chinese officials once again formally denied that China planned to divert the river. In October 2011, Jiao Yong, Vice Minister of Water Resources, declared that "technical difficulties, environmental impacts and state relations" militated against diversion.[45] Here again, New Delhi has accepted Beijing's assurances but continues to use satellites to verify Chinese actions.[46]

For India, cooperation on dam-building would at the very least entail China being more transparent on its plans, restricting itself to run-of-the-river construction, and in the case of the Great Bend dam, shelving the plan altogether. In respect of water diversion, cooperation would mean China's staying with its stated decision not to divert the waters of the Yarlung. What are the incentives for China to be cooperative in both cases?

While it is true that China is in a position, both geographically and politically, to do whatever it pleases, there are domestic and international reasons for being cautious. Domestically, we note that while dam-building and water diversion have their supporters, they also have critics and dissenters, both at the decision-making and popular levels. For a number of economic, environmental, and political reasons, ambitious dam-building and water diversions are running into difficulties. China certainly has the funds to support dam-building and river diversion, but these projects will be costly. The long-term financial viability of these projects is also an issue, including operational and maintenance costs and the costs of externalities such as environmental damage. Environmental degradation and its attendant health and social consequences are increasingly salient concerns in China. Much of the growing environmental dissatisfaction in China arises from the country's breakneck industrialisation. It also arises from large-scale dam and river projects. The Three Gorges Dam is a case in point, but the eastern and central routes of the South-North Water Transfer Project, which have already been completed, have had significant environmental costs too.[47] There are political fears attached to dam-building and more so to water diversion. These include worries in the southern provinces that they may lose water to the north. A number of local communities along the diversion have already complained about the economic, environmental, and health costs to them when the benefits will largely go to the cities and towns of the northeast.[48]

China must also factor in the international diplomatic and political costs of building large dams upriver and particularly of diverting large volumes of water. If India is affected by China's water policies, Bangladesh is likely to be even more seriously affected. Beijing has slowly cultivated better relations with Dhaka and must weigh the consequences of alienating Bangladeshi opinion. So far, Bangladesh has been silent on the issue, at least with China. Dhaka's focus has been the sharing of the Ganges waters with India, and it has reserved most of its hydrological ire for New Delhi. However, China cannot count on Bangladesh continuing to turn a blind eye to developments on the Brahmaputra and allowing New Delhi to lead the diplomatic charge against Beijing.

Besides Bangladesh, Beijing must worry about the impact of its India policies on various Southeast Asian countries that are downstream on the Mekong and Salween, on which it has also constructed a series of dams.[49] While Chinese leaders have sought to reassure its Southeast Asian neighbours, the construction of a massive dam on the Brahmaputra or ambitious water diversion will frighten them. Southeast Asia is already fearful of China's new assertiveness on its territorial quarrels with Japan, the Philippines, and Vietnam in the East and South China Sea, respectively. Beijing's decision to ignore New Delhi's concerns on dams and diversion would further alarm the countries of Southeast Asia, which are much weaker than India.

In addition, India, Bangladesh, and Southeast Asia's worries could well be exploited by the US and could drive these countries closer to Washington. Since 2011, US authorities have increasingly spoken out against China's stand on the East and South China Sea territorial disputes. Chinese leaders must consider how far they can push India and Southeast Asian countries on river waters. While these countries all have strong economic and in some cases cultural, political, and diplomatic ties to China, Beijing must be mindful of antagonising them too much.

The case of the Myitsone Dam in Burma is a case in point. Burma's decision in 2011 to suspend the project, the cooling of relations with China, and the political and diplomatic opening that resulted for the US and other Western countries as well as India are a cautionary tale for Chinese leaders. China has mounted a vigorous campaign to refurbish its image in Burma and to reinvigorate the dam project, but the setback on the Myitsone Dam indicates that smaller, seemingly dependent countries can turn against China if pushed too hard.[50]

In short, China and India so far have cooperated on water, at least insofar as neither side has made decisions that would force the other's hand. China has held off on building a dam at the Great Bend and a diversion of the Yarlung. It has also begun to share some hydrological data with India. India has accepted Chinese assurances on water and has not internationalised its concerns. The great possibility ahead is to jointly tap the hydropower of the Yarlung in an ecologically responsible way and to move towards integrated basin development.

Five broad conclusions

As these chapters demonstrate, there is no easy path ahead for China and India in dealing with the bilateral challenges arising from their development path. Differences over trade imbalances, finance and investment, environmental challenges including climate change, energy and other natural resources, and shared river waters are not susceptible to quick and easy solutions. However, if the current state of bilateral relations is any indication for the future, Beijing and New Delhi are keen to fashion a closer and more enduring relationship and construct mechanisms for problem-solving and long-term cooperation.

We end here with some broad and general conclusions about the possibility of cooperation between China and India, drawing both on the chapters in the volume and the discussions held during the conference in Singapore.

First, traditional security and geopolitical concerns, on the one hand, and cooperation in economics, environment, energy, and water, on the other, are interrelated. None of our authors feel that China and India can afford to ignore security and geopolitics and isolate those concerns altogether from cooperation in other areas. Security and geopolitical differences engender mistrust, which sets limits to cooperation in economics, environment, energy, and water. On the other hand, Chinese and Indian leaders have over time pinned their hopes on the functionalist argument that cooperation in "low politics" will soften differences in "high politics". Thus, while security and geopolitics mistrust can set limits to cooperation, cooperation is important for the material benefits it brings and for its melioration of high politics differences. Zhao makes the important point that China and India for too long focused their diplomatic attention on settling the border conflict. Our analysis shows that it is important to pay attention to the high *and* low politics tracks and make progress in both even if one track sees quicker progress than the other.

Second, cooperation appears most likely in economics, followed by the environment and energy, and lastly water issues. International trade rules and the opening of the two economies have made the exchange of goods a relatively routine matter. The level of investment between the two countries is low, but both sides seem more open to capital flows from the other than in the past. Cooperation in international institutions also seems feasible, though China may break ranks with India in the coming years as its economy matures. While there are cooperative possibilities in the environment and energy, the record up to this point is not a strong one. Environmental degradation and growing energy demands could well force the two governments and business communities to consider cooperation more seriously, but again there are signs that on climate change China could break ranks and that on energy both countries may go their own way unless they look at newer areas of collaboration (shale gas and oil, new nuclear reactors, and the development of smart cities). With regard to water, China and India already have cooperated to a degree. China has thus far not altered the flow of water downriver and after discussions with India has agreed to share hydrological data. Cooperating beyond this, for instance on joint hydro-power projects and a comprehensive and integrated basin development plan, seems out of reach at the present.

Third, domestic politics and capability are key limiting factors in cooperation. Both leaderships are attentive to the political costs of cooperating. Neither can be seen to be "soft" on the other given that there are oppositional forces – in China within the Communist Party, and in India in the form of other political parties vying for power. These forces could well stoke nationalism and dissatisfaction to their advantage by portraying cooperation as appeasement or strategic ignorance. The media in both countries – social media in China, and the press and television in India – complicate the ability of both governments to carry through cooperation.

Cooperation is also limited by state capacity. China is not thought of as a weak state, but there are areas where it is weak. Ho, for instance, argues that China lacks an understanding of international river water norms and conventions, and in the absence of water treaties with neighbouring states it has little experience of cooperative accords. India by contrast has agreements with Bangladesh, Bhutan, Nepal, and Pakistan. On the other hand, India is much more fundamentally a weak, low-capacity state, one that finds it difficult to take tough decisions internationally as well as domestically and to enact and implement policies. Ignorance about the other country and the workings of its political institutions, bureaucracies, business communities, and civil society organisations places another limit on cooperation. This ignorance is compounded by a lack of communication across national boundaries between these various sectors of Chinese and Indian society.

Fourth, China–India cooperation in these four areas will require leadership at the highest levels. While the chapters do not squarely address the importance of leadership, the conference discussions in 2013 repeatedly drew attention to this factor. Since 2013, both countries have seen the rise to power of two reputedly strong leaders, Xi Jinping and Narendra Modi. Xi seems to be on the verge of political dominance to a degree unseen in China since Deng Xiaoping, and Modi is the first Indian Prime Minister to have won an absolute majority in parliamentary elections since 1984. Both leaders are ambitious for themselves and their countries. Both have asserted themselves on China–India relations. Xi took a decision to offer India US $20 billion in investment, and to woo India on the New Development Bank, AIIB, and the silk routes. Modi overruled his bureaucracy on the New Development Bank as well and has committed his government to various economic deals with China, including the setting up of Chinese industrial parks and allowing Chinese investments in infrastructure in India. Most recently, in 2015, the two leaders agreed upon memoranda of understanding (MOUs) and agreements worth $22 billion.[51] Looking ahead, Xi and Modi will have to continue to push for cooperation in the face of bureaucratic, political, and social resistance.

A final broad conclusion is that, on the whole, our Indian authors are more enthusiastic and optimistic about the possibility of cooperation. This may reflect India's greater need for cooperation, as the weaker party. It may also reflect the fact that Indian analysts pay far more attention to China than Chinese analysts pay to India, and that they have therefore thought through the advantages and feasibility of cooperation more than Chinese counterparts.

We end with the thought that there are rational, measured, and practical policy options for the two powers as they rise to power and influence. China and India want not just a satisfying and secure existence for their people but also dignity and respect and perhaps some of the glory of the past when they were in positions of global pre-eminence. Satisfied, secure, and accorded the status they so much crave, China and India together could be an enormous force for regional and global stability. These chapters taken together suggest a way ahead. It will take all the sagacity and strength of the countries' leaderships to turn promise into reality.

Acknowledgement

We wish to record our thanks to Varigonda Kesava Chandra and Libby Morgan Beri for their valuable inputs in this chapter.

Notes

1 Nargiza Salidjanova, "China's Foreign Exchange Reserves and Holdings of U.S. Securities", *USCC Economic Issue*, 2, 21 March 2014, http://origin.www.uscc.gov/sites/default/files/Research/USCC%20Economic%20Issue%20Brief_China%27s%20FX%20Reserves%20and%20Treasury%20Holdings.pdf.
2 Dhiraj Nayar, "How to Bridge India's Infrastructure Gap", *LiveMint*, 18 February 2015, http://www.livemint.com/Opinion/3YpBrQ1Fc9Yk7zlVEImblL/How-to-bridge-Indias-infrastructure-gap.html.
3 Dilasha Seth and Yogima Seth Sharma, "China Offers to Finance 30 per cent of India's Infrastructure Development Plan", *The Economic Times*, 20 February 2014, http://articles.economictimes.indiatimes.com/2014-02-20/news/47527235_1_india-s-infrastructure-development-plan-infrastructure-sector.
4 Jason Burke, "India and China Announce Trade Deals During Xi Visit to Delhi", *The Guardian*, 18 September 2014, http://www.theguardian.com/world/2014/sep/18/india-china-trade-deals-xi-delhi.

5 Seth and Sharma, "China Offers to Finance 30 per cent of India's Infrastructure Development Plan".
6 Ibid.
7 Ibid.
8 Amitendu Palit, "Paranoid about the Deficit", *Indian Express*, 23 September 2014, http://indianexpress.com/article/opinion/columns/paranoid-about-the-deficit/2/.
9 Between 2001 and 2012, India filed 120 complaints against China, out of a total of 648 complaints against Beijing. See Umair H. Ghori, "The Dumping Dragon: Analysing China's Evolving Anti-dumping Behaviour", International Trade and Academic Research Conference, London, November 2013, p. 116, http://epublications.bond.edu.au/cgi/viewcontent.cgi?article=1669&context=law_pubs. India is the leader in filing complaints against China.
10 Palit, "Paranoid about the Deficit".
11 "President Obama Says China Open to Joining Trade Partnership", *Marketplace*, 3 June 2015, http://www.marketplace.org/topics/world/president-obama-talks-trade/president-obama-says-china-open-joining-trade-partnership.
12 See, for instance, Aurelia George Mulgan, "Japan, US and the TPP: The View from China", *East Asia Forum*, 5 May 2013, http://www.eastasiaforum.org/2013/05/05/japan-us-and-the-tpp-the-view-from-china/.
13 Mulgan, "Japan, US and the TPP: The View from China." On China and India's views of the TPP, see Amitendu Palit, *The Transpacific Partnership, China and India: Economic and Political Implications*, Abingdon: Routledge, 2014.
14 "India, China for Early Conclusion of IMF Quota", *Business Standard*, 27 September 2013, http://www.business-standard.com/article/markets/india-china-for-early-conclusion-of-imf-quota-reforms-113092700455_1.html.
15 "IMF Says Yuan on Path to Inclusion in SDR Basket", *Reuters*, 16 April 2015, http://www.reuters.com/article/2015/04/16/imf-g20-china-idUSL2N0XD1LI20150416.
16 "France's Lagarde Bids to Lead IMF after Strauss-Kahn Resignation", *CNN*, 25 May 2011, http://edition.cnn.com/2011/WORLD/europe/05/25/france.lagarde.imf/.
17 Lee Glendinning and Graeme Wearden, "Dominique Strauss-Kahn Resigns as Head of IMF", *The Guardian*, 19 May 2011, http://www.theguardian.com/world/2011/may/19/dominique-strauss-kahn-resigns-imf.
18 "India Says 'Difficult' to Appoint Non-European to IMF", *Emirates 24/7*, 25 May 2011, http://www.emirates247.com/business/economy-finance/india-says-difficult-to-appoint-non-european-to-imf-2011-05-25-1.397307.
19 Alan Beattie, "Lagarde Wins China Official's Backing", *Financial Times*, 28 June 2011.
20 Raghuram Rajan, Governor of the Indian Reserve Bank, ends his term in 2016, two months after Christine Lagarde ends her term as Managing Director of the IMF. Rajan was Chief Economist of the Fund from 2003 to 2006. Speculation has surfaced on whether or not Rajan would be a candidate to replace Lagarde. See "RBI Chief Rajan Brushes off Talk of Top IMF role – Paper", *Reuters*, 8 April 2015, http://in.reuters.com/article/2015/04/08/india-rbi-rajan-idINKBN0MZ08N20150408.
21 New Delhi has already nominated the banker K.V. Kamath for the chairmanship of the New Development Bank. See "Private Banker KV Kamath Named First BRICS Bank Head", *Reuters*, 11 May 2015, http://in.reuters.com/article/2015/05/11/brics-bank-chairman-idINKBN0NW0FI20150511.
22 Raj M. Desai and James Raymond Vreeland, "What the New Bank of BRICS is All About", *Washington Post*, 17 July 2014, http://www.washingtonpost.com/blogs/

monkey-cage/wp/2014/07/17/what-the-new-bank-of-brics-is-all-about/; Prashant Jha, "BRICS Bank: How PM Got Big Powers to Accept India's Idea", *Hindustan Times*, 9 August 2014, http://www.hindustantimes.com/allaboutmodisarkar/bank-on-modi-what-pm-got-for-india-from-brics-summit/article1-1240877.aspx.

23 "India Can Choose to Take Part in Any Silk Road Project: China", *The Economic Times*, 15 April 2015, http://articles.economictimes.indiatimes.com/2015-04-15/news/61180125_1_indian-ocean-maritime-silk-road-south-china-sea; "China's Proposed Maritime Silk Road (MSR): Impact on Indian Foreign and Security Policies," *Centre for China Analysis and Strategy*, July 2014, http://ccasindia.org/issue_policy.php?ipid=21.

24 "Ready to Link Our Silk Route Plans With India's 'Spice Route' and 'Mausam' Projects, Says China", *NDTV*, 5 April 2015, http://www.ndtv.com/india-news/ready-to-link-our-silk-route-plans-with-indias-spice-route-and-mausam-projects-says-china-752448.

25 David Biello, "Everything You Need to Know about the U.S.–China Climate Change Agreement", *Scientific American*, 12 November 2014, http://www.scientificamerican.com/article/everything-you-need-to-know-about-the-u-s-china-climate-change-agreement/.

26 See Press Information Bureau, Prime Minister's Office, Government of India, "Joint Statement on Climate Change between India and China during PM's visit to China", 15 May 2015, http://pib.nic.in/newsite/PrintRelease.aspx?relid=121754.

27 The White House, "Fact Sheet: U.S. and India Climate and Clean Energy Cooperation", 25 January 2015, https://www.whitehouse.gov/the-press-office/2015/01/25/fact-sheet-us-and-india-climate-and-clean-energy-cooperation.

28 Silvio Marcacci, "7.7 Million Renewable Energy Jobs Worldwide In 2014", *Clean Technica*, 21 May 2015, http://cleantechnica.com/2015/05/21/7-7-million-renewable-energy-jobs-worldwide-2014/.

29 Ibid.

30 Smiti Mittal, "India's Solar Power Potential Estimated At 750 GW", *Clean Technica*, 29 November 2014, http://cleantechnica.com/2014/11/29/indias-solar-power-potential-estimated-750-gw/.

31 India's present renewable energy capacity is 31,692.14MW. See Utpal Bhaskar, "NTPC to Buy 15,000MW of Solar Power through Reverse Auction", *LiveMint*, 21 May 2015, http://www.livemint.com/Industry/zC1OSDPTl64L1S6BKnGAXJ/NTPC-to-buy-15000MW-of-solar-power-through-reverse-auction.html.

32 Ibid.

33 For a detailed and careful reconstruction of the Sudan case, where both China and India were heavily involved, see Luke Patey, *The New Kings of Crude: China, India, and the Global Struggle for Oil in Sudan and South Sudan*, New Delhi: HarperCollins Publishers India, 2014.

34 See the conclusion in Patey, *The New Kings of Crude*, pp. 263–274 in particular.

35 Anthony Fensom, "China: The Next Shale-Gas Superpower?" *The National Interest*, 9 October 2014, http://nationalinterest.org/feature/china-the-next-shale-gas-superpower-11432.

36 On China's shale oil, see US Energy Information Agency, "Technically Recoverable Shale Oil and Shale Gas Resources: An Assessment of 137 Shale Formations in 41 Countries Outside the United States", 13 June 2013, http://www.eia.gov/analysis/studies/worldshalegas/. On the figures for China's shale oil reserves, see Vello A. Kuuskraa, Scott H. Stevens, and Keith D. Moodhe, "World Shale Gas and Shale Oil Resource Assessment", a report prepared for U.S. Energy Information Administration at the U.S. Department of Energy, Washington, DC, 17 May 2013, pp. 1–7.

37 On India's shale gas, see "World Shale Gas Resources", *Geology.com*, http://geology.com/energy/world-shale-gas/.
38 On India's shale oil reserves, see Vello A. Kuuskraa, Scott H. Stevens, and Keith D. Moodhe, "World Shale Gas and Shale Oil Resource Assessment", pp. 1–7.
39 See Andrew Koch and Shelby McNichols, "Tarapur," Monterey Institute of International Studies, http://cns.miis.edu/archive/country_india/nucfacil/tarapur.htm, March 1999.
40 "China Produces First AP1000 vessel", *World Nuclear News*, http://www.world-nuclear-news.org/NN-China-produces-first-AP1000-vessel-1106144.html.
41 On China's smart cities plans, see for instance Kang Yanrong, Zang Lei, Chen Cai, Ge Yuming, Li Hao, Cui Ying, Jeanette Whyte, and Thomas Hart, "Comparative Study of Smart Cities in Europe and China", White Paper, EU-China Policy Dialogues Support Facility II (PDSF), March 2014, p. 10, http://euchina-ict.eu/wp-content/uploads/2015/01/Smart_City_report_draft-White-Paper-_-March-2014.pdf. On India's plans, see NASSCOM, "100 Smart Cities," http://www.nasscom.in/100-smart-cities-program.
42 See Stephanie Pappas, "Why Asia's Glaciers Are Mysteriously Expanding, Not Melting", *Live Science*, 12 October 2014, http://www.livescience.com/48256-asia-kara koram-glaciers-stability.html; and Richard Harris, "Melt Or Grow? Fate of Himalayan Glaciers Unknown," *NPR*, 24 April 2012, http://www.npr.org/2012/04/24/151206843/melt-or-grow-fate-of-himalayan-glaciers-unknown. For the view that the glaciers are melting, see the research of Chinese scientists cited in Jane Qiu, "Tibetan Glaciers Shrinking Rapidly: Comprehensive Survey Reveals Influence of Prevailing Winds", *Nature*, 15 July 2012, http://www.nature.com/news/tibetan-glaciers-shrinking-rap idly-1.11010. For a balanced, measured view see United Nations Environmental Programme (UNEP), "Measuring Glacier Change in the Himalayas", September 2012, http://na.unep.net/geas/getUNEPPageWithArticleIDScript.php?article_id=91.
43 Quoted in Sujay Mehdudia, "We Trust China's Promise on Dam: Manmohan", *The Hindu*, 5 August 2011, http://www.thehindu.com/news/national/we-trust-chinas-prom ise-on-dam-manmohan/article2322266.ece.
44 "No Plans to Divert Brahmaputra: China", *The Times of India*, 25 October 2006, http://articles.timesofindia.indiatimes.com/2006-10-25/rest-of-world/27788942_1_brahma-putra-yellow-river-liu-jianchao.
45 "China Rules Out Brahmaputra Diversion", *The Hindu*, 13 October 2011, http://www.thehindu.com/news/international/china-rules-out-brahmaputra-diversion/arti cle2532283.ece?ref=relatedNews.
46 "Satellite Imagery Allays Fears of China's Diversion of Brahmaputra Waters", *The Times of India*, 17 July 2011, http://articles.timesofindia.indiatimes.com/2011-06-17/india/29669506_1_brahmaputra-river-run-of-the-river-satellite-imagery.
47 On the dissatisfaction over the Three Gorges Dam, see Michael Wines, "China Admits Problems with Three Gorges Dam", 19 May 2011, *New York Times*, http://www.nytimes.com/2011/05/20/world/asia/20gorges.html?_r=0.
48 See for instance Carla Freeman, "Quenching the Dragon's Thirst: The South-North Water Transfer Project—Old Plumbing for New China?" China Environment Forum, Woodrow Wilson International Center for Scholars, http://www.wilsoncenter.org/pub lication/quenching-the-dragons-thirst-the-south-north-water-transfer-project8212old-plumbing-for and Jennifer Duggan, "China's Mega Water Diversion Project Begins

Conclusion 217

Testing", *The Guardian*, 5 June 2013, http://www.theguardian.com/environment/chinas-choice/2013/jun/05/chinas-water-diversion-project-south-north.

49 On China's relations with Southeast Asian countries over its river water projects on the Mekong, see Selina Ho, "River Politics: China's Policies in the Mekong and the Brahmaputra in Comparative Perspective", *Journal of Contemporary China*, 23/85, pp. 1–20. Also see Evelyn Goh, *Developing the Mekong: Regionalism and Regional Security in China–Southeast Asian Relations*, Adelphi Paper No. 387 (London: IISS, June 2007).

50 Sri Lanka, after the presidential elections in 2015, has also undertaken a review of its projects with China.

51 See "Business MoU/ Agreements signed at India–China Business Forum during PM's visit to Shanghai (May 16, 2015)", Ministry of External Affairs, Government of India, 16 May 2015, http://www.mea.gov.in/bilateral-documents.htm?dtl/25248/Business+MoU+Agreements+signed+at+India+China+Business+Forum+during+PMs+visit+to+Shanghai+May+16+2015.

Index

Afghanistan 145
Africa: competition in 187–188; investment in 31; oil fields 137; trade 55
agriculture: climate change impact on 116, 122–123; ecological 96–97, 205; greenhouse gas emissions 114–115; India 33n4, 75, 145, 146, 147–148; tariffs 76; water use efficiency 150, 153, 159
Ahluwalia, Montek Singh 44
AIIB *see* Asian Infrastructure Investment Bank
Aiyar, Mani Shankar 138
Aksai Chin 3
Angola 154, 206
anti-dumping cases 59, 79, 156, 200
APEC *see* Asia Pacific Economic Cooperation
Arctic Council 157, 177
arms acquisitions 6
Arunchal Pradesh 3, 11, 167, 178n5, 185, 188, 191
ASEAN *see* Association of Southeast Asian Nations
Asia Pacific Economic Cooperation (APEC) 10, 60, 61, 152, 201
Asian Development Bank 134, 185
Asian Infrastructure Investment Bank (AIIB) 10, 44–45, 202, 203, 213
Association of Southeast Asian Nations (ASEAN) 10, 60, 61, 62, 78, 85
Australia 118, 120, 158

Bali Action Plan (BAP) 108
Bangladesh: India's trade balance with 76; riparian relations 172, 173, 175, 193, 194, 210, 212; vulnerability to climate change 147
Bangladesh–China–India–Myanmar (BCIM) Economic Corridor 81–82, 85
banking 24–25, 27, 84
BASIC countries 102, 105, 111, 123, 170
BCIM Economic Corridor 81–82, 85
Beijing Olympics (2008) 27
Bhat, T.P. 55
Bhutan 54, 212
Biba, Sebastian 189
biofuels 131, 146, 147–148, 149
biomass 121–122, 146, 157, 158, 205
biotechnology 85, 122, 205
Bo Xilai 30–31
border incidents 3, 6, 14n21; *see also* territorial disputes
border negotiations 5, 6
bourgeoisie 23, 33n5
BP 133, 134
Brahmaputra (Yarlung Tsangpo) River 32, 167, 168, 175, 182; benefits of cooperation 177; Chinese policies towards 187–189; climate change impact on 116; dams 9, 101, 169, 174, 188, 189, 191, 208, 209, 210; diversion plans 169, 170, 185, 188, 208, 209; Himalayan glaciology 172; Indian concerns 183; joint development 192, 211; sharing of hydrological information 11, 173–174, 177, 180n29, 190–191, 208; volume of water flow 185
Brandler, Andrew 78
Braudel, Fernand 52–53
Brazil: BASIC 102, 111; IMF head selection 202; IMF quotas 43, 50n21;

India's trade balance with 76; Itaipu dam 177; New Development Bank 202; steel production 101; trade 62
BRICS countries 31, 38, 41, 43, 102, 105, 201; G20 process 62; international financial institutions 43, 48; investment in resource-rich economies 144; New Development Bank 10, 44, 45, 48, 202
Burma (Myanmar) 54, 81, 154, 155, 191, 206, 211
Burundi 180n30
business models 150, 151, 156–157

Cambodia 172, 191
Canada 109, 120, 158
capitalism 21, 25, 32
carbon emissions 8, 10, 95, 108–110, 204; domestic policy responses 116–118; economic development 22; global governance 153; international cooperation 97–100; scenarios 129n69; *see also* greenhouse gas emissions
carbon trading schemes 117–118
CDM *see* Clean Development Mechanism
chemicals 69–73, 139
Chevron 136
China: carbon emissions 8, 95, 98, 99, 109, 110; climate change cooperation 8, 98–100, 108–129, 157–158, 203–204; Communist Party 23, 25, 30–31, 207, 212; ecological civilisation 96–97; economic development 21–22, 23–25, 27–33; energy 7–8, 93–94, 130–143, 145, 152, 154–159, 204–207; financial cooperation 37, 39–41, 42–45, 50n24, 198–199, 201–203; food security 123; fossil fuel production 95, 96; IMF quotas 43, 50n21; industrialisation and urbanisation 93–95; Kargil incident 13n15; long peace 2–7; low regard for India 193; mercantilism 154; new areas of competition 7–9; obstacles to environmental cooperation 100–102; opportunities for cooperation 1–2, 9–11, 211–213; political interruption of business exchanges 45–46; public opinion 33n1; rising power of 38–39, 48; scenarios for cooperation 102–104; tense relations with India 187–188; trade 7, 39, 52–66, 67–90, 199–201, 203; water 8–9, 167–181, 182–197, 207–211
China National Petroleum Corporation (CNPC) 134, 136–137, 154–155, 206, 207
China Petroleum & Chemical Corporation (Sinopec) 136, 137
'Chindia' concept 38, 85, 86, 89n46, 102, 103, 188
CII *see* Confederation of Indian Industry
class conflict 23, 25, 31, 33n5
Clean Development Mechanism (CDM) 118–119, 204
climate change 8, 10–11, 108–129, 139, 203–204; adaptation 157–158, 159, 205–206; Clean Development Mechanism 118–119, 204; domestic policy responses 116–118; energy demand 112–114; food security 122–123, 205; Himalayan glaciology 167, 171–172, 183, 185–186, 195, 208–209; India 147, 153; international cooperation 97–100; low-carbon development 116, 119–120, 121–122, 124; resource nexus for India 147–149, 159; shared agenda 60; South-South framework for cooperation 119–121; US–China–India trilateral partnership 62; vulnerability to 115–116; water pressures 167, 176; *see also* carbon emissions
CNPC *see* China National Petroleum Corporation
coal 94, 96, 97, 113, 158; China 132, 133; India 145, 151
'common but differentiated responsibility' 10, 98, 100, 111, 124n1, 124n7
comparative advantage 55, 68, 86, 100, 104, 200
competition 112, 170, 187–188; economic 52; energy 32, 135, 137–138, 139–140, 154, 158, 206; geopolitical 41; market 96; new areas of 7–9; psychological 100; strategic 103; trade 54–55, 56, 59–60
Confederation of Indian Industry (CII) 79–80
confidence-building measures 5, 6, 41, 49n14, 193

220 *Index*

conflict 13n9, 38, 103; climate change 116; economic 22; geopolitical 112; potential for 1; water 183–184, 193, 194
Congress Party 3
ConocoPhillips 137
consumer goods 23, 26, 27, 67
consumption 83, 103, 130; China 33; ecological civilisation 97; energy 93, 94, 131, 133, 135, 145, 146; India 29; mineral resources 144; water 167, 184–185
cooperation 1–2, 11–12, 38–39, 170, 206; climate change 8, 60, 97–100, 108–129, 203–204; economic 22, 31, 33, 37–51, 52, 103–104, 198–203, 211–212; energy 105, 136–140, 154–159, 204–207, 212; financial 37, 40–41, 42–45, 46–48, 50n24, 198–199, 201–203; 'five principles' 63; food security 123; international context 40–42; mutual investment 37, 39–41, 46–47, 48, 63; obstacles to environmental cooperation 100–102; opportunities for 9–11, 211–213; regional 60–61; scenarios for 102–104; science and technology 139; trade 55–56, 57, 59–61, 82–86, 200–201; water 168, 171, 173–174, 176–177, 182, 190–195, 207–211, 212; *see also* diplomacy
Copenhagen Accord (2009) 108, 109, 111, 124n7
corruption 21, 25, 30, 35n47, 78
Cultural Revolution 3
currency depreciation 76–77

Dalai Lama 6, 100, 170, 193
dams: China 9, 11, 101, 168, 169, 174–175, 188–189, 194, 208, 209–210; conflict over 183; critics of 209–210; India 170, 191, 193; Myitsone Dam 211; Pakistan 185; Tibet 176
Das Gupta, Ashin 53
debt 24
Deng Xiaoping 3, 5, 212
developing countries 41–42, 63; carbon emissions 98, 100, 111; climate change 108, 111, 124, 204; economic regionalisation 61; industrialisation 127n58; international financial order 42–43, 48
Dhar, Biswajit 199

diplomacy 5; energy 137, 138; 'peripheral diplomacy' 195; water 171, 173, 175, 176, 178, 208
domestic politics 3, 30–31, 103, 212
drought 147, 148

East Asia Summit (EAS) 61
EC *see* ecological civilisation
ecological civilisation (EC) 96–97, 103
economic growth 7, 21, 22, 31; carbon emissions linked to 98, 109; China 5, 33, 41, 98; Chinese internal water disputes 187; energy security 130, 131; imbalanced 38, 39; India 25–26, 27, 32–33, 41; international economic order 44; projections for 112; resources 144, 145–146; trade patterns 71–72; water scarcities 184, 185
economics 1–2, 11–12, 21–36, 188, 198–203, 211–212; BRICS 41; economic integration 4–5; financial cooperation 37, 40–41, 42–45, 46–48, 50n24, 198–199, 201–203; mutual investment 37, 39–41, 46–47, 48, 63; scenarios for cooperation 103, 104; *see also* trade
Ecuador 137, 154, 206
elections 30, 36n52
electricity 113, 121, 132, 133, 135–136, 146
Emissions Trading Schemes (ETSs) 118
employment 28
EnCana 137
energy 1–2, 130–143, 212; Chinese approaches to energy security 131–135; clean energy investment 119–121; climate change mitigation pledges 108; cooperation 11, 32, 154–159, 204–207; demand for 7–8, 112–114, 122, 145, 150, 152–154; distributed infrastructure 150, 151, 156–157; energy efficiency targets 117; exports 134; fossil fuel production 95, 96; future research 140; global governance 152, 153–154, 157; government frameworks for cooperation 138–140; greenhouse gas emissions 114–115; household consumption 145; imports 113–114; industrialisation and urbanisation 93–95; resource nexus for India 147–149, 159; Strategic Economic

Dialogue 81; supply constraints 150–152; targets 131; US–China–India trilateral partnership 62; *see also* carbon emissions; oil; renewable energy; resources
Engels, Friedrich 25, 33n5
engineering 89n51
environment 1–2, 93–107, 203–207, 212; climate change 8; constraints against resource exploitation 144, 147; dams 210; ecological civilisation 96–97; obstacles to cooperation 100–102; Strategic Economic Dialogue 81; sustainable use of water resources 194; Tibet 175–176; water issues 175; *see also* carbon emissions; climate change; pollution; resources
'equitable utilisation' 170, 174, 179n16, 183
equity: climate change 123, 124n1, 129n74; social 21; water 176, 178, 191
ETSs *see* Emissions Trading Schemes
European Union (EU): carbon emissions 95, 99, 109, 118; clean energy investment 120; future scenarios 103; international financial institutions 202; steel production 101; trade 61, 62, 76, 156
exchange rate 26, 28
exports: China 27, 28, 31, 54, 56–57, 68–69, 74–75, 83; energy 134; ICT 85; India 31, 52, 56–59, 65n25, 68, 70–73, 76–78; oil 105n4; pharmaceuticals 84; trade balance 76–78

FDI *see* foreign direct investment
Federation of Indian Chambers of Commerce and Industry (FICCI) 79–80
financial cooperation 37, 40–41, 42–45, 46–48, 50n24, 198–199, 201–203
financial crisis 3, 37–38, 41, 67, 202
financial policy: China 23–25, 28; India 34n23; international financial order 40–41, 42–45, 47–48, 201–203
fiscal stimulus 28, 29
Five-Year Plans (FYPs) 131, 168, 169, 185, 188
flooding 147, 170, 172, 208
food security: climate change impact on 122–123, 205; global governance 151; resource nexus for India 146, 147–149, 159; water scarcities 167
foreign direct investment (FDI) 26, 58, 78, 200; *see also* investment
foreign exchange reserves 26, 27–28, 31, 45
fossil fuels 95, 96, 104, 114–115, 122, 139; Chinese approaches to energy security 131, 132, 133; India 146; *see also* coal; gas; oil
France 109
free trade agreements (FTAs) 9–10, 52, 62, 75, 81, 85, 86, 201
Free Trade Area of the Asia-Pacific (FTAAP) 201
fruit industry 80
Fukushima Daiichi nuclear power accident 132
FYPs *see* Five-Year Plans

G7 102
G20 62, 102, 105, 201, 202; clean energy investment 119–120; Indian presidency 154; international financial order 43, 44, 48
Gandhi, Indira 3, 25
Gandhi, Rajiv 5, 34n23, 203
Ganges River 167, 172, 173, 175, 193
Garver, John W. 48n4
gas: China 133; competition over 154; cooperation 32, 136, 138, 156, 206; imports 130; India 145, 147, 149, 151
GDP *see* gross domestic product
geopolitics 41, 102, 123, 211; as barrier to research cooperation 206; Cold War 54; economic competition 112; obstacles to environmental cooperation 100; Trans-Pacific Partnership 200–201; water conflicts 193; *see also* politics
Germany: carbon emissions 109; clean energy investment 120; energy consumption 94; manufacturing 72; rise of 48
glaciers, Himalayan 116, 167, 171–172, 180n22, 183, 185–186, 195, 208–209
GMS *see* Greater Mekong Subregion
Gobel, Christian 36n53
governance: energy 134–135, 140; resources 150, 151–152, 153–154, 157; scenarios for cooperation 102

222 Index

Gramsci, Antonio 174
Great Bend dam 188, 209, 211
Great Leap Forward 3
Greater Mekong Subregion (GMS) 191–192
greenhouse gas (GHG) emissions 93, 94–95, 97–98, 105, 114–115, 116–117, 119, 158; *see also* carbon emissions
gross domestic product (GDP) 40, 52, 113; China 21, 48n3; India 27–28, 48n3, 116; projections 112
Guha, Atulan 55

Hazare, Anna 35n47, 36n51
higher education 89n51
Himalayan glaciology 116, 167, 171–172, 180n22, 183, 185–186, 195, 208–209
Hu Jintao 30, 56, 82, 174, 175
Huawei 45–46, 58, 79
hydropower 32, 104, 133–134, 168, 173, 183, 188–189; Chinese agreements with Russia 180n29; cooperation 177, 204, 205; ecological civilisation 97; India 148, 191; joint development 105, 194, 211, 212; obstacles to environmental cooperation 101

IC *see* industrial civilisation
IEA *see* International Energy Agency
IMF *see* International Monetary Fund
import-substituting industrialisation 54
imports: China 56–57, 67, 71; coal 145; energy 113–114, 130, 131, 132, 151, 154; India 26, 52, 56–57, 58, 71, 73–74, 79–80, 135; oil 7–8, 105n4, 138, 145; pharmaceuticals 84
India: bourgeoisie 23; carbon emissions 8, 95, 98, 99, 109–110, 129n69, 153; China's low regard for 193; climate change cooperation 8, 98–100, 108–129, 157–158, 203–204; ecological civilisation 96–97; economic development 21–22, 25–33; energy 7–8, 32, 93–94, 130, 135–140, 145, 204–207; financial cooperation 37, 39–41, 42–45, 50n24, 198–199, 201–203; food security 123; fossil fuel production 95, 96; IMF quotas 43, 50n21; industrialisation and urbanisation 93–95; long peace 2–7;

new areas of competition 7–9; obstacles to environmental cooperation 100–102; opportunities for cooperation 1–2, 9–11, 211–213; political interruption of business exchanges 45–46; resources 144–164; rising power of 38–39, 48; scenarios for cooperation 102–104; tense relations with China 187–188; trade 7, 39, 52–66, 67–90, 199–201, 203; vulnerability to climate change 147; water 8–9, 167–181, 182–186, 190–195, 207–211
Indonesia 55, 76
Indus River 167, 171, 172, 173, 175, 185, 193
industrial civilisation (IC) 96
industrial parks 84
industrial zones 86
industrialisation 93–95, 97; carbon emissions 98; China 54; import-substituting 54; India 22; 'leapfrogging' by developing countries 127n58; social stability 103; technologies 101; water scarcities 184
inequalities 21
inflation 29
information technology (IT) 100, 102, 104; economic complementarity 188; market access 58, 80; trade cooperation 55–56, 68, 83, 84, 85; *see also* technology
infrastructure: Asian Infrastructure Investment Bank 10, 44–45, 202, 203, 213; China 28, 33; collaboration 41; energy 150, 151, 155–156, 159, 206, 207; 'five principles' 63; foreign direct investment 58; India 31, 33, 78, 80–81, 198–199, 213; mutual investment 46; 'One Belt, One Road' initiative 10; Strategic Economic Dialogue 81; urbanisation 103
intellectual property rights (IPRs) 120
interest rates 29
Intergovernmental Panel on Climate Change (IPCC) 114–115, 172, 186, 209
International Energy Agency (IEA) 131, 134, 139, 152, 157, 160n5
international financial institutions 41, 42–43, 47–48, 63, 201–203
International Monetary Fund (IMF) 42, 43–44, 45, 48, 50n21, 201–202

International Renewable Energy Agency (IRENA) 205
investment 9–10; in China 28, 33; clean energy 119–121; competition 60; energy 32, 155–156, 159, 207; in India 26, 29, 31–33, 58, 80–81, 84, 198–199, 200, 213; international economic order 44; mutual 37, 39–41, 46–47, 48, 63; resource-rich economies 144
IPCC *see* Intergovernmental Panel on Climate Change
IPRs *see* intellectual property rights
Iran 136, 145, 154, 206
Iraq 134, 145
IRENA *see* International Renewable Energy Agency
irrigation 146, 149, 168, 174, 181n46
Israel 171, 184
IT *see* information technology

Jaishankar, S. 65n24
Japan: Asian Infrastructure Investment Bank 45; carbon emissions 110; China–Japan relationship 1; clean energy investment 120; coal imports 134; energy consumption 94; energy governance 135; Fukushima Daiichi nuclear power accident 132; manufacturing 72; oil imports 138; regional cooperation 60; steel production 101; territorial disputes with China 210; trade 62, 76
JEG *see* Joint Economic Group
Jiao Yong 209
joint development 158, 191–193, 195, 212
Joint Economic Group (JEG) 81
Jordan 171

Kalecki, Michael 33n5
Kalirajan, Kaliappa 84
Kamath, K.V. 214n21
Kargil incident 5, 13n15
Kashmir 4, 5, 7, 185, 199
Kazakhstan: energy 137, 145, 154, 155, 158, 206; water 173, 180n29, 192–193, 208
Kenya 155
Khurshid, Salman 58
Kondapalli, Srikanth 13n15
Krishna, S.M. 209
Kyoto Protocol 10, 97

LAC *see* Line of Actual Control
Lagarde, Christine 43, 202, 214n20
Lao Dan 96
Laos 172, 191
Large Industrial Houses (LIHs) 23, 25–26, 32
Latin America 55, 187–188
leadership 212–213
'leapfrogging' 119, 127n58
legislation 25–26, 32, 36n51
legitimacy 29–30
Li Keqiang 6, 28, 183, 194–195; development projects 86; investment 31; trade 9, 80, 81, 82, 83; water cooperation 174
liberalisation 27, 32, 55, 67, 72
Libya 145
licensing 67
LIHs *see* Large Industrial Houses
Line of Actual Control (LAC) 3, 6, 49n14
Liu Jianchao 209
local government 23–24, 25, 28
long peace 2–7
'Look East Policy' 54, 61
low-carbon development 116, 119–120, 121–122, 124, 154

Ma Kai 138
Mahindra & Mahindra 86
Malacca Straits 52, 53
Malaysia 55, 60, 76, 184
Mallet, Alexandra 122
manufacturing 56, 58, 59, 68, 71–72; China 74, 114; comparison of India and China 87n16; economic complementarity 188; energy efficiency 153; future trends 83; improvement in Indian 84; India's economy 22, 75; India's National Manufacturing Policy 145; India's weakness in 7, 67, 74, 77–78, 200; industrial zones 86; small manufacturers in India 25
Mao Zedong 3
Mark, Karl 25, 33n5
market access 57–58, 59–60, 62, 80, 81
Mauritius 203
Mausam initiative 203
Mekong River Commission (MRC) 172–173, 191

224   Index

Memoranda of Understanding (MOUs) 213; climate change 158, 195, 204; energy 155, 156, 206; science and technology cooperation 139; trade 80, 81, 83–84; water 11, 173, 174, 177, 183, 189, 190–191, 195
mercantilism 54–55, 150, 153–154, 159
middle class 27, 29, 83
Middle East 8, 138, 156
military policy 4, 6
mineral resources 144, 146, 157
modernisation 1, 4, 28, 31
Modi, Narendra 10, 203, 212–213; climate change 204; investment 31; manufacturing policy 84; smart cities 207
Motuo Dam (Great Bend) 188, 209, 211
MOUs *see* Memoranda of Understanding
MRC *see* Mekong River Commission
multilateralism 41–42; climate change 111, 123; resources 144; trade 55, 60, 61–63; water 178
Myanmar (Burma) 54, 81, 154, 155, 191, 206, 211
Myitsone Dam 211

Namibia 158
Natarajan, Jayanthi 129n74
Nath, Kamal 65n25
national security 168
Nehru, Jawaharlal 3, 47
Nepal 194, 212
New Development Bank 10, 44, 45, 48, 202, 203, 213
Nigeria 145, 154, 206
'no-harm rule' 170, 175, 176, 179n16, 179n17, 183
non-tariff barriers 47, 57, 65n24, 79
nuclear deterrence 4
nuclear energy 132, 158, 207

Obama, Barack 99, 204
oil: competition 154; cooperation 32, 136–137, 138, 139, 155–156, 158, 206–207; demand for 7–8; exports 105n4, 134; global governance 152; imports 7–8, 105n4, 113, 130, 138, 145, 151; obstacles to environmental cooperation 101; pipelines 145, 155–156, 159, 206, 207; prices 94; reserves 95, 96; resource nexus for India 147, 149; trade in 135

Oil & Natural Gas Corporation (ONGC) 136–137, 154–155, 206
'One Belt, One Road' initiative 10, 203
O'Neill, Jim 38
Ong, Lynette H. 36n53
ONGC Videsh Ltd. (OVL) 136, 155, 207
optimistic view 38, 48

Pakistan 4, 13n15, 145; China's nuclear cooperation with 158; China's support for 6–7; riparian relations 171, 172, 173, 175, 185, 193, 194, 212; trade 54; war with India 5
Palit, Amitendu 199, 200
Paraguay 177
PAT *see* Perform, Achieve and Trade scheme
Patey, Luke 207
Paul, Mahua 55
Perform, Achieve and Trade (PAT) scheme 117, 118, 153
pessimistic view 38
pharmaceutical industry 47, 56, 72, 80–81, 82, 83–84, 86, 200
Philippines 55, 210
pipelines 145, 155–156, 159, 206, 207
Poland 109
politics: bilateral relations 82; domestic 3, 30–31, 103, 212; 'high' and 'low' 211; hydropolitics 170–171, 172, 184, 185; India 25, 30, 36n52; political interruption of business exchanges 45–46; political stability 21; rivalry 103, 104; *see also* geopolitics
pollution 8, 10–11, 94; economic development 22; water 183, 184
poverty 25, 83, 113
power equipment 78, 79
private sector 22, 41
privatisation 21, 24
protectionism 46–47, 60, 68, 79–81, 200
protests 3, 30, 34n15, 36n53
Punjab 4

Rajan, Raghuram 214n20
Ramesh, Jairam 49n5, 89n46, 111
Rao, Narasimha 5, 26, 54
Rao, Nirupama 65n25
raw materials 56, 58, 65n25, 68, 70–73, 77, 100, 134

RBI *see* Reserve Bank of India
RCEP *see* Regional Comprehensive Economic Partnership
REC *see* Renewable Energy Certificate
recession: China 24, 25, 28, 29–30, 33; India 27, 29; world 67
Regional Comprehensive Economic Partnership (RCEP) 10, 60–61, 85, 201
regional cooperation 60–61, 85, 152
'regional public goods' 122
regional trade agreements (RTAs) 80, 81, 85, 86
renewable energy 98, 100, 101, 104; CDM projects 118–119; China 120, 133–134; climate change adaptation 157, 206; cooperation 105, 159, 204–205, 206, 207; development goals 139; distributed infrastructure 151, 156; low-carbon development 121–122; resource nexus for India 147–149; scenarios 128n69; *see also* solar energy; wind energy
Renewable Energy Certificate (REC) 117, 118
research cooperation 206
Reserve Bank of India (RBI) 29
resources 95, 103, 133, 144–164, 170; basic needs 144, 146, 150, 153; border regions 105; demand pressures 150, 152–154; domestic policies 150–151, 152–153; ecological civilisation 97; economic growth 144, 145–146; environmental constraints 144, 147; equity 129n74; global governance 150, 151–152, 153–154, 157; obstacles to environmental cooperation 101; prices 94; resource nexus for India 147–149; supply constraints 150–152; *see also* energy; water
run-of-river (ROR) projects 169, 191, 209
rupee 26, 76–77
Russia: carbon emissions 109; energy 154, 156, 206, 207; future scenarios 103; G20 62; IMF head selection 202; IMF quotas 50n21; New Development Bank 202; oil 138; river diversions 173; steel production 101; water agreements with China 180n29

SAARC *see* South Asian Association for Regional Cooperation
Salman, Salman M.A. 181n45
Saudi Arabia 76
Schlesinger, James R. 134
science and technology (S&T) cooperation 139
SCO *see* Shanghai Cooperation Organisation
SDRs *see* special drawing rights
sea level rises 116, 208
security 1, 188, 211; long peace 2–7; water as a security issue 183–186
SED *see* Strategic Economic Dialogue
services 75, 102, 114, 188
Seychelles 203
shale gas 132–133, 207
Shambaugh, David 181n38
Shanghai Cooperation Organisation (SCO) 138–139, 192
Sharma, Anand 58
Sikkim 82
Silk Road *see* 'One Belt, One Road' initiative
Silk Road Fund 203
Singapore 55, 76, 184
Singh, Manmohan 8, 30, 63, 82; competition and cooperation 59; economic relations 52; fiscal stimulus 29; investment 31; RCEP 61; water 167, 174, 195
Singh, Swaran 111
Sinopec *see* China Petroleum & Chemical Corporation
smart cities 207
SNWTP *see* South-North Water Transfer Project
social stability 103
SOEs *see* state-owned enterprises
soil erosion 147
solar energy 32, 98, 104, 105; China 120, 133–134, 205; climate change adaptation 158; ecological civilisation 97; India 117, 120, 121–122, 148, 156, 157, 205
South Africa: BASIC 102, 111; clean energy investment 120; IMF head selection 202; New Development Bank 202; trade 76
South Asian Association for Regional Cooperation (SAARC) 193

South Korea: carbon emissions 109; energy governance 135; free trade agreements 62; implications of China's WTO entry 55; India's trade balance with 76; oil imports 138; steel production 101
South-North Water Transfer Project (SNWTP) 169, 179n9, 188, 210
South Sudan 145, 155
Southeast Asia 54, 55, 61, 192, 208, 210
Soviet Union, former 4, 54; *see also* Russia
special drawing rights (SDRs) 42, 43, 201
Spice Route 203
Sri Lanka 54, 76, 203
Srivastava, Leena 109–110
state capacity 212
state-owned enterprises (SOEs) 21–22, 23, 117
steel 101
Strategic Economic Dialogue (SED) 40, 44, 50n24, 57, 81, 82, 111–112, 121, 201
strategic partnership 102, 104
Strauss-Kahn, Dominique 43, 202
subsidies 79
Sudan 136, 137, 154–155, 206
summits 5–6, 41, 43, 48, 203
sustainable development 123, 129n74, 144, 176, 178
Sutlej River 11, 167, 172, 174, 175, 177, 185, 190–191
Syria 136–137, 155, 206

tariffs 26, 76, 77, 79, 132
Tata Consultancy Services (TCS) 56, 84
taxation 23–24
technology 83, 85, 86; clean energy 120–121, 205; climate change adaptation 157, 158, 206; industrialisation 101; renewable energy 105; science and technology cooperation 104, 139; Strategic Economic Dialogue 81; *see also* information technology
telecommunications 45–46, 58, 75, 79
territorial disputes 38, 41, 103, 104, 182, 188, 210; *see also* border incidents
territorial integrity 170
territorial sovereignty 170, 171, 182, 191
terrorism 3, 6, 192
Thailand 55, 76, 172, 191

Tibet 3, 6, 82, 100, 193; environmental concerns 175–176; separatists 103, 104; water 167, 175–178, 182, 185–186, 188, 208
tourism 105
TPP *see* Trans-Pacific Partnership
trade 5–6, 31, 52–66, 67–90, 188, 199–201, 211–212; complementarity 67, 68–73; decline in 7, 179n18; energy 135–136, 139, 207; future trends 82–86; growth in 7, 13n19, 37, 39, 46, 56, 67, 82; historical background 52–54; imbalance 67, 68, 73–78, 82, 86; institutional efforts at trade promotion 81–82; international economic order 44; international trading regime 84–85; managing competition and cooperation 59–60; multilateral system 61–63; new bilateral economic relationship 55–58; opportunities for cooperation 9–10; optimistic view 48; outward orientation 54–55; protectionism 79–81; regional cooperation 60–61; trade deficit 7, 57–59, 65n25, 67, 73–78, 100, 199–200, 203
Trans-Pacific Partnership (TPP) 61, 62, 85, 200–201
Transatlantic Trade and Investment Partnership (T-TIP) 61, 62, 85
transparency: dams 174; investment 47; pricing 79; trade 58, 59, 62
transport 10, 100, 115
trust: climate change cooperation 112, 124; lack of 38, 58, 59, 100, 173, 193; water cooperation 173, 182, 208
T-TIP *see* Transatlantic Trade and Investment Partnership
Turkey 101, 180n30

Ukraine 101, 109
unemployment 29
UNFCCC *see* United Nations Framework Convention on Climate Change
United Arab Emirates (UAE) 76
United Kingdom 109, 120
United Nations Convention on the Law of the Non-Navigational Use of International Watercourses (UN Watercourses Convention) 168, 172, 175, 179n17, 180n30, 187

United Nations Framework Convention on Climate Change (UNFCCC) 97–98, 108, 111, 124n1, 204
United Nations Security Council 38, 63
United States (US): Asian Infrastructure Investment Bank 45; carbon emissions 95, 98, 99, 109; China–US relations 1, 4, 44; clean energy investment 120; climate change cooperation 203–204; commodities 78; energy consumption 94; energy governance 135; free trade agreements 52; future scenarios 103; IMF quotas 43; India–US Joint Clean Energy R&D Centre 158; India–US relations 4, 195; international financial institutions 201, 202; manufacturing 72; mercantilism 154; oil imports 138; renewable energy 104; rise of 48; shale gas 132; Southeast Asia relations 210; steel production 101; trade 54, 62, 156; Trans-Pacific Partnership 200–201; US–China–India trilateral partnership 62; water 9
urbanisation 83, 93–95, 97, 105n2, 113; economic growth 130; social stability 103; water scarcities 184, 185

Vajpayee, Atal Bihari 39, 81
Venezuela 145
Vietnam 4, 76, 145, 172, 191, 210
Vishwanath, T.S. 79–80

Wang, Tao 122
waste 146
water 1–2, 32, 167–181, 182–197, 207–211, 212; Chinese policies on transboundary waters 186–187; Chinese policies towards the Brahmaputra 187–189; climate change adaptation 158, 206; cooperation 11; demand for 8–9, 146, 169, 184–185; diversion plans 169–170, 173, 179n9, 185, 188, 208, 209–210; food security 146; global governance 152; Himalayan glaciology 167, 171–172, 180n22, 183, 185–186, 195, 208–209; hydropolitics 170–171, 172, 184, 185; India 147; as a political and security issue 183–186; prospects for cooperation 190–194; resource nexus for India 147–149, 159; Strategic Economic Dialogue 81; vulnerability to climate change 116; 'water rationality' view 168; water use efficiency in agriculture 150, 153, 159; *see also* hydropower
Watson, Jim 122
Wen Jiabao 28, 82, 111; China–India Finance Dialogue 50n24; energy security 138; trade 37, 39, 56; water 8, 167, 176, 189
wind energy 98, 105, 120, 133–134, 204–205
Wittfogel, Karl 177, 181n46
World Bank 42, 45, 48, 49n13, 201, 202; energy projects 134; hydropower 133; Partnership for Market Readiness 118; water management 183–184, 191
World Trade Organisation (WTO) 43, 60, 61, 85; anti-dumping cases 200; China's accession 5, 55, 63, 67, 83; Ministerial Conference 62; trading norms 200

Xi Jinping 6, 28, 203, 212–213; APEC 10; BRICS cooperation 41; carbon emissions 99; 'five principles' 63; investment in India 32, 80–81, 84, 199; 'peripheral diplomacy' 195; trade 13n19
Xie Zhenhua 111
Xinjiang 3

Yangtze River 178n8, 179n9, 184
Yarlung Tsangpo (Brahmaputra) River 32, 167, 168, 175, 182; benefits of cooperation 177; Chinese policies towards 187–189; climate change impact on 116; dams 9, 101, 169, 174, 188, 189, 191, 208, 209, 210; diversion plans 169, 170, 185, 188, 208, 209; Himalayan glaciology 172; Indian concerns 183; joint development 192, 211; sharing of hydrological information 11, 173–174, 177, 180n29, 190–191, 208; volume of water flow 185
yuan 201–202

Zangmu Dam 169, 188, 189
Zhang Xiaoqiang 40
Zheng Bijian 51n34
Zhou Enlai 3
Zhu Rongji 21, 24, 35n35, 37, 39, 56

eBooks
from Taylor & Francis

Helping you to choose the right eBooks for your Library

Add to your library's digital collection today with Taylor & Francis eBooks. We have over 50,000 eBooks in the Humanities, Social Sciences, Behavioural Sciences, Built Environment and Law, from leading imprints, including Routledge, Focal Press and Psychology Press.

Choose from a range of subject packages or create your own!

Benefits for you
- Free MARC records
- COUNTER-compliant usage statistics
- Flexible purchase and pricing options
- All titles DRM-free.

Benefits for your user
- Off-site, anytime access via Athens or referring URL
- Print or copy pages or chapters
- Full content search
- Bookmark, highlight and annotate text
- Access to thousands of pages of quality research at the click of a button.

Free Trials Available
We offer free trials to qualifying academic, corporate and government customers.

eCollections

Choose from over 30 subject eCollections, including:

Archaeology	Language Learning
Architecture	Law
Asian Studies	Literature
Business & Management	Media & Communication
Classical Studies	Middle East Studies
Construction	Music
Creative & Media Arts	Philosophy
Criminology & Criminal Justice	Planning
Economics	Politics
Education	Psychology & Mental Health
Energy	Religion
Engineering	Security
English Language & Linguistics	Social Work
Environment & Sustainability	Sociology
Geography	Sport
Health Studies	Theatre & Performance
History	Tourism, Hospitality & Events

For more information, pricing enquiries or to order a free trial, please contact your local sales team:
www.tandfebooks.com/page/sales

www.tandfebooks.com